rive

"Future generations will marvel at Manal al-Sharif, whose voice is laden with quiet dignity even at its most urgent. Her gripping account of homegrown courage will speak to the fighter in all of us."

—Deborah Feldman, *New York Times* bestselling author of *Unorthodox*

"[*Daring to Drive*] should shock you even if you think you already have a pretty good handle on conditions for women in Saudi Arabia."

—Meghan Daum, *The New York Times Book Review*

"An astonishing, humble, truthful book, more illuminating than a hundred newspaper stories."

—Azadeh Moaveni, author of *Lipstick Jihad*

"There are vignettes of laughter and love . . . [and] glimpses of rich, vibrant Arab life. . . . A testament to how women in Muslim countries are helping change their culture, one step at a time."

—*New York Journal of Books*

"Remarkable."

—*Jewish Journal*

"Eye-opening . . . [and] compelling."

—*Christian Science Monitor*

"A captivating read. Manal al-Sharif refuses to hide her scars, unveiling what she endured and sacrificed to become a professional who has fearlessly pushed the boundaries of tradition."

—Elena Gorokhova, author of *Russian Tattoo*

"Remarkable. Manal al-Sharif invites us to ride with her to bend the arc of history towards equality and justice."

—Rula Jebreal, international bestselling author of *Miral*

DARING
to DRIVE

A Saudi Woman's Awakening

Manal al-Sharif

SIMON & SCHUSTER PAPERBACKS
New York   London   Toronto   Sydney   New Delhi

Author's Note: This book is based on my personal recollections. I have endeavored to be as accurate as possible, but I do not claim to be a historian or religious expert. In most cases, I have removed names or used only first names. Any errors or missing details are unintentional. My apologies for any mistakes in these pages.

Simon & Schuster Paperbacks
1230 Avenue of the Americas
New York, NY 10020

First Simon & Schuster paperback edition June 2018

SIMON & SCHUSTER PAPERBACKS and colophon are registered trademarks of Simon & Schuster, Inc.

For information about special discounts for bulk purchases, please contact Simon & Schuster Special Sales at 1-866-506-1949 or business@simonandschuster.com.

The Simon & Schuster Speakers Bureau can bring authors to your live event. For more information, or to book an event, contact the Simon & Schuster Speakers Bureau at 1-866-248-3049 or visit our website at www.simonspeakers.com.

Interior design by Lewelin Polanco

Manufactured in the United States of America

1 3 5 7 9 5 10 8 6 4 2

Library of Congress Cataloging-in-Publication Data

Names: Sharif, Manal, 1979– author
Title: Daring to drive : a Saudi woman's awakening / Manal al-Sharif.
Description: New York : Simon & Schuster, 2017.
Identifiers: LCCN 2016041017 (print) | LCCN 2016050553 (ebook) | ISBN 9781476793023 (hardcover) | ISBN 9781476793047 (ebook)
Subjects: LCSH: Sharif, Manal, 1979– | Women—Saudi Arabia—Biography. | Women political activists—Biography. | Women automobile drivers—Saudi Arabia—Biography.
Classification: LCC HQ1730.Z75 S47 2017 (print) | LCC HQ1730.Z75 (ebook) | DDC 320.082/09538—dc23
LC record available at https://lccn.loc.gov/2016041017

ISBN 978-1-4767-9302-3 (hardcover)
ISBN 978-1-4767-9303-0 (pbk)
ISBN 978-1-4767-9304-7 (ebook)

To Mama & Abouya:
Sorry that we have not been thankful
for everything you gave us or taught us;
we didn't know it was all you had.

To Abdalla and Hamza:
Question the rules, not yourself.

To the forty-seven women drivers of 1990:
You are my idols.

"The best of you are those who are best to the women."

—PROPHET MUHAMMAD, Peace Be Upon Him

"Don't be afraid. Fear won't prevent death, it prevents life."

—NAGUIB MAHFOUZ

"My problem isn't forgetting, my real problem is having excessive memories."

—GHAZI ALGOSAIBI

Contents

DARING
to DRIVE

1

A Country of One King and Millions of Queens

The secret police came for me at two in the morning. The second knock on the door quickly followed the first. They were loud, hard knocks, the kind that radiate out and shake the doorframe. My five-year-old son was asleep, but I was awake still, sitting up with my brother.

Startled, my brother jumped up and rushed to the entry. I stayed slightly behind, feeling the night air rush in as he pulled open the door. It was May, so the air was warm but still pleasant, not oppressively hot. And it was dark. My lone porch light had burned out weeks before and I hadn't bothered to replace it. I thought about the light, I wondered whether the sudden noise would have woken my son— small thoughts passing through my mind in those seconds before everything changed.

In the shadowy darkness, all we could see were men, crowding around my front stoop, pressing forward. They had no uniforms, nothing to identify them. When my brother asked them who they were, there was silence. Finally, one of them spoke. "Is this Manal al-Sharif's house?"

My brother didn't hesitate. "Yes," he answered, his voice firm.

"She needs to come with us right now. They want to see her at the Dhahran police station." My brother did not have to ask why. That previous afternoon I had been pulled over by the traffic police for the "crime" of driving my brother's car. The specific citation was "driving while female." My brother had been sitting beside me, in the passenger seat, and then had sat next to me again for five hours inside the Thuqbah traffic police station, a two-story, nondescript concrete government building with a sturdy fence all around and a detention room where drivers could be held for hours or even days. There was only one detention space in the station, and it was only for men. I'm quite sure that I was the first woman ever to enter the Thuqbah station. It took the police several hours, including a call to the commander and a visit to the local governor's house, just to produce a paper for me to sign. The paper was a promise to never again drive on Saudi lands. I refused to sign, but they persisted. When my brother read the piece of paper, he realized I would only be admitting to having violated Saudi custom, because there are no specific Saudi statutes or lines in the traffic code that forbid women from driving. All they could accuse me of was disobeying the *orf,* or custom. I signed, and we were released. My brother and I took a taxi home, thinking that the incident was over, thinking that we had stymied the system, that in some small way, we had won.

We returned to my town house to find the TV on. There were pizza boxes on the coffee table, and three of my friends were clustered in my small living room with their laptops and smartphones. As I walked in, my sister-in-law started crying, and my friends rushed over and hugged me, shouting that they couldn't believe the police had let me go. One friend had even started a Twitter hashtag, #FreeManal, after I'd texted him from the car when the police first pulled me over. Everyone was talking at once, telling me to look at this tweet or that Facebook page or this news feed. In the six hours, the news of my arrest had gone viral. But I couldn't look at anything. I was exhausted, physically, mentally, and emotionally. All I wanted to do was to take a shower and go to bed. But it is against every Saudi custom to ask guests to leave, so I sat and we talked about winning our first battle, about having proved that there is no traffic code explicitly banning women from driving. When they finally left, they were still so excited and happy—and so was I, thinking, Well, now no one can stop us.

But then it was 2:00 a.m. and there were men at my door and my elation from the day was gone. As soon as I heard the words "Dhahran police station," I was terrified. My brother slammed the door shut and locked the bolt. There was a pause. Then the knocking started again.

—

My town house was not in the holy city of Mecca, my childhood home of twisted streets and thronging pilgrims, off-limits to all non-Muslims. Nor was it set amid the gleaming towers and sky bridges of the Saudi Arabian capital of Riyadh, high on a desert plateau. It was tucked in perhaps the most Western enclave in the entire kingdom, the pristine Aramco (Saudi Arabian Oil Company) compound in the Eastern Province, originally designed by Americans working for John D. Rockefeller's company, Standard Oil, which had helped found Aramco. Today, Aramco is the Saudi state oil company and the world's largest daily exporter of oil, sitting atop 260 billion barrels of petroleum reserves. It is also the world's wealthiest company, with a net worth estimated as high as $2.5 trillion. And it was my employer. When the Americans sold Aramco to the Saudis in the 1970s and 1980s, part of the agreement required the Saudis to continue to employ women.

The Aramco compound has long been a world unto itself. With lush green golf courses, lawns, palm trees, parks, and swimming pools, it looks very much like a perfect Southern California town. Inside the gates of Aramco, Saudi rules do not apply. Men and women mix together. Women do not have to be veiled or covered. We celebrated holidays like Halloween, when everyone dresses up in costumes. And unlike every other place in Saudi Arabia, inside the Aramco compound, women can drive. There are no prohibitions, no restrictions. They simply slip behind the wheel and start the engine. And there are protections. Not even the local city police or the Saudi religious police are allowed to venture onto Aramco-controlled land. Aramco has its own security and fire departments. It handles its matters internally, like a separate, sovereign state inside the Saudi kingdom.

But the Saudi secret police, I learned that night, could still enter.

I turned to face the sliding glass doors at the edge of my living room. Unlike the traditional Saudi way of covering one's house the way most families cover their women, I have never liked curtains. I always wanted the light streaming in. Now one of the men stood with his face pressed against the bare glass, his damp breath spreading like fog before the dry desert air sucked it back up again. He said nothing, and he did not move. Only his eyes slowly scanned my room. That night, he did not move from that glass door, did not release his face the entire time. Like the others, he was dressed in civilian clothes. That, however, is the hallmark of the secret police. They do not wear uniforms. They do not even identify themselves as police. They have other jobs, other identities. Yet they are woven through society at every level, and their sole purpose is to inform. They are employed by the kingdom to monitor citizens and to enforce the rules.

From behind the door, my brother began pushing back. "Don't you realize it's two in the morning? People are asleep here. Besides, we've only just come from the Thuqbah traffic police station." He wanted to imply that the matter had already been resolved. But there was no reply.

My brother paused and then raised his voice a little louder. "Who are you people? Unless you have an arrest warrant, we won't leave. If you want something, come back in the morning. You don't show up in the middle of the night and talk about bringing us to the police."

This was an understatement. In Saudi Arabia, our legal code is referred to not as "laws," which devout Saudi Muslims believe can be given only by Allah; we use another word that translates into English roughly as "system." The system says that no one can be arrested for a minor crime between the hours of sunset and sunrise. The same system also says that you cannot arrest anyone without a statement from a judge, unless the authorities consider you a threat to national security. But the men outside said nothing. After a few minutes had passed, they started knocking again.

I was standing now in my living room, wearing sweatpants and a Mickey Mouse T-shirt. I had nowhere else to go. It was a small house: a living room, a tiny galley kitchen, one bedroom, and a balcony, all of 750 square feet. Enough for my five-year-old son and me. I was divorced; under Saudi rules, without a husband, my father was my official male guardian. I could not work, attend school, or travel without his permission. But he lived in Jeddah, on the other side of the country.

I didn't know if the men could force open the door and come in and take me. I still didn't even know exactly who "they" were, but I realized I had to tell someone what was happening. I dialed a female Saudi journalist. I'd reached out to her when I'd first become interested in proving that women could legally drive. Even though it was the middle of the night, she answered the phone and told me she'd get me a lawyer. She gave me the number the lawyer would be calling me from. A few minutes later my phone rang. A woman named Suad al-Shammari, who identified herself as a lawyer, was on the line. The first thing she told me was to record our phone call, so I recorded the call with my iPhone as we spoke.

"Who are they?" she asked. "Are they religious police? Representatives from the traffic police? Do they have any kind of warrant?"

I told her that I didn't know. "They're still outside knocking," I said.

Suad talked with me for nearly twenty minutes. She told me that unless these men were from the national security division and I was wanted as a terrorist, they weren't allowed to come in the middle of the night and tell me to leave my home. She suggested I call the local police and ask if a warrant had been issued for my arrest. If there was no warrant, I should not go with them. "Send them away," she said. "Don't leave with them." So, as I listened to the men rapping their fists against my front door, I dialed 999 to speak with the police. A man on the other end of the line assured me there was no warrant for my arrest.

Almost as soon as I hung up, my phone rang again. This call was from Kholoud, a women's rights activist, who had already been tweeting about my arrest the previous afternoon. In the confusion, I didn't know that at that very moment one of my colleagues from Aramco, Omar al-Johani, was hiding behind a bush very close to my house. He had read Kholoud's tweets about my arrest and knew the street where I lived. He drove around until he saw the cars and the security guards. Now he was tweeting about the men surrounding my door. Kholoud was following him online. "Manal," she said calmly, "I want you to do something. I want you to go with these guys. It will bring them shame if we announce that they've taken you from your house in the middle of the night. This is a violation of your rights. We should expose them."

I didn't like the idea of going *anywhere* with these people. I didn't want to leave my son and I still didn't know exactly who was outside. But I kept thinking about what Kholoud had said. I decided to pray. I went upstairs. In the hallway leading to my small bedroom. I performed two *raka'as* (the full cycle of an Islamic prayer, spoken while standing, sitting, and prostrating) and asked for God to show me the way. It was now nearly four in the morning. In a little over an hour the sky would be streaked with the first hint of desert sun. I felt something inside me say, "Go, Manal. You'll be okay."

I composed myself, walked downstairs, and opened the door. Not everyone outside was a stranger. I recognized one man, Fahad, as an Aramco official; he held up his company ID card as proof. He started speaking to me but the whole time his eyes and his face were turned away, so that he was looking only at my brother. "We just need you to come to the Dhahran police station," he said. "You'll sign some papers and then be released. I am a colleague, so you can trust me. I will be there with you, I will not leave you. I will bring you back."

I didn't trust him. I called Aramco security. The man on the other end assured me, "This guy works for us. He will escort you to the police station." My brother insisted upon accompanying me as well, although all the men outside wanted me to go alone, without him, which should have convinced me that something was wrong. In Saudi society, a woman needs her official guardian (usually her father or husband) or a *mahram*—a close male family relative whom she cannot marry, such as a father, brother, uncle, or even a son—to accompany her on any official business.

Even a woman in labor will not be admitted into a hospital without her guardian or at least a mahram. Police cannot enter a home during a robbery, and firefighters are forbidden from entering a home during a fire or medical emergency if a woman is inside but does not have a mahram present. In 2014, Amna Bawazeer died on the campus of King Saud University when school officials refused to allow male paramedics to enter the female-only school after Amna collapsed from a heart ailment. The same story repeated itself in 2016 at Qaseem University when male paramedics were not allowed on campus to treat a female student, Dhuha Almane, who subsequently died. It is not a stretch to say that death is preferable to violating the strict code of guardianship and mahrams.

I went back inside and put on my abaya, the swirling black cloak that covered my entire body, except for my hands and the tips of my feet, as well as a hijab, a head scarf, that covered my hair, my ears, and my neck, everything except my face. Then I made one last phone call to Atika Shubert, a female reporter for CNN based in London, who had interviewed me a week earlier. Atika promised that she'd put the news that I'd been taken from my home on CNN's international website. If she did that, I trusted that I would not simply disappear.

I walked out holding my brother's arm, I hadn't even looked at my sleeping little boy or kissed him goodbye. I wanted to believe that this was a formality, that I'd be back in time to wake him, feed him breakfast, get him to school, and then head to work. At most, I told myself, I would only be gone a couple of hours. At this time of night, it was less than ten minutes from the Aramco compound to the Dhahran police station.

As soon as I stepped outside I counted the people there. There were nine of them: seven men, two women, and five cars. Once I passed through the doorway, the two women—female Aramco guards, fully covered except for a small slit for their eyes—muscled in beside me. I knew they worked for Aramco because over their abayas they were wearing the company's standard issue khaki-colored coats with a large badge on the chest. They were most likely part of the contingent of female guards who manned the checkpoint at the women's gate into the compound. When veiled women entered Aramco, these guards were the ones who uncovered their faces to verify the women's identities. They could gaze upon any other woman's face, know her identity, without ever revealing their own.

They walked uncomfortably close, as if they were ready to grab me and hold me down if I tried to escape. I got into the back of one of the cars—not a police car but an Aramco company car. The women didn't follow me in. I was alone, except for two men. My brother sat in the front, and Fahad, the Aramco official, drove. No one spoke. I looked out the window at the blackness, felt the car hum along the road. Five minutes passed, then ten. I could make out none of the familiar landmarks in Dhahran. We were not heading into the city. We were driving east. Everything else left my mind except for one question: "Where are you taking us?"

———

I never set out to be an activist. I was a religious girl, born and raised in Mecca. I started covering myself with abayas and niqabs before it was even required, simply because I wanted to emulate and please my religious teachers. And I believed in a highly fundamentalist version of Islam. For years, I melted my brother's pop music cassette tapes in the oven because in fundamentalist Islam, music is considered *haram,* meaning forbidden. The first time I ever heard a song, I was twenty years old. It was the Backstreet Boys' "Show Me the Meaning of Being Lonely," and I still remember almost every word.

The only thing I did at a young age that was somewhat rebellious was to get a job. I had a bachelor's degree in computer science, and I was hired by Aramco as an information security specialist. I got married young, at age twenty-four, and had a son. Then I got divorced, which is fairly common; some published statistics estimate that the divorce rate inside Saudi Arabia is as high as sixty percent. Both my parents were divorced when they married. But once I turned thirty, I started to do daring things on my birthdays. On my thirtieth birthday, I was working in the United States, in New Hampshire, and I went skydiving. The next year, I bought a ticket to Puerto Rico and spent thirty-six hours traveling alone. And back in Saudi Arabia in 2011, when I turned thirty-two, I decided that I would start driving.

I learned the proper rules of driving when I was working and living in the States—I got a New Hampshire and then a Massachusetts driver's license. But in Saudi Arabia, I never got behind the wheel, except inside the Aramco compound. Saudi women rely on drivers, usually foreign men, some of whom have never taken a driving test or had any kind of professional instruction, to ferry them from place to place. We are at their mercy. Some families are wealthy enough to employ their own personal driver, but many women rely on an informal network of men with cars who illegally transport female passengers. Women carry lists of these private drivers in their phones, and we call and call until we find one who's available. Or we take a taxi—taxis and their drivers are at least registered and licensed by the traffic police— but the taxis are old and many of the men who operate them don't bathe, so the stench is often overwhelming. My friends would text me if they found a clean taxi driver, and I would text them.

Almost every woman I know has been harassed by a driver. They make comments about our appearance or about conversations they overhear; they demand more money; they touch you inappropriately. Some women have been attacked. I've had drivers make all sorts of inappropriate comments and tape my calls when I've used my cell phone, even drivers who don't speak Arabic, thinking maybe they could blackmail or extort me. Then there are the cases of drivers who sexually molest the children they are hired to drive to and from school.

It is an amazing contradiction: a society that frowns on a woman going out without a man; that forces you to use separate entrances for universities, banks, restaurants, and mosques; that divides restaurants with partitions so that unrelated males and females cannot sit together; that same society expects you to get into a car with a man who is not your relative, with a man who is a complete stranger, by yourself and have him take you somewhere inside a locked car, alone. Even women who have personal drivers cannot depend on these hired men. Some don't show up, others disappear entirely. The Saudi men call women "queens," and say that queens don't drive. Women often mock this title by saying "The kingdom of one king and millions of queens." Or they post a photo of Great Britain's Queen Elizabeth driving her Jaguar, saying "Real queens drive their own cars."

One night in 2011, I had a doctor's appointment after work in Khobar, outside the Aramco compound. When I left the medical office at nearly 9:00 p.m., I called all the drivers I knew to ask for a ride home, but none was available. They were off-duty, or busy driving other Saudi queens. When the clinic locked its doors, I started making my way down the streets. There were plenty of men in their cars out that night, and they all saw me, walking alone, my face uncovered. (Most Saudi women cover their faces.) It was an invitation for them to harass me, and they did. Some cars whizzed past; others slowed to a crawl. The drivers honked their horns and screamed slurs and cruel names and other vile things. I kept looking straight ahead, but it was terrifying. I called my brother, but his phone was turned off.

One of the cars followed me. There were shops lining the street, but it was night, so they were closed. And they were all set back, with wide parking lots in front. This guy would slowly pull his car into one of the lots. Then he'd lower his window and look at me, as though inviting me to get in. I'd keep walking, and he'd pull into the next parking lot, lower his window, and look at me again. I was so mad. I felt violated, all because I couldn't find a driver and I couldn't do what he could: drive myself home. When I passed by what must have been a construction site, I picked up a loose rock from the ground and held it in my hand. As soon as he saw me with the rock, he shot me a furious look and sped off, tires squealing. But I threw it anyway, as hard as I could, toward him and his car. Then I stood there in the street, tears running down my face, crying like a little girl. I'm not a girl. I'm a woman, I'm a mother, I'm educated, I had a car that I bought and had been making payments on for four years—it was sitting with its stone-cold engine, parked next to my town house—but I still couldn't stop things like this from happening to me.

In Saudi Arabia, harassment isn't a criminal offense. The authorities, especially the religious police, always blame the woman. They say she was harassed because of how she looked or because of the way she was walking or because she was wearing perfume. They make you the criminal.

When I got home that night, I poured out my complaints on Facebook: the degradation of having to find a driver, of always worrying about being late, or being left somewhere, of trying to cobble together a patchwork of rides from relatives and drivers whose numbers I hoarded in my phone. I ended my post by promising to drive outside the Aramco compound on my birthday and take videos and upload them to YouTube. David, one of my American friends from New Hampshire, wrote on my Facebook wall "trouble-maker," and I replied, "no, history-maker." But even then, I didn't believe myself. I thought I was bluffing.

——

Fahad, the Aramco government affairs man, the person who had promised to bring me home, who had told me over and over that we were going to the Dhahran police station, had lied. But I couldn't call him a liar to his face. Instead, in what I hoped was a calm voice, I asked where we were going. He had said the Dhahran police station, I reminded him.

He brushed off my question, saying, "Yeah, yeah. Well, they waited so long at Dhahran and you didn't come, so now they've asked for you to go to the Khobar police station." His style was smoother and softer than that of the religious police, who used to carry sticks for beatings and now just scream and yell at women. But the message was the same: it was my fault for not grabbing my bag and my abaya and going straight away with a group of strange, unidentified men at two o'clock in the morning.

Khobar is a sprawling city with almost 1 million residents. Like most newer Saudi cities, it is a collection of skyscrapers and shopping malls, located on what was an ancient port bordering the Persian Gulf, which we call the Arabian Gulf. In the West, it is perhaps best known for the 1996 Khobar Towers bombing, when a massive bomb hidden inside a tanker truck by extremists killed nineteen American military service members.

The sky was just turning light with the first streaks of pink as we arrived at the station. It was a big, cinder-block building on King Abdullah Road, not far from the waters of the gulf. I had already passed this very same station in my car two days before. That day was the only other time that I had driven on public roads inside the kingdom.

Inside the station, everyone was nice to me at first—even solicitous. They asked my brother and me if they could get us juice or water, maybe some coffee. They apologized for bringing us in so early. "We just need to finish this paperwork," they said. "We will let you go just after we finish this paperwork." My brother and I were led into a small room with one window. There was a desk and some chairs and a very large picture of King Abdullah framed and hanging on the wall, looking down at me.

The man from the police station started off by saying that they didn't want to scare me, and he began with the simplest of questions: "You are Manal al-Sharif?" I nodded. Then he turned to my brother and asked him some questions as well.

It was hard to tell how much time had passed. Eventually, a young man entered and offered me a sandwich and orange juice, but I refused to eat. I tried to cooperate with the questioning as much as I could, hoping that they'd get what they needed and let me go home to my son.

There was a second man in the room, sitting behind a desk. He too began to speak. He wanted to know who was behind the Women-2Drive group, of which I was the public face and one of the leaders, and also whom I had spoken with in the foreign press. He asked me about my relationship with Wajeha al-Huwaider, the woman who had filmed me driving. Wajeha was a well-known activist in Saudi Arabia, but I had no idea about the depths of her troubled relationship with the government. The second man would ask me questions, and then the first man would ask me questions, over and over. I kept smiling the whole time.

All of a sudden, the man behind the desk closed the interrogation file. He looked at me and said something very much like, "Come on, Manal. You know the king is going through a very difficult time with the Arab Spring and all the things that are happening in the region. Why would you add more burdens to the king? Don't you love the king?" And there right in front of me was the king's picture, staring down at me with that half-smile.

In Saudi Arabia, your patriotism is measured by how much you love the king. The king is revered like a father, and we are considered his daughters and sons. And out of all the Saudi kings, Abdullah is the king I have loved instead of feared. He is the only one to start opening doors for women, to speak up for women or to allow more freedom of speech and freedom of the press. So it was not hard for me to tell the interrogator, "No, of course, I love King Abdullah so much. I wouldn't want to do anything that would cause him any more burdens."

The interrogator nodded and said that the problem wasn't so much with me driving, it was with me posting my video on YouTube and talking to the foreign media and causing so much fuss.

I tried to follow his lead and started apologizing. I told him that if my participation in the Women2Drive campaign was what was causing all these problems, I'd just stop. I told him that I never imagined I'd have all these problems with officials, and I was so sorry. My purpose, I added, "was not to inconvenience anyone."

He nodded and then left. My brother and I were alone. Fahad, the Aramco guy, was already gone. Just as the first interrogator had finished, Fahad had stuck his head into the room and said: "I think you're fine now. Sorry, I have to go to work. It's seven a.m. and I have to report to my office." He told me we could take a taxi back, or call him and he would come pick us up.

I sat in silence with my brother, texting the girls who were putting up the feeds on Twitter. I asked them to please stop tweeting about me and my arrest, telling them that I did not want any more attention. It was just something minor, I added, just the video that was the problem. I would be released soon.

About thirty minutes passed and then another man came in. The first thing he did was order my brother to leave. My brother was swiftly escorted out and, in his place, they ushered in a woman. She was called the prison guard. No name, just "the prison guard." She was fully veiled in a black abaya and black niqab with black shoes, black socks, and black gloves on her hands. Even her bag was black. I couldn't even see a glimpse of her face, just a thin slash through the cloth where the whites of her eyes glowed. She sat next to me, saying nothing. Her gloves were so old and worn that there were holes in the fabric and along the seams where the threads had come loose. I could see down to her dark skin. Her bag was old too, battered, with a strap that was barely hanging on. But then I stopped looking at her because the new interrogator was not done.

He took my bag with my wallet, my cell phone, and everything I had. My papers and my identity were gone. Even my ability to tell time was gone; there was no clock in the room. On any other morning, I would know when my neighbors began to move about their houses, when the Aramco buses would begin their morning loops around the smooth asphalt streets of the compound. I would know when my five-year-old son woke up. On this morning when he opened his eyes, he would discover that his mother was gone.

Now I was truly frightened.

———

The new interrogator asked me all the same questions, what's your name, what's your age, where do you work? He continued to ask me for the names of the people I had talked to in the foreign media. Everything was the same as the previous rounds of questioning, except he spoke in a harsher tone. Then he left and I sat there, with my silent guard, waiting.

Then another man came in. He sat down right in front of me, and the first thing he said, in a concerned voice, was, "Tell me your story." So, I told him my story again, and he listened, and then he left the room. I didn't know until much later that all of this was a standard pattern: to use multiple interrogators, to alternate between cajoling and being sympathetic and then firm and harsh, to repeat the same questions again and again, to keep the detainee waiting. Each time, they were trying to see if I would change my story. Would there be inconsistencies? Would I inadvertently say the wrong thing or give something away?

I don't know if I would call myself a calm person by nature, but the effect of having been up for more than twenty-four hours, of having eaten so little, and of having expended so much adrenaline, first in the car and then at the traffic police station the previous afternoon, made me calm and methodical. My story was my story. It did not change.

At some point, one of my interrogators had brought in a copy of *Al Yaum* newspaper. He held it in his left hand, his fingers gripping the paper like a vise, until it buckled and creased around the edges. With his free hand, he pointed to my picture and the headline about my arrest on the front page. Afterward, he threw it on the desk. He wanted the names of people involved with the driving campaign. I gave him only two names, names he already knew: Bahiya al-Mansour, the girl who had started the Facebook event for Women2Drive, and Wajeha al-Huwaider, the activist. (Both were later picked up and interrogated as well.) But I kept my answers short, as King Abdullah's bespectacled face gazed down from his portrait. Then once more the prison guard and I were left alone.

It was work to keep my body in the chair. I had never thought of sitting as tiring, but it was taking every muscle in me to keep myself in that position, to keep my head from folding over into my lap. I hadn't been to the bathroom yet, and I knew that at some point soon, it would be time for midday prayers. I kept asking this woman if there was a place I could go for some privacy.

Suddenly the silence broke. There was big flurry of activity. The door opened, people motioned, speaking in fast, clipped Arabic, without any of the usual pleasantries or greetings: "Come with us." I followed and found myself in another area, surrounded by a lot of men. My face was uncovered, and I was the only woman, except for the prison guard, who followed mutely along.

I started speaking, asking, "Where is my brother? Where is my bag? What's happening?"

We were led to a metal door and motioned through. I could hear the metal close hard behind us. I kept asking the guard: "Why are we in here? What's going on?"

She was as terrified as I was. I could hear her voice shaking as she said, "I don't know."

The room was the filthiest thing I had ever seen. It was crawling with cockroaches, their hard shells racing across the floor and up the walls, the scurrying of their legs making a low, clicking sound. The room stank of piss and sweat and every foul odor possible to imagine. I took small breaths through my hand, my stomach clenching in revulsion. There was another, smaller room attached. It had no door, but it was supposed to be the bathroom. There was no toilet, just a hole in the ground and human shit all over the floor.

On the floor, amid the cockroaches, was a sponge mattress. Nomadic Arabs don't have traditional beds, just these roll-up mattresses. Even now, when many people live together in one house, we often sleep on these mattresses at night and then roll them up for the daytime. This was a small mattress, and it was filthy, shiny with sweat and dirt that had been worn into the covering. There was nowhere else to sit. We were inside the detention room of the Khobar police station, and I did not know for how long. I felt tears well up in my eyes, but I shut them. I was not going to cry in this place. I was not going to cry in front of this woman.

Finally, the woman told me her name. Halimah. I kept saying to her, "Halimah, what did I do? Where is my brother? What's going on? Why did they take my bag?" I was like all those interrogators, but in reverse.

Halimah kept saying, "I don't know."

I started banging on the metal door, my fist pounding and then stinging. "Please, please, where's my brother?" I would call out. "Can I just talk to my lawyer? Can I talk to my son?"

I stood for a long time, but I was so tired. I had been awake for the better part of two days. My head was throbbing, and I had to sit down on that disgusting mattress. I had to close my eyes. But I started talking to Halimah. I asked her about her husband, I asked if she had children. She told me that her husband was a security guard. Being a security guard is usually the lowest form of work that a Saudi man can accept. Most guards work long hours and earn low wages, maybe 1,500 riyals a month, which is only about $400, not even enough to pay rent in most places. Halimah said she had two kids. She told me their names, but in my exhaustion, I forgot them. I asked her question after question, the way you try to forget about your own situation by involving yourself in someone else's.

As she spoke, I looked at my fancy shoes and my fancy, well-made abaya, which cost the equivalent of her husband's salary for at least one month. The bag that they had already taken from me would have cost her husband three months' wages. Her phone was an old phone, black and white, the kind that could only hold about ten messages before it ran out of storage. I looked at her and thought of her having no other options than to work in this place, thought of what must have driven her to take this job. Sitting in that cell, I pitied her, even more than myself.

Suddenly the door was wrenched open. Two guards told me to come out, and as I walked through the doorway, they told me to show my hands. One of the men was holding a large roller covered in blue ink, which he proceeded to slide across my hands until they were thickly coated. He told me to press my fingers and hands to a series of papers, first my thumbs, then my fingers, then my whole hand. Because I am a woman, it was taboo for him to touch my skin. Methodically, I followed his instructions. I placed my hands on the papers, and when I looked up, I recognized one of the other men in the room—the head of the Khobar police station. He had also been present at the Thuqbah traffic police headquarters when they had detained me the day before.

I looked straight at him and asked, "What's going on? Why are you doing this?"

"You ask yourself, Manal al-Sharif," he said. "You put yourself in this position!"

2

Cockroaches and Prison Bars

could not tell you if I stayed in that police room with my sticky, ink-stained hands for a long time or for a short time, if many minutes had passed or only a few. My entire sense of time had vanished. Eventually, another man entered and said that we were going upstairs. He carried the stack of rustling papers with my handprints on them. He was talking in brisk, overlapping sentences to me, but really to no one, rattling off a list of bureaucratic instructions and observations. It was like being thrust into a conversation where I only knew a few words of the language. I felt my mind grasping for a familiar phrase. "We need to send your papers to the governor's house. It's out of our hands, we can't do anything. They'll take care of your papers there. We'll need to send you there."

I was not going home.

There were two guys waiting for me, in civilian clothes with a civilian car—a white Toyota Camry with fabric seats. A man in a uniform handed them my papers and told the two men to open them once they were inside the car. They acted like they were in a hurry, sliding into their seats, facing forward. Around their heads, held in place by a black band, they wore the traditional Saudi *shemagh,* the red-and-white checked cloth that identifies Saudi men. But their shemaghs were draped in such a way that I could not see their faces. If I were to pass them on a street or in hallway at some point in the future, I would not be able to recognize them.

Halimah came with me, trailing slightly behind with her ripped gloves and her bag with the nearly broken strap. She sat next to me, completely silent, clutching her bag on her lap. They had given her my cell phone and my ID but had returned the rest of my bag to me. In the bright sunlight, I could see that her abaya was dirty. She looked even poorer than she had inside the police station.

I asked the men if I could perform my afternoon prayers. They ignored me. I asked again, and they very curtly told me that I could do my prayers "when we get there." The entire time that I had been at the police station, I had convinced myself that I was not a criminal, just a regular person merely being brought in for an interrogation, that I'm not someone who would be sitting next to a woman whom they would all call "my prison guard." But now, in that silent car, it was hard to keep pretending.

It was afternoon and because it was May, it was neither hot nor cold. Springtime in the eastern part of Saudi Arabia is quite beautiful. In the green, watered spaces, flowers were blooming. I knew that it was around 2:00 p.m., because I saw all the government workers streaming out of their offices at the end of their workday. It was crowded; we were just another car joining the commuter stream. We had vanished by blending in.

Usually when I'm riding in the car, I read a book. I am a voracious reader. I keep a book beside my bed on the nightstand, in my office, even in the bathroom. But I didn't have a book then. So, as the man from the prison drove, I started reading whatever I could see out of the car windows. I read the names of the shops and stores along the streets; I read the billboards, the road signs. I read while we were entering Dammam, the city where I had lived for four years when I was married. I was still reading signs when we arrived at one that read Dammam Central Prison. A solid concrete wall and a checkpoint loomed before us. I was being sent to jail.

They had taken me from my house at 4:00 a.m., without warning, without allowing me to call a lawyer, without a warrant. I had begged the men who had interrogated me to let me call my son, but they didn't allow me to call anyone. It was as if I had disappeared. And they could detain me indefinitely. It was done. There are people in jail in Saudi Arabia, even women, who have languished there for years without a trial or a sentence.

I started yelling at the two men in the front seat. "Where are you taking me? Sir, please talk to me, where are you taking me? It's my right to know where you are taking me."

They remained silent.

"You can't just do this, I am not a criminal!" I screamed. "How could you take me to jail without papers, without a ruling, without being sentenced in the court?"

Not a word. I looked at Halimah. "Halimah, say something, do something," I pleaded. But she just clutched at her bag balanced on her knees, not making a sound.

If any of them had shouted back at me, that would have been more merciful. I had never been to jail. All I could think was that if I went in there, I would never get out. I thought about my son. Would I ever see him again? I thought about my job, knowing that after this, I would surely lose it—a job that I had fought so hard to get and keep. I was the only woman working among so many men, not just working beside them but proving that I was better than them. I thought about the scandal that being jailed would bring to my family.

The car stopped. The driver rolled down his window and asked the security guard where the women's prison was.

I tried to think. I had to get a message through to Halimah. When I had left the house in such a rush, I hadn't checked my bag. I didn't even have a pen or paper to write on. But then I realized that I did have a piece of paper in my bag. I had been planning to go to apply for a driver's license with one of the female activists, but we couldn't find a taxi to take us to the licensing office. Instead, I had gone off driving on the streets with my brother after work. When I ended up at the Thuqbah police station and one of the policemen had accused me of driving without a Saudi license, I had pulled out the paper and said, "This is my application. Give me my driver's license." Now, ironically, those papers were still sitting in my bag. I just needed a pen. I dug around and the only thing I had was an eyebrow pencil. It was good enough. I wrote on the driver's license application, "Help. Get me Muneera's number from my phone." Muneera is my sister-in-law. As we drove on, I reached over and squeezed Halimah's hand and showed her the paper. I had to be careful. The men could see us through the rearview mirror. They could hear anything that we said. But I had to get her to read the note.

She didn't say anything. She didn't even look at me.

We reached yet another gate that led to a parking lot and a building. But the driver didn't park in any of the spaces; he drove up and stopped next to the door. The two men left the car and went inside carrying my papers. This was my chance. I had to get in touch with someone. I didn't know where my brother was, and the only phone number I could remember was my dad's, but I wouldn't call him. He did not even know about the campaign for women to drive. But my sister-in-law, I could reach her.

I turned to Halimah. This time, I reached out and took hold of both her hands, and said, "Halimah, I need your help. I need to call my family." I kept talking to her. "Please, Halimah. They are inside. No one will know. I just need to make a call from my phone or send a text message to my sister-in-law. Just so they know where I am. Please."

Her eyes looked at me through the tiny slit, and she said, "I'm really, really sorry." Her voice sounded like she was in pain. She said that she did not know they were bringing me here. She had only been told to accompany me so that I would not be alone with two men. But, she said, "I cannot give you your phone."

I kept pleading with her. "I have a child," I said. "You have two kids, I have one kid. You know, you understand."

But she told me that if she gave me my phone, she would be fired. She had instructions that she could not violate. "If I break them," she said, "I will be in so much trouble. I cannot afford to lose my job."

I kept begging her the entire time that we waited, but she did not relent. When the men came back, they opened the car door and told me to come with them. I tried to resist. I said, "No, I'm not going with you, I want to call a lawyer. You can't just put me in jail with no charges."

But they replied that I was coming with them. If I refused, they said, "We will have to drag you inside by force."

I dragged my feet the whole way inside to a very big room with an office on one end. The first thing I noticed was the ceramic tile on the floor. It was the exact same black-and-white pattern that had covered the floors of my old school in Mecca. Decades before, when the kingdom built all its government and school buildings, it must have used these tiles on every floor. They might have looked new back then, but now they just looked worn and old.

There were two men at the entrance, sitting on a row of chairs, the kind you see in airport terminals, where the seats are connected. They were holding papers. I was told to go toward the office and wait on a sofa away from the desk. Then they ushered me in.

My papers were handed to a man in a uniform sitting behind the desk. His name, Musaad, had been engraved on a small wooden nameplate. I later learned that he was the deputy head of the prison. The man in charge of the prison was on vacation, which is how I came to be standing in Musaad's office. He did not cover his head. He had a short beard and a mustache, and when he saw my papers, pure disgust crossed his face. He looked at my papers, then up at me. I started to wonder what those papers said.

"So you're the infamous Manal al-Sharif," he said, eyeing me from behind his desk. "Aren't you ashamed of what you did?"

"Is driving a car something shameful?" I answered back.

The same Saudi newspaper that the interrogator had showed me earlier in the day lay open in front of him. Musaad held it up, pointing to my picture with my face uncovered and my colorful hijab. He was shouting now: "How could you go out like this? Your face is uncovered, you're not even wearing a black hijab." He raised his voice still louder, as if he had an audience but lacked a microphone, so that his words bounced out of the small office and out over the long expanse of tiles. "You've shamed your religion, you've shamed your tradition, you've shamed your country. You deserve what's happening to you."

"Sir," I said, "there must be a mistake, you cannot put me in jail."

His look told me that of course he could.

"Can I at least talk to my son?" I asked. "He doesn't know I'm here."

"Now you ask about your son? You didn't ask about your son when you drove? You didn't ask about your son when you started your woman-to-drive group?" He was still sitting, while I was standing before him, my face uncovered, because I refuse to cover my face. So he had to look at my expression as clearly as I had to look at his. I think that irritated him more than anything, having a woman dare to stand before him with an uncovered face.

He continued to scold me for at least half an hour as if I were an errant child. I did not get angry or aggressive. I remained respectful, polite. All through the interrogations, I had been cooperative, I had given them information. I knew that I could not get angry, that I could not fight back, because against all these men, I would lose. I kept saying, "Please, sir, you cannot put me inside without me being able to call my lawyer and my family. I don't know where they took my brother, I don't know why I am here, and my family doesn't know that I am here." He kept shouting, "No, no, no. Later you will talk to your family, you cannot talk now," although sitting next to him on the desk was a phone.

I was standing, trying to stay upright despite my exhaustion, when I remembered something that one of my friends had told me. She is an activist and has been detained, but she has never been jailed. Once I asked her what her secret was. She said, "It's easy, we're women." And then she showed me. She made her shoulders start to shake and tears come to her eyes. "Give them two tears, say you are sorry, and they will pity you and let you go," she said. I kept thinking about what she had told me, but for me, there were no tears in my eyes.

I cannot cry in front of men. In 2002, I started working for Aramco, and for the first six years, all my colleagues were men. In 2008, a new girl joined our section. She always cried; the slightest criticism or comment that she found hurtful would bring her to tears. I remember my boss saying to me, "I wish she had ten percent of you, Manal. I never see you cry." And it's true; my nightmare is to have a man see me crying. Even my ex-husband would say, "I might show you mercy, if I were to see you cry." But if I want to cry, I cry alone. Or I can cry in front of women. They understand. It is okay if they see my tears.

At this moment, though, I was pushing myself to cry. I thought if I could at least cry a little and say, "Please, sir, can I talk to my son?" he would take pity on me and allow me to make that phone call.

There were so many things that I wanted to tell Musaad. I wanted to say, "I'm not a criminal. I'm a good person. This country should be proud of someone like me. I am the first woman to work in information security for the state oil company. I've been assigned to work in a very sensitive and important department. My company is very proud of me. I've been written about in the newspaper for my work, and I've done interviews with magazines. I do not deserve to be standing here being shouted at by you."

I finally managed a few tears, enough for Halimah, who had been standing silently off to one side, to reach over and take my hand in hers. She stroked it, the way a mother strokes the hair of a distraught child. But seeing my eyes well up only made the prison deputy director meaner. He kept saying nasty, hurtful things, loud enough so that anyone nearby could hear: the two soldiers in his office, the guard, my escort to the prison, everyone.

Then in the middle of his tirade, his phone rang. I could hear the name of the man on the other end, it was the head of the Khobar police station. He was the one who had told me that I had done this to myself. The two men talked and then Musaad closed his office door. He looked at me, and he said, "Don't worry, you'll be here for a couple of days." Then he used the Arabic phrase that means "just pinching your ear." In school, if you forgot your homework or you misbehaved, the teacher would pinch your ear. In Arabic, "pinching your ear" basically means "teaching someone a lesson."

I started pleading with him again, "Please, can I just get my sister-in-law's number from my phone?"

And this time, he said, "Okay, you can open your phone."

Halimah gave it to me, and while everyone was talking (I type very fast), I typed two text messages. One was to my friend and colleague Ahmed, who had been tweeting from the Women2Drive account. I told him, "I'm in Dammam Women's Prison. Tweet about it." The other message was to my sister-in-law, who was with my son. I also told her I was in prison. And I asked her to find me a lawyer. Even though I had talked to a female lawyer before I was taken from my house, in Saudi Arabia at that time, women weren't given licenses to practice (the first licenses for female lawyers were issued in 2014). I would need a man if I was going to get out of Dammam Women's Prison.

At that moment, everyone turned back to me and the deputy director starting asking, "What are you doing?"

I said, "I'm just getting the number."

"Did you finish?"

I told him yes, and I turned my phone off and gave it back. I have a password on my phone, so I did not think that they could unlock it.

Then, carrying my bag, without my phone and my ID, I walked with Halimah and the security guard, a man, into prison. It was an old place, with high walls, and to get to the main prison we had to cross a huge yard that was all dirt. No tiles, no walkways, just bare earth. On the other side of the yard was a huge metal gate, and next to the gate was a small, enclosed space for a guard with a weapon. And in the distance were towers all around the prison.

I entered through another building. The door was damaged, almost broken, there were no windows, and the seats were filthy. Someone told me to sit down. I was still insisting on making a phone call. Mussad had told the security guard that I could use a phone once I was inside the women's jail, but that I could not make a call from my phone. Inside the jail, I could pay money and buy a phone card, ten or twenty riyals' worth. (Interestingly, some of the Saudi men who are detained are allowed to keep their phones.)

I bought a card and the guard then asked me how many cards I wanted for food.

"I'll be leaving tomorrow," I said. "I don't want anything."

He kept saying, no, no, no, you will need it inside. So I bought a small coupon book for 100 riyals. It looked like the booklet that we used to buy as kids in school to pay for our breakfasts. It was full of yellow cards, and I stuck it in my bag.

We walked from this admission room closer toward the prison itself, passing through two gates. At the smaller one, the male guard had to leave. We were entering the place where only women could pass.

On the other side of the gate was a hallway. The moment I stepped inside, I covered my nose and mouth against the stench of urine and shit. It smelled like a giant bathroom. On one side, the wall was thick Plexiglas. This, I would learn, was the place where visitors were permitted. There were no chairs to sit down: everyone pressed up against the Plexiglas. There were small holes on each side, but none of the holes matched up. You could shout some conversation, but nothing could pass easily back and forth.

Halimah took my hand in her thin, worn glove. Then she handed my papers and my phone to the internal prison guard. She looked at me and said, "May God protect you." Then she added, "You will be fine."

She turned and walked back through the doorway, back to the outside world. Even though she was called a "prison guard," she was not an actual guard inside a jail. When they shut the door behind her, I felt as if more than a door was closing. I felt as if it was the last time that I would see the outside or see someone from the outside world. My hope closed along with that door.

I didn't know that was there was basically no cell phone service in jail. The coverage was very weak; it came and went. The two texts that I had sent did not go through. Had I known that at that moment, I might have cried for real.

——

I was alone now with a new female guard, who was little more than a girl, certainly younger than me. She was not wearing an abaya. She was dressed in a long skirt and a long-sleeved blouse, with her hair twisted tightly and wrapped around at the back of her head in a style of bun. She took my papers, the papers that had followed me from the Khobar police station to jail, and pointed at a place where I was supposed to sign. On the paper there was a line for charges. In the blank space, someone had written "driving while female."

After I signed, the guard looked at my paper and asked me, "Why are you here in this jail?"

I looked at her and said, "Guess."

She said, "You are Manal al-Sharif?"—she already knew my name—and then added, "They brought you here? For driving a car?" She asked each question as if she couldn't believe it, couldn't believe that I was standing there, couldn't believe that I was being sent to her jail for driving a car.

I decided that this was the opening I needed. I told her that I was to be allowed one phone call before I entered the jail. She looked at me and said, "No. Who told you that?" I explained that Musaad had told me to ask the prison guard when I got inside. I showed her that I had already bought my calling card.

The prison had one small room with an old landline phone for prisoners. Each woman was allowed one call per month. I kept insisting that I could make a call. Finally, the guard called the main section, and someone must have told her that it was okay. I used my phone card to call my sister-in-law.

She was upset and relieved at the same time. She kept asking, "Where are you?" I told her that I was fine, that I was in Dammam Central Prison and to tell my friend Ahmed to tweet about it. She replied, "What's 'tweet'?" She had no idea what Twitter was. We went back and forth a few times, and finally I said to her, "Just tell Ahmed to tweet, and he will understand." And I told her to find me a lawyer. Then the call was over. I hung up the receiver with its long cord. There was nothing else I could do.

I wasn't going to be getting any more special favors. The guard looked at my bag and told me that I could not take it with me. She took it, along with my ID and my phone, and told me to follow her through a back door. In an apologetic voice, she said, "You will not like this." I didn't understand what she was talking about.

We entered another foul-smelling area and she said, "Take off your clothes." I thought I had misheard her.

I said, "Excuse me?"

She told me again to take off my clothes and to bend over.

"All my clothes?" I asked. "Even my underwear?"

"Yes, even your underwear."

It is hard to convey just what an extreme indignity this was. If you are raised as a traditional Saudi woman, you cannot bear being exposed. It is the greatest shame possible. Women do not uncover themselves even for doctors. When I was in the hospital giving birth to my son, the only time I felt embarrassed and uneasy was when the doctor came in and I had to take off my underwear. The doctor was another woman, and still I felt extremely uncomfortable, even though I was in labor. Submitting to this examination, bending over to have this strange prison guard with her gloved hands check the most intimate parts of me was the most humiliating thing I had ever experienced.

When it was done, she told me to put on my clothes.

All my frustration and rage spilled over. I starting shouting at her, saying that this could not be happening, and I vowed that I would have her exposed.

She looked at me and said very calmly, "You have to leave here first. Only then can you start threatening to expose us."

Those words stunned me into silence.

We stepped back into the processing office where another woman was waiting. Her name was Zahrah, which means "flower" in Arabic. She was also wearing a skirt; apparently that was the uniform for the prison guards. She was short and heavy and was carrying an enormous chain of keys. She was to lead me to jail.

We exited the administration area, leaving behind the offices and the tiny room with the old phone, and another that was like a workshop with sewing machines, and a holy room set aside for prayers. We passed through a very small yard. The top should have been open to the sky and filled with blazing afternoon desert light, but instead there were two layers of metal netting, each overlaying the other. It was like being fenced in on all sides. We came to another room with a metal mesh ceiling, but in this one there were ropes stretching from wall to wall. They were the clotheslines. Women could go into the bathroom, wash their clothes in the same sinks as they used for the toilets, wring out the water with their hands, and then hang the clothes up to dry on the rope lines. The room was only open one hour a day.

Then we arrived at the cellblock itself, behind a heavy, noisy gate. The individual cells ran along a corridor lined with bars, and as I stepped inside, I could see faces pressed into each open space. There's nothing to do in jail. It's like watching your life in slow motion. The boredom—the complete nothingness—makes you want to kill yourself. You come up with anything to fill the space: even a new cockroach crossing the wall will be something to talk about. So, at the sound of the gate opening, all the prisoners rushed to the bars and started looking. The noise was so loud: the sounds of them pushing against bars, pushing against each other, the screech of everyone talking at once, "*Jadid, jadid,*" Arabic for "new one."

I desperately wanted to cover my face.

For more than a decade, I'd fought with my family, fought with my ex-husband, fought with my society not to cover my face. My face is my identity. No one will cover it. I'm proud of my face. If my face bothers you, don't look. Turn your own face away, take your eyes off me. If you are seduced by merely looking at my face, that is your problem. Do not tell me to cover it. You cannot punish me simply because you cannot control yourself.

But now, passing through this crush of women, I wished I were veiled. I didn't want to be seen. Not in this place. I was not a criminal. I did not do anything wrong. I just wanted to throw back my head and scream. The pain was almost overwhelming.

We have a phrase in Arabic: "He swept the floor with my dignity." I felt like my dignity was being wiped on that foul-smelling, hard concrete floor.

Zahrah got out one of her many keys, walked to the door of one cell, and opened the lock. She pulled the bars behind me, and that was it.

The women inside crowded around, speaking in broken Arabic. "You're Saudi? You're Saudi?" they asked. They were mostly housemaids and domestic workers from Sri Lanka, the Philippines, Indonesia, Somalia, and India. They were all speaking over each other. It was like being in an aviary with flocks of every type of bird, screeching and calling and beating their wings. Out of 168 inmates in the prison, only seven were Saudi, and four of these were not even prisoners, they were merely in temporary detention. There is no detention center for women, so the authorities jail them instead.

A women in a black hijab made her way toward me. She was dressed the way many Saudi women do inside their houses, and when she spoke to me, it was with a Saudi accent. "Come with me," she said, taking my hand. We walked to a room with twelve bunk beds and white fluorescent lights flickering from the ceiling. Ropes, sagging with clothes, were strung all around. It felt like standing in a closet. The walls were covered in plastic bags, filled with partly eaten bread, plastic spoons, and more clothes. Still more clothes were stuffed under the beds. The beds themselves were draped in fabric, like a curtain, because that was the only way to sleep: no one ever turned off the harsh, faintly buzzing lights overhead. Their tubes glowed day and night. There was only one tiny window at the top of the room, closed off with tight iron bars so that only the littlest bit of light and no fresh air drifted in. The room smelled damp, like a carpet that has been flooded with water; like food; like diapers, because there was a newborn baby; like hair oil and creams; like sweat, days of sweat that had not been scrubbed off in a long time.

And everywhere, there were cockroaches. Thousands and thousands of cockroaches scurried across the floors, the walls. Cockroaches on the bed, on the floor, on the food.

The Saudi woman was named Nuwayer. Her bed was the first on the right. She told me, this is my bed, please sit down. I didn't know if I should trust her, but I sat. She had small eyes and was maybe a little older than me. I couldn't see her hair, but it looked like it was in two braids. She was wearing a black dress with flowers on it, and she had a big scar running down her face. I never asked her how she got that scar. I have scars myself, from my childhood, so I never ask people about theirs.

She started asking me questions: Why are you here? What happened? She couldn't believe that I had been brought to this prison for driving a car. She refused to believe it. After a while, there was nothing more I could say. How could I prove that I was not lying?

Finally, I looked at her and I said, "Nuwayer, I'm so, so tired. I haven't slept for two days." I didn't care about eating anymore.

She said, "It's okay, just sleep in my bed."

I could see the cockroaches climbing over everything. In the outside world, if I saw one cockroach, I used bleach, disinfectants, anything to kill them and clean every surface they'd touched. I hated cockroaches that much. Also, cockroaches usually run away when they see people: they scurry off into dark corners when you turn on the light. But here, they just crawled, heedless of the light, over everything, under everything. As I was talking to Nuwayer, I felt them on top of my head, trying to crawl up the hem of my abaya. I kept batting them off, shrieking, "Cockroach! Oh, cockroach!" And Nuwayer was so kind, so calm. She told me that I would get used to them.

Nuwayer told me to take off my abaya, but I insisted on leaving it on. I was still hoping to leave, if not by the end of this day, then by the next day. But first I had to sleep. I must have basically fainted on her bed. It was so noisy: the women, the kids, the crying newborn, the click click click of the cockroaches on the floor, the walls, the plastic. But I slept. Not peacefully though. It was like when you have been swimming in the ocean for too long, and when you lie down at the end of day, all you can feel is the pitch and roll of the waves all over again. As I slept, I felt my day all over again: the pain, the humiliation, the indignity. I dreamed of crying in front of a man who did not care. I dreamed of a girl pushing her rough, gloved hands over me and in me. In my sleep, I tried to push these thoughts away. I tried to think of my son. I tried to think of my sister-in-law telling me on the phone that he was okay, that his father had come and gotten him.

It turned out that I didn't need to call anyone in my family to tell them where I had gone. The newspapers, the television, the radio, and the Internet had already done it for me. By the time I'd fallen asleep, all of Saudi Arabia knew that Manal al-Sharif, the woman who drove, was in jail.

3

Dirty Girls

I was born on the floor of our cramped apartment in the city of Mecca on April 25, 1979. My mother was alone, except for my older sister, who was barely much more than a toddler herself. My father had been out when she went into labor, and under Saudi rules and customs, my mother could not be admitted without her male guardian or a mahram to accompany her to the hospital. There were no exceptions. She couldn't even call for help because our apartment had no phone.

I was fortunate to be her fifth child, and the third to survive; her body knew how to have children. When she heard my first cry, she asked my sister, "What did I bring into the world?" And Muna, who had been able to talk since she was about one year old, looked at me on a towel, covered in blood and afterbirth, and said simply, "Ne'ama." Ne'ama is the name of one of my cousins from my mother's side, and in Arabic it means "bliss." My sister knew I was a girl and had named me. But my older cousin Saadiya, from my father's side, changed my name to Manal. She said that Ne'ama was an uncommon name in Saudi and warned that kids would make fun of me. She was right, and she spared me a lot of bullying in school. So it was that my parents' children are a matched set, Muna, Manal, and Muhammad—but my mother and father always called me "Ne'ama."

My mother was Libyan. She was born in 1947 in a hospital in Alexandria, Egypt, where her father had moved his family during the Italian colonial period. But she always considered herself Libyan. Her family was prestigious, proud, and wealthy. At one point they were responsible for overseeing the Ottoman Empire's vast treasury in North Africa. This is where the family name came from: *bayt al mal* was what the Ottomans called the minister of finance at the time. My grandfather was a successful merchant and owned property across a vast swath of territory between Libya and Egypt. When he moved to Egypt, he was given the honorific nickname of Sheikh of the Maghareba, or chief of the Moroccans, a loose reference to the many peoples of North Africa living to the west of Egypt. My mother was raised in a lavish house in the port city with servants and attendants and every material comfort a girl of that era could imagine, everything except love.

My father was born poor in the village of Tarfa'a in Wadi Fatima, a valley less than twenty miles outside Mecca. No one ever recorded the date of his birth, although we all believe he was born ten years before his official government age. When he was required to get a national ID and a driver's license, the state simply assigned him the first day of the month of Rajab. Most undocumented people have that date as their birthday—there is a joke that on the first of Rajab, you can say happy birthday to half of the Saudi nation. Growing up, all of my girlfriends' parents were also listed as being born on that date. It is as if you suddenly told half of America that their birthday is going to be on July 1.

My father never knew his own father, who died before he was born. He never spoke of his father or his lineage, although it is also a noble one. Nearly everyone in the Fatima Valley belonged to a single tribe, the Ashraf (plural of al Sharif) tribe. Our tribe can trace its origins back to the Prophet Muhammad (Peace Be Upon Him, hereafter

PBUH); we are the descendants of his grandson Hassan, the child of Muhammad's youngest daughter, Fatima, and her husband, Ali bin Abi Taleb, known as the Fourth Caliph, who was also Muhammad's cousin (Peace Be Upon Them). The influence of the al-Sharif tribe has been felt across the Arab world. In the last century alone, al-Sharifs have governed the Hejaz region of the Saudi kingdom, and have ruled as kings in Iraq, Yemen, Jordan, Morocco, Syria, and Palestine.

My own father, whom we always called Abouya, which means "my father" in his native Hejazi dialect, never went to school. He is illiterate, although he has memorized all the basic phrases for the prayers. But he is curious. He would often listen to the radio and he followed and argued about politics and sports. Once I could read, I would read him the newspaper and a few times tried to teach him how to read and write. My mother had been to school through the fourth grade, so she could read enough to fill out our school registration forms, which she did with a fierce determination.

My parents would never have met if not for Islam. As young men, my father and his elder brother, Uncle Sa'ad, moved to Mecca to work. My dad had a car that he used to ferry pious Muslims back and forth between the airport outside the bustling port city of Jeddah and the sacred places of Mecca. He was busiest during the month of the hajj, the once-in-a-lifetime visit required of all able Muslims to the holiest place in the Muslim world, the Grand Mosque of Mecca and the dark granite Kaaba, literally "the cube," which stands inside. The Kaaba is revered in Islam as the first house of worship, built by the Prophet Ibrahim (PBUH), who is known to Christians and Jews as Abraham. It is the place toward which all Muslims face when they perform their five daily prayers. When a Muslim dies, tradition dictates that for burial his or her face must be turned toward the Kaaba. The rest of the year, my father drove other pilgrims who traveled to the city to observe lesser rites; devout Muslims believe a prayer in the presence of the Kaaba is worth a hundred thousand prayers elsewhere.

My father, Massoud al-Sharif, first laid eyes on my mother when she came from Egypt with her family to perform the hajj. It was as if their meeting was fated. My father was divorced, and so was my mother. When she returned home, he flew to Alexandria, showed up at her house, and asked her father for permission to marry. Her father said yes.

Years later, Abouya would say he married my mother for her beauty, and she was indeed very beautiful. Mama, in turn, would say that she married my father to escape the stepmother she hated: her own mother had died when she was only four years old. But perhaps she wanted to escape from everything. Not once did I hear her wish blessings on her father's soul, something that Islamic religion and culture require of children after the death of a parent. "God does not wish mercy upon my father," she used to say, whenever his name was mentioned. "He robbed me of my son, and my education too."

During her first marriage, Mama had given birth to a son, Essam. But when her marriage dissolved, Mama had to leave her baby behind: her father would not allow her to return to his house with a child. Mama saw her elder son just one time in all those intervening years, in 1990, during a visit to Libya, when Essam was about twenty-one years old.

My grandfather had also refused to allow Mama to continue her education past the fourth grade because Egyptian schools were mixed. Once she turned ten, my grandfather would not allow her to learn in the presence of boys.

So Mama left her life of comfort and even opulence in Alexandria to marry a Saudi man with no education and a menial job, to live in a walk-up apartment without regular running water or a telephone. My mother, however, refused to live like a typical Saudi woman. She refused to stay shut up in the apartment. She would go out alone, without her guardian or a mahram. She refused to have no means of employment, so she sewed, which had been her childhood hobby. She sewed dresses for my sister and me, and she made clothes for her friends and acquaintances, earning her own small income independent of my father. It was our mother who took us to get vaccinated at the health clinic, who decided where we could go, what we could do, and what was safe. And it was our mother who was determined that each of her children should receive an education. She was the one who went by herself to enroll us in school, first primary school, then middle school, and then secondary school. She even registered my younger brother in the boys' school, something almost unheard of for a woman.

I remember how the school guard at the boys' primary school stopped her at the gate and barred her from entering, but Mama refused to move until the deputy administrator came out to see her. Again and again, he tried to dismiss her and send her on her way, his tongue clucking against the roof of his mouth, repeating that my father had to be present to register my brother. But my mother refused to leave, and finally, the deputy administrator relented. Almost twenty-five years later, he came to my mother's funeral and told my brother that Mama was the reason why he received an education. Hearing this story for the first time, my brother broke down in tears. My mother's persistence is the reason all three of her children graduated from university at the top of our classes. Today, my sister is a medical doctor, my brother a petroleum geoscientist, and I have a bachelor's degree in computer science.

In other ways, my mother did become a more typical Saudi woman. She gave up the colorful head scarves and bright clothes that she had worn in Egypt, covering herself in the shapeless black abaya. And she tolerated another aspect of being a Saudi wife: my father was free to beat her. Not all Saudi wives are beaten; as far as I know, none of my aunts were. But that did not matter in our home. For decades, until 2012, Saudi Arabia had no domestic violence codes to protect women or children. And that meant parents could also beat their children.

I considered Abouya's bamboo cane the sixth person in our home. The cane was a familiar sight in almost any house in Mecca; very few of my friends were fortunate enough not to know its sting. Abouya replaced his bamboo cane every autumn, to coincide with the beginning of the new academic year. As we covered our new school notebooks in paper wrapping, he covered his new cane in brightly colored chrome tape, and hung it up menacingly for all to see. He didn't beat us because we were lazy at school; the three of us always ranked among the top students, not only in our classes and our school but in all the schools in Mecca. I had a box of certificates and trophies, yet I was beaten regularly, for reasons that I still do not understand. If one of us knew we were about to be beaten, at first we used to hide the cane, but the trick never worked on Abouya. If he couldn't find the cane, he would use the water hose from the bathroom. We soon learned that the lashes from the hard, thick rubber hose were far more painful than those of the bamboo.

When Mama beat us, she used her bare hands. She slapped us and pinched the inside of our thighs, and when we outran her or managed to scramble away, she threw anything within easy reach: a slipper, a plate, even her sharp, pointed sewing scissors. I have two scars on my forehead and a third under my left eye that will forever remind me of my mother's furious beatings. When a photographer suggested to me that we hide those three scars using Photoshop, I refused. He couldn't understand why, and told me gently, "You're strange. Women usually want me to hide every flaw on their face, and you're asking me to do the opposite!" In fact, to this day he can't comprehend why I am so adamant. But my view is that while there are some scars that we might wish to hide because the spiritual or mental pain they represent is far greater than the physical pain caused to us at the time of injury, there are also some scars that we want to see whenever we look in the mirror. Because these scars serve as a valuable reminder of our past. My scars teach me that I am stronger than what caused them.

Whenever I look at the scars on my face, I feel a renewed sense of resolve that my children should have a happy life, full of love and encouragement, free from screaming, scolding, and neglect. That they should never endure a single act of physical violence.

One of my favorite Arab fairy tales is about a young prince who took lessons from a tutor. Those lessons were designed to prepare him for his future as king by educating him in literature, wisdom, and governmental affairs. One day, at the start of his lessons, without cause or warning, the tutor slapped the small prince hard across the face. Years passed. The prince grew up and became king. On the day he ascended the throne, the newly crowned king asked for his old tutor to be brought before him. Angrily, the king asked the tutor, "Do you remember the day you slapped me without reason?" He continued, "I've never forgotten that day. Now, I will take my revenge. But first, tell me, why did you do such a thing?"

"Your Majesty," the tutor replied. "I knew that one day you would become king, and I wanted you to taste injustice when you were young. For he who has already tasted injustice will never force others to suffer the same." The story ends with the coda that the king remembered that slap whenever his power might have led him to rule with oppression, and instead he always ruled with justice. It is too soon to say how many of my generation may have learned to despise injustice as a consequence of the beatings, verbal abuse, and general cruelty that we suffered as children. But I know that I have, and I know that I will carry that lesson with me always.

——

The five of us—Abouya, Mama, Muna, Muhammad, and I—lived in a neighborhood of downtown Mecca called Al-Utaibiyyah. Just outside the city, in a nearby cave, the Prophet Muhammad (PBUH) received the first revelations of what would become the Koran, which to Muslims is the final word of God. If you tell almost anyone in the Islamic world that you are from Mecca, they will exclaim, "You are a neighbor of God's house." Even the water that bubbles up from the Zamzam spring inside the Grand Mosque is said to have traveled to Mecca directly from paradise. We were a quick twenty-minute walk from the Grand Mosque, a mere five minutes by bus. But almost no one would want to live in our neighborhood. Our section of Mecca was ringed by slums, and some of what happened there—foul language, bad manners, and trouble—spilled over onto our streets. It was commonplace to hear an insult, followed by a frenzy of beating and punching, biting, and pulling hair. Inside the slums, more serious fights could spark in a second. A brief argument, a flash of weapons, and then one man would inflict a deadly injury upon another right in front of anyone passing by. As a result, my parents would never allow my sister and me to wander the streets. My brother could only go out to buy food and then had to come right back. And the entire time, my mother would be waiting by the window for his return, afraid.

There were about sixty-six slums in Mecca when I was growing up. They had nothing: no running water, no basic infrastructure, no real sanitation, no schools, just makeshift places to study the Koran. One of my good friends from school lived on the edge of one of them. I was never allowed to go into her house; instead, I could walk with Mama to meet her to exchange something like a schoolbook or schoolwork. Even as Mama and I walked toward her neighborhood, we could smell the horrible odor of the common toilets and waste in the gutter. The kids and teenagers in the streets said all kinds of vulgar things, although my friend was very polite. Many of these teenagers would buy small bottles of cologne for about five riyals and then drink them for the alcohol. There were also drugs. Every time I went with Mama, she would walk very fast, rushing past the awful sights, sounds, and smells. Sometimes we brought food from our kitchen to the family, and when it was date season, they would sometimes tell us to bring our date box, which they would fill with lush, plump dates that they had picked on a date farm. But we never stayed.

Although non-Muslims are forbidden to enter Mecca, the city is the most diverse in the entire Saudi kingdom, home to untold numbers of Muslim immigrants, legal and illegal. There are parts of the city where you will not hear one word of Arabic spoken. Each nationality has its own community and its own varied reasons for staying. Some arrived to build buildings and study the Koran. Others came as merchants or even refugees. There are enclaves of people from Egypt, Syria, Nigeria, Indonesia, Bangladesh, Pakistan, India, Burma, Turkey, and Yemen, all trying to get by. In various corners of the city, Nigerian men wash cars and Nigerian women sell dried seeds, stored in huge turbans on their heads, or come and work in houses for next to nothing. We had a Nigerian woman who cleaned and did washing and ironing for about 400 riyals, or about 105 dollars a month, and we were a family that didn't have running water all of the time.

A sizable number of immigrants came because they wanted to study *Ilm* (which translates as "religious knowledge," a key concept in Islam) and the Koran, in the place where both began. Generations ago, before the kingdom was founded, these people were able to remain, and eventually they became Saudi citizens. But in the decades since, hundreds of thousands more have come for the annual hajj or for study and then have simply stayed behind, melting into the city. It is possible to have two families from the same country, and the one that arrived earlier might have Saudi citizenship, while the later arrival must retain its original nationality. Yet many pilgrims still want to stay: even the people who are deported seem to find a way to return. When I was a child, one house in the city might hold forty people, all crowded in together. In some ways, the Dammam Women's Prison was like a microcosm of the underside of Mecca, a cacophony of languages and nationalities all wedged together inside a single, tiny space.

We couldn't afford to move to a nicer section of the city; the rent there would be at least two or three times more. So we stayed indoors. The apartments we lived in were always small. We would have a sitting room for eating, studying, and watching TV, which was also where we slept, on mattresses that we stacked up against the walls in the daytime. In one apartment, my brother, sister, and I slept on the sitting room floor, my dad slept on a bed in the sitting room, and my mother slept in the hallway. In another, my father had a bed in the bedroom, my brother and I slept on the bedroom floor, my mother still slept in the hallway, and my sister slept in the guest room. But compared to some families, we had plenty of room. My uncle, who was wealthier than my father, had nine kids, and they all slept together. We couldn't believe that there were places in the world where kids had their own rooms like we saw in the movies. Private space was largely unheard of. If you fought with a sister or brother, you couldn't go off to your own room and close the door. If I wanted to be by myself, I might go to the balcony. When I got a little older, I had a portable, plastic storage closet. I used to put it together in the middle of the sitting room and cover the top with sheets to make a curtain, so I would have part of the room for myself. I could write and read and be by myself, until my brother would come along and demolish it.

Saudi houses and apartments are usually filled with people: children, aunts and uncles, all kinds of friends and relatives. Neighbors might knock on the door and come in with food, or send their kids back and forth. My mother was known for her North African couscous. My cousins loved my mother's cooking so much that when she made this dish, she would make two pots, and Abdullah, Uncle Sa'ad's older son, would come over to get one. My uncle's house would always be crowded with an endless cycle of coffee and tea and snacks put out for arriving guests. Often, the adults would kick the children out of the rooms because we made so much noise. We would be sent up to the roof to play soccer. Sometimes we would play in the streets. My parents wouldn't have allowed it, but they never knew. Those are nearly the only times I can remember running around in the streets.

But my uncle and his wife rarely came to visit our house, even though for a number of years we lived right across the street. Nor would my mother go to theirs. She would only send them her couscous pot. The only one of my father's relatives who made my mother feel welcome was my father's oldest sister, Aunt Zein, who was named after an al-Sharif queen and was nicknamed "peace dove." Even then, my mother would not visit her house when my uncle and his family were expected to be there.

——

Family mattered most during the yearly celebration of Eid al-Fitr, the happy end to the monthlong dawn-to-dusk fast of Ramadan. Eid was my favorite holiday. It began at sundown with nighttime shopping, perhaps for fabric for new clothes or shoes, but always ended at Shara'a al-Halawiyyāt, the nickname we had for a street in the Thieves' Market filled with confectionery vendors, literally the "sweets street." Beneath the glittering lights and decorations, we would stroll past stall after stall of vendors in white robes, colorful vests, and Aleppo turbans, listening to each seller as he promised the softest, sweetest sweets: "Turkish delight as you can't find it anywhere else. Whoever chooses to eat any kind except this will break his teeth!" Amid the bustle of the market, the *saqa'*, or water carrier, would wander by, offering copper cups of cold water to quench the thirst of those who had neither eaten nor drunk during the fasting days.

After we passed by the chewy *halawa*, or Turkish delights, there were all kinds of other tempting sweets and candies set out for the holidays: *al-limoniyyah*, a colored sugar candy with a piece of almond in the center, and *al-loziyyah*, toasted almonds with a sugar coating. My favorite and the most expensive of all were Mackintosh's chocolates, sold in a white aluminum tin with pink edges. A man in the famous red uniform and black hat of Britain's Queen's Guard clasped the hand of his smartly dressed female companion and beamed out at us from a picture on the tin's lid. Mama didn't allow us to eat Mackintosh's sweets—they were for guests only—but we always managed to pilfer one or two while her attention was elsewhere.

Eid was a time to make our apartment beautiful, to bring the mattresses and stuffed cotton cushions to the upholsterer to be refurbished, to take down the curtains and wash them. My mother prepared the cups for tea and coffee and infused the rooms with the scent of aloewood, which was too expensive to use any other time of the year. We always spent the night of Eid baking *ma'amoul*, a shortbread cookie stuffed with nuts, and *ghureeba*, a buttery cookie. All these years later, the smell of freshly baked cakes and cookies still takes me back to the Eids of my childhood. After we finished baking, Mama applied henna to my palm and my sister's, and wrapped them in plastic bags before we slept. We didn't untie the bag until Eid prayers.

Mecca is the only city in Saudi Arabia in which the holy month of Ramadan and the day of Eid al-Fitr are welcomed with a twenty-one-cannon salute, a custom that survives from the days of the Ottoman Empire, and one of the few Meccan traditions that was not undone by the rising Wahhabi-Salafi militancy, which promotes a fundamentalist reinterpretation of Islam. On the actual day of the holiday, my father would take us to Mecca's Masjid al-Haram, the Grand Mosque—to attend al-Mashhad, the Eid prayers. We wore our special Eid clothes, and Mama made sure to carry with her a portion of the sweet halawa and a bundle of small change to distribute to the children we passed as we left the mosque after praying. When we arrived home, Mama arranged our own plate of halawa and prepared tea and Arabic coffee with cardamom for any guests who would stop by. She distributed the freshly baked cookies to our neighbors.

That day, we would begin the formal holiday celebration with an Iftar feast, literally a breaking of the fast, at Aunt Zein's, then on the second day at Uncle Sa'ad's, and on the third day at our apartment. But while during the first two days my aunt and uncle's rooms were crowded with cousins and relatives, my mother was not among them. And on the third day, although friends and neighbors came by, none of our relatives ever gathered in our apartment, and not one of my father's family ever knocked at our door. I never asked Abouya why this was, but I could see the hurt in my mother's eyes. "Mama," I finally asked her, "why does no one visit us?"

"Because I'm *gharība* [foreign]," came her curt reply.

I was a child, so I didn't understand the complexity of this particular situation. My mother felt shunned, but in truth my father's family had not rejected her. Before my father had married my mother, he had been married to the sister of his brother's wife. The friction that my mother felt came largely from the severing of those multiple ties. And so my mother isolated herself, even though most of my father's family appreciated her generosity, her many talents, and her perfect etiquette. It was not until her death, not until my father's extended family came to pay their condolences, not until I was long grown, that I began to understand any of this. For all of my childhood, I felt like an outcast.

On the second day of Eid, and despite Mama's objections, we always went with Abouya to eat breakfast and lunch at the house of Uncle Sa'ad, my father's older—and only—brother. The atmosphere in his house was very different from Aunt Zein's. Because money was tight, Mama bought my sister and me only one dress each for Eid; in fact, often she sewed them herself. I wore this dress on all special occasions throughout the whole of the following year, since I would outgrow it by the time the next Eid came around. Invariably, when I entered Uncle Sa'ad's house, one of his older daughters would say with a sneer, "Oh look, the same dress as yesterday!"

The youngest of Uncle Sa'ad's daughters, Amal, was the same age as me. Though she always wore a new dress on the second day of Eid, she never said anything about my "repeated" dress and remained my friend throughout my childhood. Usually on the holiday, the younger children would go up to play on the roof, where the girls would show off their new dresses: Amal's was always a touch more lavish than everyone else's. Together, the girls and boys would also play a tag game known in Arabic as Shar'at, where one child chases the others, and those who are tagged before reaching the "safe wall" are forced out to wait until the next round. Other times, Amal and I would sit quietly and draw and paint and read comic books.

In the final part of the celebration at my uncle's house, *eidiyyāt*, money given as gifts to celebrate Eid, would be handed out. At Aunt Zein's house, the eidiyyāt was given out first, tucked into small bags that my aunt would press into my palm and my brother's when we walked through the door. (Eidiyyāt varies in amount, from anywhere from five riyals to more than one hundred. Favored children receive more eidiyyāt from their relatives. Aunt Zein was always very generous with me.)

I remember early on at my uncle's, I got my small purse and hung it over my shoulder in preparation for the gift giving. Then my

uncle's older daughters called the children to gather around in a circle, where one by one my cousins would push the eidiyyāt into their
outstretched palms. They called every name, except for mine and
my brother's and sister's. At first, I assumed that they simply forgot
us. But each year it was the same, until I stopped taking my purse at
all. Then there came the year when I thought I understood the reason. My sister had inherited the same milky, fair complexion as my
mother, a feature not usually found within my father's family; among
his tribe tanned skin prevails. As we entered my uncle's house that
year, I had heard other women asking in curious voices, "Who are
these girls?"

If someone asks about a child—boy or girl—it is customary in
Saudi culture to refer to them in relation to their father. You only
mention their mother's family if you want to belittle them. To the
question, "Who are these girls?" I was expecting my cousins to answer, "The daughters of Uncle Massoud." But instead my female
cousins replied, "The daughters of the Egyptian." They of course
knew my mother's name and that she was Libyan, not Egyptian. But
they had learned to say that my sister and I were "the daughters of
the Egyptian."

———

Saudi families, almost universally, reflect a contradictory combination of extreme intimacy and extreme segregation and impene-
trable privacy. We sleep in common rooms and travel in and out
of each other's apartments, but we keep our windows covered, and
indeed often have no windows that face the outside world. In many
houses, men and women live on different sides, and enter and exit
via different doors. We are a culture of peeking, where women peek
from behind windows or on the other side of doors to see who might
have come to visit. We do have apartments with balconies, but those
apartments were designed by Egyptian civil engineers and others
from cultures that ring the Mediterranean Sea. In those countries,
people gather on balconies, sip their dark, aromatic coffee, and call

down to passersby on the streets, whether friends or the vegetable seller. They do not live in the dusty, blazing, dry, desert heat of the Saudi kingdom. In Mecca, we did not sit on our balconies. Women might use them to spy on the surrounding streets, watching cars or other vehicles, but we did not socialize on our balconies. We called down to no one, drank nothing. Our own balcony stored an extra water tank. I would sometimes flatten myself against it to watch kids playing below, but even as a child, I considered balconies a useless waste of space.

More often than not, we were not taught the rules of our lives, we simply absorbed them. Just as our first day of Eid was always spent at Aunt Zein's house, just as my father always brought the same sweet fried dough balls (*halwa al-zalabya*) and the same sesame sweets called *halwa tahiniyya* from a shop named Abu Nar, the most famous halawa store in the whole of Mecca, and just as my aunt always prepared sweet vermicelli with sugar and cardamom, and set out plates of white cheese, olives, and Indian-style mango pickle and the same Meccan dishes of *debyāza*, *fūl mabakher*, and *khobz al-shreek* bread, we always sat in the same arrangements.

Aunt Zein lived with her husband, Uncle Hamed, and six of their children on the first floor of a two-story house. Their eldest child was a professor of Islamic studies at a university and lived on the second floor with his own wife and family. They had two sons, Hammam and Hossam, who were close in age to my brother and me, as well as to Zein's youngest daughter, Hanan, and to Amal, uncle Sa'ad's youngest daughter. When we were small, we would all crowd in together around one *sofra,* a plastic sheet that we spread on the floor, picnic-style, to eat our way through the Iftar spread. My older female cousins, the other daughters of my uncle Sa'ad, never joined us. They didn't want to share our *sofra* with us. They sat in a separate area and ate at a separate sofra to avoid mixing with Aunt Zein's older sons, their male cousins, teenagers and men whom they could presumably marry. As a small girl I was annoyed with this and wondered why all the cousins didn't just sit together. I made a promise to myself that I would never sit separately from my favorite cousins, nor would we stop playing soccer and riding bikes together when I came to visit.

But when I was twelve, Hammam and Hossam were banned from my life with no warning and no explanation. We could not say so much as hello to each other; I never got to say goodbye. Today, if I passed them on the street, I would not even recognize the men they have become.

———

Unwritten Saudi rules determined far more than my holiday celebrations, they cast a shadow over nearly my entire childhood.

In our apartment in Al-Utaibiyyah, we had a neighbor with a twelve-year-old son. He would often come to visit us along with his mother and his sisters. But once he came alone, and while the mothers were elsewhere, he asked me to take off my underwear. I was about six years old, and I feared him from that moment on. I knew better than to mention it to Mama, but after that day, I stayed with her whenever he visited us, refusing to leave her side until he was gone. Then this boy had made the mistake of asking my sister to remove her underwear. Unlike me, Muna would not keep quiet. She told Mama right away.

Mama questioned my sister and me about the details of what had happened, but I was too shocked to speak and afraid that she would hit me because of what this boy had asked me to do. I denied that he had asked me to remove my underwear.

The usual custom would have been to wait for my father to return home from work and have him deal with the issue, but Mama's patience would not allow it. She pulled her abaya over her head and dragged my sister and me by our hands to the neighbor's home. My mother found the boy and started screaming. He yelled back, and although they battled with words alone, to me standing there it seemed dangerously close to physical fighting. "I swear to God," my mother warned him, "if you ever approach either of my daughters again—in the building or on the street—I will cut off your male parts and hang them round your neck!"

The boy hadn't in fact touched us; his advances had been verbal only. But Mama said that if it were not for the *sitr*—the veil of protection—of Allah over us, things could have been much worse. Afterward, she made a promise between herself and God. Believing that He had kept us safe, that He had allowed us to retain our precious and all-important virginity, she vowed that she would fast every Monday and Thursday for the rest of her life. Mama adhered to these two days of fasting without fail. It was only when I heard of my mother's vow that I became fully aware to what extent a girl's virginity determines her fate in Saudi society.

Although Mama never told our father what had happened, my sister and I lived out the rest of our childhoods under a kind of house arrest. We were never again allowed to play with our neighbors' children in the corridor between the apartment doorways or on the roof of the building. The most we were permitted to do was to open the *shara'ah*, a small window in the front door, so we could watch the other children play, and perhaps occasionally use a water gun ourselves from behind this narrow window. Whether or not he ever knew about our neighbor, Abouya was equally strict; he permitted us only to enter two houses in Mecca: Aunt Zein's and Uncle Sa'ad's.

It did not matter even when our family moved from one apartment to another. No matter where we lived, the rules were always the same and absolute. But they only applied to Muna and me. Mama and, later, Muhammad were free to leave. So, for hours on end, Muna and I would be locked in the apartment, alone.

We did all kinds of crazy things. The apartment did not have water all the time, so whenever the water did come on, Mama told us to fill up the tank on the balcony and then to turn off the water once it was full. One time we didn't turn off the water, and the tank overflowed, sending water all over the balcony. We quickly realized that with the right preparations, we could have our own outdoor pool. We put down a towel to trap the water and keep it away from the drain and then took off our clothes, until we were wearing nothing but our underwear. Like little mermaids, we went water skiing on the water on the balcony floor. Another time, I got out of the shower with my wet, long curly hair. There was a small opening, a type of window, on the balcony, and I could slip my head through it and dangle my hair down toward the ground. Anyone looking up would have thought that there was a dead body on the balcony, its lifeless head hanging above the street.

We spent hours, days, and weeks like this alone, particularly in the summers, when there was no school and nothing to do. At least once a week, no one was here at all when Mama went off to the Grand Mosque to conduct her fast, give her gifts, and keep her pledge to Allah in thanks for Him keeping us safe. To amuse ourselves while she was out, we smoked the small, expensive cigarettes that my uncle had given my father as a gift and that my mother had hidden away because my father smoked other brands. One time, we put oil in our hair and then decided to play a game we had invented. We lit candles and I danced around my sister singing, "Happy birthday to you" and waving a candle. Suddenly the candle fell from my hands onto her oiled hair. We both started screaming. I remembered a safety program from TV about a spray that put out fire. I ran all around the apartment looking for the spray. I found a can of Raid and started spraying it, but Raid was not a fire extinguisher. It was designed to kill insects. My sister lost all her hair. Mama was furious. The beating she gave me afterward almost killed me.

Perhaps the worst of all was the time Muna announced that she was going to do a trick. She started climbing up the door and asked me to hand her the broomstick. I gave her the stick and just then she slipped. The stick went through the roof of her mouth and into her nose. We were alone, and she was bleeding everywhere, but we had no phone and we were locked inside, so all we could do was wait. Muna bled until Mama came home. She was rushed to the hospital and they stitched the hole closed, but she almost died. Afterward, I got another beating from Mama.

All those years of confinement with one another also meant that my sister and I would often fight between ourselves. We fought in the house, at school, anywhere. Muna was very strong, and I was very thin, so she had the advantage. One time at school I was eating breakfast and Muna and her friends were cleaning the paintbrushes after doing watercolors. Muna said, "Watch me" to her friends and then walked up and spilled the dirty brush water all over my face in front of everyone. I grabbed my orange-colored drink and splashed it on her face in return. Then Muna grabbed my hair, pulled me from my seat, and dragged me over to the dirt, where she started pummeling me. No one stopped her. Finally, after she walked away, the older sister of one of my friends took me to the bathroom and washed my face. I couldn't tell my teachers what had happened because Muna was my sister. I couldn't tell my mother because if I told her, Mama would give me a second beating, probably worse than Muna's. I learned to keep my mouth shut and take whatever came.

———

There was one pain that my sister and I shared, a moment of such deep wounding that the scars will never fully heal. The story of these wounds begins with my older female cousins, the same ones who mocked my single dress and my "Egyptian" mother. "Dirty girls," they said of my sister and me. "They still haven't been circumcised."

I knew *circumcision* was a fearful word before I knew its meaning. I had once seen an elderly woman named Hasaneyya visiting my uncle's house: my cousins told me that she was the one who performed "circumcision" on girls. If my sister or I failed to behave properly during our visits, we were told, "Be careful, or we will call Aunt Hasaneyya to come and circumcise you." Today, my body still clenches at the mention of her name.

One morning, I woke to hear my sister crying in front of the closed bathroom door, making a sorrowful appeal to my father, who was on the other side. When I came over to her she told me, in between sobs, "There are two women in the sitting room with Mama. They've come to circumcise us."

I still didn't understand what circumcision was, but my small mind realized it was something connected to weeping and wailing. I started to cry alongside my sister, and as my father emerged from the bathroom, we grabbed his long, loose robe and hung on in a state of utter hysteria. Abouya dragged us to the sitting room, where Mama sat with two dark-skinned women. They were swathed in black and smelled strongly of aloewood. They had deep long scars on their cheeks and liquid kohl painted around their eyes. A black case sat before them. I wondered to myself if circumcision was what had caused their sunken facial scars. My father asked them quietly to leave the house, and despite my mother's objections, they did so. But the idea did not leave with them. Instead, it returned, in the guise of a man.

I was eight years old. It was a normal morning during the first days of the summer vacation, and I remember I was wearing a long, yellow *jalabiya* with embroidered red roses and green leaves, which Aunt Zein had given to me. I had taken out my stories and my coloring books and was sitting on the floor in front of the television screen. In the fall, I would be starting third grade.

We heard the doorbell ring, and my brother and I raced to answer it. Two men and a woman stood outside. I knew the first of the men, Abdulaleem, an Egyptian barber and a friend of my father; the second man was his son. I had never seen the woman before.

I remember what happened next as if it were yesterday: it was painful and degrading and left deformities that serve as a constant reminder.

The actual event was over quickly. My sister disappeared, hiding herself in a place where she believed no one could find her. Mama took my brother into the other room, while I stayed with my father, the two men, and the woman. It didn't take me long to grasp what was going on: my circumcision, after all this time, was about to become real. Sitting in that room, I recalled everything I knew about circumcision thus far: my sister's wailing; my cousins' threats; the sunken scars on the faces of the women swathed in black.

In one swift motion, the barber's son grabbed me by my shoulders, the woman opened my legs, and I began to cry and scream hysterically. My father brought the water hose from the bathroom, the same hose that he used to beat us when he could not find his bamboo cane. He stood in front of me, threatening to whip me if I didn't stop resisting. I stopped struggling.

The "operation" was performed in a few snips with a single pair of scissors and no anesthetic. The blood flowed red and wet down my legs. In that moment—and forever after—I wished with all my heart that I had kept on screaming and struggling, because the sting of the water hose was infinitely less than the agony I experienced that morning.

When my circumcision was completed, they found my sister. Because the scissors used during my procedure were blunt and a bit dull, they had managed to cut only the upper part of the clitoris. On my sister, they used a sharp razor blade. They removed everything.

Soaked in sweat and salty tears, and overcome with humiliation and searing pain, I hid my face under the covers and slept as if I had been knocked unconscious. At one point I felt a hand under the duvet. It reached toward my wound, and I sprang out of bed in fear. The hand belonged to the barber, who was clutching an ointment to smear on the wound. I ran, feeling nothing except the warm blood gushing from between my thighs. Very soon after, I lost consciousness.

I bled for three days; my sister told me afterward that my face turned yellow. They couldn't take me to the doctor: although there is no official rule banning female circumcision, female circumcision can still be treated as a crime in many Saudi hospitals. If my circumcision had been reported, the barber could have been charged.

After the three days of heavy bleeding, an end of sorts came to the trauma. My parents were out, and the old lady was there once again, but this time she was sitting by my head. The barber asked my sister to bring him a needle and thread from my mother's sewing machine.

(My sister told me afterward that she hid all the needles once she realized his intention and brought only the thread.) He used the thread to tie five knots in various places on my most private areas. I don't recall if it was painful or not, since I was almost delirious; my sister later told me what had happened. Either the knots or simply time or perhaps some combination of the two stopped the bleeding, and slowly I began to regain my health. But no one removed the thread afterward. The knots the barber tied that day caused lifelong deformities on the most intimate part of my body. Beyond the physical pain, I also could not forgive my parents, nor has my sister to this day. Almost none of my friends were circumcised. Mama and Abouya had made Muna and me unlike all the other girls.

Sometimes, I wonder how things would have been if the dark-skinned women that my mother brought to the house had succeeded in their task. Then my sister and I would have been subject to pharaonic circumcision, which is far worse than the agony of what we endured. Pharaonic circumcision has been practiced since the time of the pharaohs in Egypt and is common in twenty-seven different African countries, as well as Yemen and parts of Iraqi Kurdistan. It completely removes both the girl's clitoris and her labia. Then the vaginal opening is stitched shut to leave only a small opening for the exit of menstrual blood. Most activists call the procedure female genital mutilation. That is the far more accurate description.

Some years later, I asked Amal whether Aunt Hasaneyya had circumcised her and her sisters. She said no, and I was shocked. Why, then, had Aunt Hasaneyya been present at their home at all? I wondered. Why had the girls of my uncle's family called me "dirty"? I felt deceived. But perhaps they had in fact been circumcised, and it was shame, anger, or pain that prevented them from talking about it.

Circumcision is not common in Saudi Arabia, although the number of girls forced to undergo it has risen in recent years. Its practice largely occurs only in certain areas: southern Saudi Arabia and the cities of Mecca, Al Qunfudhah, and Lith. Saudi sheikhs neither command it nor forbid it. The daughters of the Prophet Muhammad

(PBUH)—whose practices Muslims look to for much of their every-day guidance—were not circumcised. Rather than drawing on religious sources, advocates of circumcision adhere to social customs and scientifically unproven beliefs, which state that the procedure protects the girl from "deviant" behavior by removing her desire for sex. They also point to the existence of *hadiths,* sayings from Muhammad (PBUH), which supposedly mention a woman in Medina who performed circumcisions on girls, and whom the Prophet did not prevent from doing so. Yet when I searched for these hadiths and studied them, I found that the actual evidence is very weak and cannot support such a harsh conclusion.

So it was that a few minutes on a single summer morning forever altered two young girls' lives in about as much time as it takes to unlock a car door, slide into a seat, pull a seat belt tight, engage the engine, and back out into the street.

4

Mecca under Siege

*I*t was the day of Eid al-Adha, the feast of sacrifice, the holiest of all Muslim holidays, held to commemorate the willingness of Ibrahim (PBUH) to sacrifice his first-born son, Ismail, to submit to God's command. Eid al-Adha falls during the period of the hajj, the sacred pilgrimage to Mecca, one of the five pillars of Islam and a religious duty required of every able Muslim adult. We were already in Mecca, but my mother was performing the customary pilgrimage circle around the granite Kaaba. I remember clinging tightly to her, my hand tugging on her white *ihram* clothes. Mama's face was uncovered as we completed our seven circuits around the Kaaba. Even in the crowd, my mother stood tall and broad, with a pure, fair complexion and a long, full face. Her cheeks were flushed from the heat, and her body drenched with sweat. I was wearing a hijab over my dress: I was probably eight or nine. We were two drops in a sea of jostling bodies, clothed in white and circling barefoot on the cool marble sanctuary floor. The smell of sweat filled my nostrils: my ears were overwhelmed with calls of *Allahu Akbar*, spoken in accents from every corner of the globe. The sun was blazing, and some of the pilgrims poured cold Zamzam water over their heads, leaving faint trickles on the floor.

Then my mother reached down, pulling me by my small hand toward the Hijr Ismail, a rounded white marble wall adjacent to the north side of the Kaaba. Muslims believe that Hagar, the Egyptian wife of Ibrahim (PBUH), and their son Ismail are both buried there.

The days of hajj are heavily focused on purity. Men are required to dress in two sheets of seamless white cotton. The first of these, the *izār,* is wrapped around the waist, while the second is wrapped around the upper part of the body leaving one shoulder exposed. The head, too, is left bare and is shaved after a ritual sacrifice of a ram. The women are bound to the same standard of purity, and usually wear simple white robes and a white head covering. Even the Kaaba is returned to a pure state by lifting the black cloth—the *kiswah*—that usually protects the black stone structure.

My mother and I looked for a spot in which we could perform two *raka'as* of *Hijr Ismail*, the ritual recitation of phrases from the Koran accompanied by a combination of bowing and prostrating our-selves before the ancient Kaaba. All around us, people moved close to the uncovered wall of the Kaaba, touching it and seeking God's blessings. We could inhale the Kaaba's distinctive scent, a result of its daily anointing with Indian aloe and attar of rose (*ward al-Ta'ifi*). My mother pointed out a hole in the wall of the Kaaba to the woman praying beside us. "The aftermath of al-Mukboor Juhayman," she told her. ("Mukboor" translates as "put in the grave"; it is a harsh slur to speak upon a dead person.) I didn't understand what Mama meant, but I knew the word *Juhayman*. It was spoken many times in adult conversations, but always in a whisper, as if it were a bad or dangerous word.

I would later learn that the hole was from a bullet. The actual hole was relatively small, but the suffering carved out from it and from all that it represents has been much, much greater. It is a suffering that dates back to the year I was born. In November 1979, Juhayman al-Otaybi led a two-week siege of the Grand Mosque in Mecca; I was not yet seven months old. Juhayman al-Otaybi, whose name in Arabic means "angry face," was an Islamist militant and prominent member of the radical fundamentalist organization Al-Jamaa Al-Salafiya Al-Muhtasiba, "the Salafi group that commands right and forbids wrong."

The Third Saudi State was still very young, just forty-seven years old, and under the reign of its fourth monarch, Khalid bin Abdul Aziz, when the siege occurred. It began on November 20. As dawn started to break that morning, which marked the first day of the year 1400 according to the Islamic calendar, Juhayman and a band of his followers, some Saudi, as well as others from across the globe, including even the United States, captured the Grand Mosque. It was just before 5:30 a.m., at the moment when the day's opening prayers and wishes for peace had just concluded. Brandishing high-powered rifles, pistols, and daggers that they had smuggled inside coffins—many Muslim families bring the coffins of their dead relatives to the Grand Mosque so that they may perform the most merciful funeral prayers, one prayer in the Grand Mosque is the equivalent of one hundred thousand prayers offered elsewhere—the attackers chained shut the Grand Mosque's fifty-one gates and scaled its seven minarets. Looking down nearly three hundred feet, Juhayman's men had a nearly perfect view of the city and a precise vantage point from which to train their guns.

By birth, Juhayman was a Bedouin; these tribal, nomadic people have lived in the region for thousands of years. He was also an Islamic preacher. He had spent eighteen years in the Saudi national guard, where he never rose above the rank of corporal but had ample time to attend lectures on Islam. His father had been an extremely devout follower of a Sunni sect founded in the mid-1700s by Muhammad Ibn Abdel Wahhab, who preached that Islam had become corrupt, paganized, and Europeanized. He rejected what he viewed as unnecessary cultural sophistication as well as personal luxuries—including silk clothing, tobacco, gold adornments for men, and music and dancing. He wanted a return to the pure form of Islam as first practiced by

Muhammad (PBUH) and a rigorous application of even the smallest details of original Islamic law. Ibn Abdel Wahhab found an ally in Muhammad bin Saud, whose descendants would become the House of Saud, the future kings of Saudi Arabia. But the alliance partly fractured in the twentieth century. The family of Abdel Wahhab remained a powerful religious force, but the religious militia that had backed the Wahhabis and the House of Saud turned on the Saudi king after he allowed Westerners into the country. In 1929, King Abdul Aziz of the House of Saud defeated his former military allies in battle. One of the survivors of that defeat was Juhayman's father.

By 1979, Juhayman had become steeped in this highly fundamentalist Wahhabi-Salafi preaching, which joined the original Wahhabi belief in a strict interpretation of Islam that rejects modern influences with a second, radical, highly Puritanical view of Islam (Salafism) that was being formulated among extremist scholars. The result is a set of extreme Salafist beliefs that is critical of and even downright hostile to modern advancements in technology and human thought. Juhayman also increasingly became convinced that the Muslim world was nearing the fateful end of days, the great cataclysm that would destroy the globe and leave only the most devout standing. Muslims believe that before this day, the Mahdi, Islam's redeemer who would rid the world of evil, will come. Juhayman was convinced that the Mahdi had arrived in the form of his brother-in-law, who accompanied him on the siege of the Grand Mosque.

Juhayman's takeover of the mosque and its grounds caused utter confusion. Initial reports suggested that the besiegers were Iranians. Just sixteen days before, on November 4, Iranian militants had seized the US embassy in Tehran and taken more than sixty hostages. Information about conditions inside the mosque came only when an American helicopter pilot who had served in Vietnam made two passes above to snap photos. (The pilot and his crew had to convert to Islam by saying the Islamic profession of faith, "There is no god but Allah, and Muhammad is his messenger," in order to be cleared to fly over the site, since no non-Muslims are permitted. At that time the government lacked any of its own pilots capable of undertaking the mission.) The Saudis quickly realized that the man in control of the mosque was part of an extremist group whose main adherents had been detained and then released less than two years before, a man whose innocence had been vouched for by none other than Abdul Aziz bin Abdullah bin Baz (one of the nation's leading Islamic scholars and a strong proponent of this growing extremist Salafi ideology). Bin Baz had in fact preached to and had taught Juhayman in Medina, the second home of the Prophet Muhammad (PBUH).*

As the siege continued, the Saudi kingdom imposed an information blackout, even cutting telephone and telegraph communications lines to the outside world: at various points, the kingdom also falsely claimed that the siege was over. It took two weeks, the assistance of a contingent of French commandos and Pakistani special forces, a massive fire, pitched gun battles, the shelling of five of the seven minarets, and the deployment of chemical gas in the vast tunnels underneath the mosque (tunnels largely built by the bin Laden construction firm, the family of Osama bin Laden) to end the siege. A fatwa by Bin Baz was written to justify the armed attack by Saudi troops on the Grand Mosque.

---

* In 1993, Bin Baz would become the kingdom's grand mufti. Ironically, one of his most famous fatwas (religious pronouncements) was the statement that he issued against women driving cars. Bin Baz wrote, "Depravity leads to the innocent and pure women being accused of indecencies. Allah has laid down one of the harshest punishments for such an act to protect society from the spreading of the causes of depravity. Women driving cars, however, is one of the causes that lead to that." But he also fell out of favor with the extremists for his ruling that allowed non-Muslim troops to be deployed on Saudi soil during the Gulf War to help defend the kingdom from the Iraqi army. In addition, his decree was seen as allowing non-Muslim soldiers to wear the Christian cross and carry the New Testament into battle against other Muslims. That ruling remains a huge point of contention within Saudi society today. One radical cleric declared Bin Baz to be *kafir*, an infidel, and a traitor to Islam.

In the days following the takeover, the turmoil spread beyond Mecca. The American embassies in Islamabad, Pakistan, and Tripoli, Libya, were violently attacked by local mobs, incited by claims that the Americans were behind the desecration of the Grand Mosque. The US embassy in Pakistan was completely destroyed; the 137 Americans inside barely made it out alive after hiding for hours in the building's safe-room vault, surrounded by an out-of-control fire. One Marine was killed. Elsewhere in the embassy compound, a US Army warrant officer asleep in his staff apartment on his day off was also killed, his body burned by the mob.

In Mecca, the final death toll was far higher. Officially, the number of dead—including Saudi kingdom soldiers, rebels, and pilgrims trapped in the Mosque when the siege began—is listed as 270, but there are other estimates that put the number of deceased at 1,000 or more, with many of those being innocent pilgrims.

On January 8, 1980, a little more than a week after Soviet forces invaded Afghanistan, the Saudi government publicly beheaded sixty-three of the rebels who had occupied the Grand Mosque. The executions were carried out in eight Saudi cities. Juhayman was the first to die, in Mecca. But his ideology did not. It has become one of the animating forces of contemporary Islamist extremism. The Egyptian army officer who would assassinate President Anwar Sadat eighteen months later was inspired by Juhayman: by chance, his brother had been a pilgrim at the Grand Mosque during the siege. Osama bin Laden's Al Qaeda, ISIS, and even groups like Nigeria's Boko Haram are rooted in the same fundamentalist ideology that Juhayman once preached, advocating a strict interpretation of the Koran, the application of harsh Islamic law, and calls for jihad against the infidels, particularly Jews and Christians.

Until "the days of Juhayman," which is how the siege is still referred to in Mecca, Saudi Arabia had been both increasingly prosperous and increasingly modern, supported by the global oil boom, which had lifted the country out of poverty and turned it into a land of plenty. But afterward, fears of a radical Islamist tide began to pervade the country, prompting the ruling family to meet with senior religious clerics and elders to discuss how this new brand of extremism could be addressed. In an effort to appease those who had gravitated to this ideology, the Saudi state decided to embrace some of their doctrines. Juhayman and his followers might have been driven from the Grand Mosque, but now their extreme beliefs would increasingly occupy the entire Saudi nation from within.

The first group to feel the full impact were women. In the weeks after the uprising, female announcers were banned from television. Pictures of females were censored in newspapers, and the government cracked down on the employment of women. A hard-line Salafist ideology was introduced and taught not only in Saudi schools but around the world by Saudi-funded missionaries. Bin Baz would issue another fatwa, declaring that jihad against the Soviets in Afghanistan was an individual duty of every Muslim. One of those who left the kingdom to join that fight was Osama bin Laden.

Growing up in Mecca, I would hear veiled references to the days of Juhayman. We never studied the siege in school, and it was never spoken about publicly. Today it has been all but erased from the public Saudi record. Even the hole in the Kaaba has been covered up. But the legacy of Juhayman and his embrace of extreme Salafism would come to impact even the smallest details of my life inside the Saudi kingdom.

———

The first official Saudi government school for girls opened in 1964, two years after the king officially banned slavery in the kingdom. It was far from a universally popular decision. The first man to call for girls to be educated, Abdulkareem Aljuhayman, had been jailed for six months for his views. One prominent Saudi scholar implored his fellow citizens, "O Muslims, be aware; pay heed to these dangers. Stay in close ranks and work together to close those schools that have been opened to educate girls with a modern approach. These schools give the appearance of compassion, but inside them lurks strife and a plague-like affliction. The end result of these schools will be immorality and a lack of regard for religion. If you will not be able to realize their closure in the future, do not accept for them to be opened now." When the first girls' school did finally open, Prince Faisal (the crown prince and later the king) had to send soldiers to protect the students, not unlike what happened when schools were desegregated in the American South. It can be so difficult to effect change, so hard to overturn long-standing views.

It was always possible to distinguish the girls' schools from the boys'. The girls' schools had the look of detention centers, shut behind high solid walls of corrugated metal (imagine a shipping container cut into pieces) and a solid gate. The only man visible was the guard standing at the entrance. The school windows were bolted shut and covered so no outside eyes might gaze inside. Although we had a large outdoor courtyard in the middle of the school, there were no playgrounds, because girls should not run around or jump.

The school door was opened in the morning so that the students and teachers could enter; then it was locked tight with a single key. It could not be opened again unless the headmistress gave her permission. There were also no emergency exits. In 2002, fifteen girls died in a fire inside Mecca's Middle School No. 31. The city's religious police had barred the girls from exiting through the front door because they were not wearing their abayas and were thus not following proper Islamic dress code. When the school door was opened and they were finally carried out, it was as charred corpses.

Many of the girls' schools in Mecca—like No. 31—were converted houses. Unlike all the boys' schools, they had no names. We knew them only by their numbers; mine were Primary School No. 21, Middle School No. 16, and Secondary School No. 13. The female students were as invisible as their schools. At the end of the day, when cars arrived to take the students and teachers home, the guard would call each girl or woman by her father's name, never her own.

School began at 7:00 a.m. and finished around noon. Our apartment was around the corner, so unlike most of the students, my sister,

Muna, and I walked to school. All of us would stand in line until we heard the bell, then each student was expected to take the hand of the girl next to her and march into the building. We stayed in one classroom for the whole schoolday, forty girls in each room.

Inside, every school was the same, three stories. The heat in the classrooms was stifling due to old or broken air conditioners. When they worked, the feeble, battered units blew warm air into the rooms. The bathrooms were dirty and smelly, and all the mirrors had been removed or broken so that no student could stop to check her face in the reflection. By middle school and adolescence, girls' faces would be completely covered by the niqab. Before then, if we wanted to catch a glimpse of ourselves, we had to crowd around the shiny metal water coolers.

My sister was allowed to register for school when she was five years old, but soon after that the rules changed, all students were required to be at least seven years old. This is why my sister was four years ahead of me in school, although we were two years apart in age. The first day that I could be registered, my mother dressed me all in white, a white hairband, white dress, and white shoes. The school forms required that I have a certain vaccination before I could enter. Mama took me to the health clinic directly across the street to get the necessary shot. The city had just finished paving the street, and the road was covered in wet, black tar. I tripped and lay splayed on the ground. My white dress became black, and I felt the humiliation of having to start school in a dirty dress.

Each year my mother made me two school dresses, which I alternated day to day. I wore them until they were little more than threadbare rags. The style and colors were dictated by the General Administration for Girls' Education: dark green for primary school, dark brown for middle school, and navy for secondary school. Before school let out, the administration sent home a notice to the parents with photos of what the next year's uniform should look like. Mama was one of the few who followed the picture exactly, the same ugly green color material, the same ugly collar. Most of my girlfriends had pretty dresses that had been redesigned by their moms or tailors with better shades of green and nicer colors. In primary school, Mama sent me off each morning in one of the ugly dresses and my hair plaited in two braids, tied with white ribbon at the ends.

At the beginning of every day, the classes lined up in queues and listened to the morning broadcast on the school's PA system. This began with recitation of the Koran and the hadiths before moving on to a piece of wisdom for the day, or new instructions for the students if there happened to be any. We were then asked to read, in unison, Sūrat al-Fatiha—the opening sura of the Koran—and to sing the Royal Salute.

After that, teachers went up and down each line to inspect the students. Had we polished our nails, which was prohibited, or forgotten to cut them? Were any of us wearing a decorative headband or colored shoes? Or perhaps we had chosen to adorn ourselves with a forbidden accessory, like a ring or bracelet. The girls' primary schools permitted black or white hairbands, black shoes, and white socks, and anyone wearing anything else did so at her peril. In middle and secondary school, white was banned. One day in secondary school I pinned a white hairband into place as I dressed for school, only to have it wrenched from my head about an hour later by the school deputy, along with a handful of my hair.

We also grew used to surprise inspections of our bags and possessions. It was forbidden to bring anything to school other than a schoolbook or notebook. Carrying a lipstick, a comb, or a mirror to school—or even an outside book or, as we grew older, a cassette tape or a photograph—was prohibited. The school would confiscate the item, summon the student's mother, and also send a letter of warning to her guardian.

There was no room in the girls' schools for any activity that was not directly related to our academic classes—they were forbidden by order of the mufti. No sports, no theater, no music, no art appreciation, no visits to museums or historical sites, no celebrations for our end-of-year graduation. There wasn't even space for a school library.

The only permitted enrichment classes were drawing, sewing, and home economics. We were taught how to make different types of stitches, how to crochet, and how to prepare cakes and pickles: even though we were at school, the expectation was that our ultimate destination was inside a home.

I adored drawing class, though we weren't allowed to draw living creatures, only plants and inanimate objects; the Saudi clerics' interpretation of Islamic law prohibits representative art, such as drawing a person. Many times I tried to test the limits of this prohibition. My smiling fruits often enjoyed the use of human hands and feet. But my teacher usually confiscated those drawings, which ended up as shreds of paper in the wastebasket. So I stopped drawing people in my art sketchbook and started instead to draw them in my notebooks at home, which I filled with the forbidden smiling faces and bounding animals.

Inside the classrooms, school was rigid, but as soon as it came time to pause our lessons to eat, chaos prevailed. There was no set place to eat, and no one formed lines to buy food. In the beginning, I brought my own food. Each day, Mama sent me with a cheese sandwich and a drink. Then one day, one of the teachers pulled me aside and asked me if everything was okay at home with my family. I said yes. She asked why I brought my own meal rather than pocket money to buy breakfast. The only girls who brought their own food to school were the poor girls, because they couldn't afford to pay for breakfast at school. My face turned red, I was so embarrassed to think that anyone at school would consider me poor. After that, I asked Mama for pocket money and she gave it to me. But every day, I had to endure a shoving match with about one hundred girls over the small box of sandwiches for sale. I was a thin, small girl and couldn't fight my way through so I ended up with my hair pulled and no breakfast. My sister refused to help in part because I wouldn't put up a fight, but a girl named Fatin, the older sister of one of my friends, took pity on me. I'd give her my money and she would buy me food. But it was always horrible. One time they left the food next to a kerosene container, which must have leaked onto the sandwiches. The smell was awful and every bite tasted like kerosene, but they sold it to us anyway. It still amazes me that we literally fought each other to buy such terrible food.

Every girl did bring her own water, however. The school's metal coolers were old and rusty, and the water that came from them was warm and brown.

In class, we were not grouped according to our abilities but rather divided up into alphabetical groups by our first names. I was incredibly lucky to find two of my best friends in my group, another Manal and a girl named Malak. There was not enough space in our classroom for me to have my own desk, so each day I would squeeze myself into a crack between Manal's and Malak's desks and nestle between them. They were both very pretty, and the pretty girls were always favored by the teachers. Malak always arrived at school dressed beautifully with bands in her hair. Her mother even ironed her socks. The teachers would bring the pretty girls candy. They would speak nicely to them and permit them to do things that the rest of us could not. When it came time to go to the bathroom, the teachers always allowed the pretty girls to go, but depending on their mood, the other girls might be forced to stay in their seats. One time, one of the average girls wet herself after she was sent back to her seat, and the teacher yelled at her as she sobbed.

I was not one of the pretty girls. In drawing class, I spent extra time trying to make the most beautiful pictures I could so that the teacher would praise my art. I was at least fortunate to be smart, although some of my teachers disliked me because I would interrupt and ask questions. Many times, though, my good grades saved me from a harsh beating. But not always.

When it came to beatings, Saudi Arabia's schools were no better than its homes. I remember the expression uttered by many parents when they registered their children, which translates literally to: "The skin is for you, and the bone is for us." This meant that the teacher was permitted to hit the child whenever he or she deemed it necessary.

The deputy of our school had a fifty-centimeter wooden ruler, some-what shorter than a yardstick, that she carried everywhere, and each teacher brought a traditional thirty-centimeter wooden ruler with her to class. When a female student was punished, she was required to ex-tend her palm and be smacked by the ruler. But it did not stop there. Teachers might also pinch our ears and slap our faces and behinds, and pull our hair. There were also "moral" punishments, like missing the daily break or being stopped and publicly reprimanded in front of every girl standing in the morning queue.

I remember the first beating I received at school, during my first week of first grade. The teacher was named Miss Ilham, and she was an angry woman very much like my mother. She was busy at her desk when she noticed me chewing gum and called for me in a loud voice to come forward. I got up from my desk and walked dumbly to the front of the class, wondering what I could have done to be singled out: no one had explained to me that chewing gum was not allowed. As I stood, confused, there came a slap on my right cheek so forceful that it drove my face into the green chalkboard and left a chalk stain on my other cheek. Then she began to scream at me, "Gum?! Gum?! Do you have no manners at all?!"

She pointed to the wastebasket. Amid my sobbing, the gum had fallen out of my mouth and now lay like an incriminating piece of evidence on the patterned white-and-black ceramic floor. Terrified, I walked toward the wastebasket and back only to receive a second slap. "Blindness in your eyes!" Miss Ilham screamed. "The gum is still on the floor, you dishonest girl!"

I was beaten again during a science class. Saudi education con-sists primarily of memorizing and reciting, not asking and answering questions. The teacher had written on the blackboard, *The sky is blue, the clouds are white.* She would ask everyone to repeat what she had written. When it came to be my turn, I said no. I had my own ideas. I said, "But the sky is white, and the clouds are blue." The first time I said the wrong line, the teacher beat me on the hands with the ruler, and then second time as well, until I finally said, "The sky is blue, the clouds are white." After that, I learned to follow the rules without questioning them.

It was common to be beaten for getting the wrong answer. Even at home, when Mama taught me to memorize the Koran, she used beating as the instructional technique. If I refused to practice, she would beat me badly. When she taught me the first sura (verse), I wasn't able to recite it correctly. She slapped me after every mistake that I made. I would be trying to learn and crying at the same time. The beatings were enough to make anyone hate education, especially when you were too young to understand your mistakes.

At the start of sixth grade, our class didn't have an Arabic-language teacher, so the geography and history teacher taught us Arabic. But she didn't teach us the correct way to draw the letters, and so all of our notebooks were filled with horrible mistakes. When we finally got a teacher for Arabic, she collected our notebooks and was horrified. Usually when you make a mistake, such as failing to do your homework, you were beaten twice on the hands with the ruler. But this teacher said that each of us would be beaten for every mistake that we had made. Imagine all of these notebooks, filled with four lines, two sentences each, over and over, day after day. Imagine how many mistakes you can make in those four lines. I was one of the top students in the whole school, and I had made forty mistakes. I got forty beatings with the ruler; I still remember the pain. The teacher was shouting and screaming at me the whole time. All forty girls in that class were beaten that day. Everyone cried. The worst was knowing that the punishment was simply because another teacher had failed to teach us what we were expected to learn. It was for something we had not been taught, not for us having failed to do the work.

Boys were beaten too, and their beatings were in many ways worse than ours. They were taken outside and told to remove their shoes, before being forced to the ground, their feet bound together and lashed to a long stick called a *falaka*. On their backs, with their legs held up by two other boys who were tasked with holding the ends of the falaka, and the soles of their feet exposed, they would be beaten on the bottom of their feet by a teacher using a bamboo cane. My brother received his first falaka beating when he was six years old. He was a student in the pre-primary level, and was not even a full-fledged student, only what we call a "listener." He cried all day afterward and refused to go back to school the next morning. Abouya told me that he himself had stopped attending the classes of his own *kutāb*—the unofficial religious schools scattered through Saudi's rural villages— after a teacher beat him so badly with the falaka that he was unable to walk. In the mid-1990s, a Saudi boy was beaten so severely by his teacher that he later died from his injuries. Finally, after that, official beatings in Saudi schools were banned.

———

But I am grateful for school. School taught me to read, and I loved reading. I would go crazy over books. Before I started school, when only my sister could read, I would chase her around the apartment, trying to learn the letters and words from her. She would always refuse. Once I was in school, I would read my sister's textbooks, sneaking them out of her bag without her knowing. It didn't matter to me that they were textbooks; I was so desperate for something new to read. Eventually, my sister would hide her books rather than give them to me.

I would often read the same book many times because there was nothing else and I saved some of my lunch money in hopes of buying a new one. Women and girls were not allowed in the only public library in Mecca, so in the summer my dad would take me to a bookshop that sold religious books for cut-rate prices. On Saudi TV Channel 2, I watched *Sesame Street* to learn the English letters A, B, C. My sister had a book with English letters, but she wouldn't share it. Once, in the stationery store, I bought an address book along with my schoolbooks, just because the address book was organized according to the letters A through Z.

Even my heroes were from books. My absolute favorite character was Jo from Louisa May Alcott's *Little Women*. To me, she was amazing. She was a writer, rebellious, and aspired to be independent. Jo did what the boys did. She wasn't supposed to ride a bicycle wearing her big dress, but she took the bicycle and rode it anyway. I had very long hair, and it saddened me that my parents would never let me cut it like Jo did.

Another of my heroes was Mowgli, the jungle boy from Rudyard Kipling's story. He had a song in the TV cartoon that went "How beautiful it is to live in a world with no walls." I loved that line. It was how I felt when I used to go visit my grandmother in the valley where my father grew up. There all the houses had huge yards and the sun came in everywhere. Everything was open, not like our apartments in Mecca, which were always small and dark. In Mecca, even if you had a window, you had to put up a lot of shades so people on the outside couldn't see what was inside. We live in one of the most sun-drenched countries on earth and most of our lives are spent indoors, in quasidarkness.

I was also captivated by Sinbad, because he was an adventurer who traveled the world. In my world, physical activity—running, jumping, climbing—was forbidden to girls because we might lose our virginity. The only games we were permitted to play involved nothing more than singing songs and holding hands. We had one song about an open road and a closed road. When we got to the closed road, we used to hold each other's hands tight and lift them up in the air. I remember we even invented one game where we just drew squares on the ground. There was nothing else to do. But reading and studying, that was something to do. At school, in books, I could run away from the troubled house I lived in, from my family, from any problems. I remember when Mama would have a fight with Abouya, I would hear the fight with one ear, but with the other one, I would be studying, minding my own business.

If reading books had opened my mind, more years of formal, state education closed it. Even though corporal punishment was banned by the time I reached middle school, we were every bit as tightly controlled in what we thought and what we did, just in other, less outwardly visible ways. Saudi education, particularly girls' education, had become the domain of Islamist theologians.

King Saud had placed girls' education under the control of an independent educational institution called the General Administration for Girls' Education. He also established a separate supervisory body headed by the grand mufti—the country's leading religious cleric— whom he tasked with organizing girls' education, developing the curriculum that the girls would study, and monitoring the progress of girls' schools. Thus the person in charge of our state education was a bearded religious sheikh, himself the product of a religious institution.

But the worst consequence of these tight intertwinings of religion and education inside Saudi Arabia would affect boys and girls equally: the radical Islamization of our studies. Anxious to reject the pan-Arab nationalists who were coming to power in places like Egypt and Iraq, the Saudis decided to align themselves with some of the most radical of the Islamists, men who had been jailed in other nations, like Egypt, for their violent ideology. These men had found a political haven in the Saudi kingdom. Now they were also going to find a place of supreme importance in the Saudi educational system. The task of drafting the curriculum for all school stages was entrusted to leaders of organizations like the Muslim Brotherhood. Thus our books included works such as "Jihad for the Sake of Allah" by Sayyid Qutb, as well as writings by radical Islamist thinkers like Hassan al-Banna and Sayyid Abul A'la Maududi, whose ideology of violent holy war on behalf of the one true Islam is the basis for much of the religious interpretations expounded by Al Qaeda and ISIS. The Ministry of Education printed their books and taught their messages of stringent Islamist education and hatred of differences in its public schools.

There was a suffocating control over everything. Independent thought was discouraged; visual, audio, and print media were equally lacking in freedom. The censorship of books left no survivors. Political writings, historical narratives, even romance novels— any type of book considered to conflict with the prevailing extreme

Salafist doctrine—was banned. Students in other countries might rebel against this madness, but the widespread illiteracy of our parents and the manner in which we were taught—dictation without discussion, memorizing and repeating without analysis or criticism—molded and subjugated us in such a way that we became domesticated and tame. We were like captive animals that had lost the will to fight. We even went so far as to defend the very constraints that they had imposed upon us. My friends and I believed that the rest of the world, and even less observant parts of the Muslim world, were conspiring against our true Islam. I believed the words of one of the kingdom's leading Salafi clerics, who stated that our Islam "represents the last bastion of truth and virtue." And I was increasingly determined to live my life according to those principles.

5

Behind the Veil

I still remember the last beating I received from my father. I was in my third year of secondary school and he struck me so hard across the side of my head with his palm that I almost lost my hearing on one side. For hours, my ear was deaf to all sound. I don't know why he hit me.

The illogical cycle of cruelty at home and in school carried over into my interactions with my siblings. We dealt with each other with our fists, the stronger one hitting the weaker. I received my share of beatings, biting, and hair pulling from my sister, and in turn, my brother received his share of beatings from me. Then as he grew up and grew stronger, I received my share of beatings from him. But we were simply acting out what we had learned. Fear dominated our relationship with our parents. If there was no physical violence, there was a steady stream of verbal abuse, frustration, an absence of encouragement, constant intimidation, or simply total indifference.

I ran away to books and lessons to forget, but that was not always successful. One time, when I was twelve, I borrowed a romance novel— *The Empty Pillow* by Egyptian writer Ihsan Abdel Quddous—from my sister, without asking. Risqué romantic novels like *The Empty Pillow* and the Abeer series, a collection of foreign romances translated into Arabic and published in Lebanon, were banned in Saudi Arabia, but frequent trips to visit my mother's family in Egypt meant that my sister and later I were able to smuggle them back into the kingdom. When Muna discovered I had her book, she beat me and then she burned the pages before my eyes so I wouldn't be able to finish it. I remained obsessed with finding out the ending—did the young lovers find happiness or not? Only when I saw the movie based on the book, during a visit to my grandfather's house in Egypt, did I discover what had happened to the characters that had captivated my mind.

My appetite for reading led me to love writing, and here again, my visits to my mother's family in Egypt were invaluable. We were staying at my grandfather's house, where my uncle Omar was also living at the time. The oldest of my uncle's daughters was a lady we called Abla (big sister) Eftaima, who baked bread for us in a wood-burning oven. One day I saw a pile of worn-out storybooks next to her. They were hidden under layers of dust, but I cleaned off one cover to reveal the title *Al-Mughamiroon Alkhamsa*—"The Five Adventurers." I realized that my cousin was tossing the books into the fire. The bread to feed our stomachs was being baked at the expense of the pages that would have fed our minds.

I asked Abla Eftaima if I could take books from the pile. I would have been thrilled with just one, so imagine my happiness when she nodded and pushed the entire pile toward me, saying, "Take them all." I spent my summer vacation with the five adventurers: cracking codes, taking risks, outwitting the most notorious of criminals, and delivering wanted fugitives to the police. As I read, I decided that I too would write my own adventures, and this time I would be a hero, as would my favorite people from real life: my brother, Muhammad, and my cousins, Amal, Ahmed, Hanan, Hammam, and Hossam.

At that time, there were no personal computers for typing my story, no home printers to print it. Since all the riyals I'd saved from my pocket money during the year went to buy books, I didn't have the money for a new notebook, so I started tearing out the empty pages from the notebooks I had used at school the previous year. I carefully cut out the subject and date line at the top of each page. I drafted each chapter in pencil until I was satisfied, and then carefully wrote over the words in blue pen. And because I loved drawing, I began to create cartoons of the people and events in my story. My greatest moment of pride was when I set down my pen after writing "The End."

I would be moving up to the sixth grade of primary school after the summer, and was counting the days until the new academic year began. I couldn't wait to show my Arabic-language teacher, the much-loved Miss Maqboola, my story. Just a day or two after classes had resumed, I stood proudly and impatiently at her desk, waiting for her to finish correcting our homework. She looked up at me from behind her glasses and smiled. I handed her my story. I explained that I had spent my summer vacation writing it, and I hoped very much that she would read it.

A day passed, two days, a week. Every time Miss Maqboola entered the classroom, I would look hopefully at her, but there was no response beyond silence. After two weeks had passed, I walked hesitantly up to her desk at the end of class to ask about the story I had left in her care. "Miss Maqboola, have you read my story?"

Her reply was angry. "Your story? You liar," she told me. "It's not your story. You copied it from others and claimed it as your own."

The whole class was listening. My cheeks turned bright red. "Could you please return it to me?" I asked, my voice shaky and verging on tears.

"I tore up your stolen story!"

I couldn't turn around to return to my seat. I stood there, tasting the salt from my tears running down the back of my throat, but under Miss Maqboola's glare, my eyes remained frozen, unable to cry.

After that, I hid almost everything I wrote. I did not want it to be destroyed again.

The most peaceful period of my childhood occurred during a war. In the summer of 1990, Iraq's ruler, Saddam Hussein, invaded the small, neighboring, oil-rich country Kuwait. Saudi Arabia's vast northeast border straddles both Iraq and Kuwait. A state of war was declared inside our kingdom, but I was not there. We were visiting my mother's family in Egypt and Libya. At that moment, we were staying in the Libyan city of Benghazi, in the house of my oldest uncle, Muhammad. The Libyan press was strongly biased against Saudi Arabia: the newspapers wrote about an American invasion of the Grand Mosque, and I remember a caricature of President George H. W. Bush in which he was shown riding round the Kaaba on a camel led by King Fahd, the Saudi king at that time. Worried, we called my father. He told us there were no American invaders and to get our news from BBC Radio London.

This wartime was also the first time that I saw my oldest half brother. My sister, brother, and I were playing Chutes and Ladders with the children of our much older cousins (Mama was the youngest of her siblings and Uncle Muhammad the oldest, making his children the same age as Mama, and their children the same age as us). We heard the sound of a car entering through the gate and stopping. I saw Mama and my grown-up cousins run toward the door. A tall young man with suntanned skin stepped inside and stopped when he saw my mother, smiling broadly. My mother began to cry, and my cousins too. My uncle's son, Abu Bakr, followed, and when Mama hugged the young man, Abu Bakr began to cry too.

My brother and sister and I sat dumbly watching the scene, waiting for an adult to explain. I turned to Kholoud, the daughter of my cousin. "Who's this?" I asked her.

"This is Essam," she replied. It didn't make things any clearer. Why was everyone crying at the sight of Essam?

But then Mama took his hand and called to us, "This is your brother."

Mama had left Essam when he was just two years old, forced to return to her father's house in Egypt after her divorce. Now she was seeing him for the first time since that day, as a grown man. Mama's head barely reached his shoulder.

The other great event from that summer was small enough to fit in my suitcase.

In Saudi Arabia, the only house where I felt truly welcome was Aunt Zein's. She was a Saudi woman in the old style. In her home, she wore traditional Hejazi tribal clothes, not the shapeless black abaya, but a bright azure dress, open at the chest, the skin beneath it covered by a high-necked, silver-buttoned white vest. It was still possible to see the part in her hair peeking out from under the white scarf wrapped around her head. She adorned herself in jewelry: rows of engraved gold bangles stacked along her wrist, jangling and announcing her arrival like a cat's bell. Her palms and nails were permanently stained with henna. And her daughter, my cousin Hanan, had dolls.

During my childhood in Mecca, the sale of most dolls was forbidden. The only acceptable ones were shapeless cloth things without faces, toys that looked more like pincushions than dolls. There were a few Western-style dolls, but they were treated like contraband. They had to be bought under the counter and you had to know the store owner well. Once, accompanied by my mother, I had bought one such doll for five riyals, and the shopkeeper had wrapped it in layers of newspaper to hide its face and shape before we stepped out of the store.

Hanan's doll was like nothing I had ever seen. She was named Barbie, and had long, luxurious blond hair and beautiful clothes and high heels. She had a car, a bicycle, and a pink-and-white home called a Dream House. She could bend her knees if she sat down. My doll wasn't blond; her hair was short and fluffy and black. She wasn't dressed in beautiful clothes, and I couldn't bend her knees.

"Where did you buy Barbie?" I asked Hanan.

"My brother brought her for me from outside Saudi Arabia," she replied. And that was that. I would never be able to find Barbie inside the kingdom.

But I discovered that Barbie was in Egypt. That summer of the

Gulf War, my mother bought me my beautiful, blond doll. She was dressed as a skater, wearing tiny white skates and a gauzy, pale, pink-and-blue skating dress, the outlines of her legs showing through her translucent skirt. I could dress her. I could style her hair. She was the loveliest creation I had ever seen. I smuggled Barbie and my Five Adventurers storybooks into the kingdom, wrapped up and buried deep inside my suitcase.

When I returned home, I did not return to school. War over Kuwait was imminent; for six months, until the Iraqi troops were forced out, our school was closed. My grandmother—"Sitti Alwa" we called her—was ill, and Aunt Zein and my uncle Sa'ad's wife, Aziza, took turns caring for her. I asked my parents if I could stay with my grandmother and help Aunt Zein, and they agreed.

Tarfa'a is an Arabic name for the tamarisk tree that grows in desert regions, but to me, it means a small, quiet village nestled between the peaks of the lofty Sarawat Mountains in an area called Wadi Fatima. The Tarfa'a of my memories is a place largely forgotten by time. Small redbrick houses with wooden ceilings lie scattered along its sandy roads. Everyone in the village knows everyone else, because everyone is from the same family. Kinship lines entwine and wrap around like a vast network of desert tree roots. At that time, there was no electricity, no water, no sewage system, no telephone, and no grocery store at which to buy your supplies. The sole source of electricity in the village was a noisy diesel motor; it grumbled to life after dark and was shut down before dawn. Although the village was only about twenty miles from Mecca, it was difficult for me to understand the accent of the people who lived there, even my grandmother, but I tried to imitate the dialect and to fit in.

My grandmother had a house at the entrance to Tarfa'a. A green iron door in a brick wall led to a wide courtyard covered with pebbles. On the right of the door was a water tank, which was filled once a month by a delivery truck. On the left was a small, barren *sidr* tree (a species mentioned in the Koran) and an assortment of cactus plants.

A small room along the eastern wall of the house was used as a bath-room. The toilet was a large hole in the ground, covered over by a narrow opening. Each occupant had to pull a concrete slab over the top after using "the facilities."

The main house at the far end of the courtyard consisted of three rooms: my grandmother's room, which was equipped with a desert air conditioner running on water; the kitchen; and an extra room, used for storage, where she kept several mattresses and an assortment of heavy, handmade wool rugs known in Arabic as *hanābil*. Behind these rooms were a goat pen and a chicken coop. My aunt would milk the goat in the morning and boil the milk to make delicious goat's milk tea. We, the children, collected eggs every morning to make om-elets, and then gathered around my grandmother to listen to the news on the radio.

Life in the village was completely different from the world I knew in Mecca. All the village girls knew how to milk the goats, bake slightly sour, brown *khabeez* bread, and prepare Arabic coffee and tea. No one wore abayas; instead both women and girls wore the kurta, a long and brightly colored dress with long sleeves and a fitted waist. On their heads they wore a *sharshaf*, a type of scarf, either pink or white, tied to reveal their faces and the initial strands of their parted hair. I liked to copy the village girls by wearing a *sharshaf*. So great was my desire to fit in that I even came close to piercing my nose; I wanted to wear a stud in my nostril like my aunt and the rest of the village women and girls.

My cousin Amal joined us, and Aunt Zein's daughter, Hanan, came from time to time as well. Every day after *Asr* prayer in the after-noon, the women of the village met at my grandmother's house. After brushing out the rugs in the courtyard, they set down mattresses along the walls and an assortment of *mirāki*—big, hard pillows—to lean on while they sat. While they set up, my aunt busied herself pre-paring refreshments: coffee with ginger, tea flavored with herbs, and a dish of salted biscuits and dates.

We as girls were not allowed to sit with the women; instead, we would go off with the children who had accompanied their mothers to play. On these days, we always played in the same place, an area behind my grandmother's house called *Shi'ab*, a local term meaning a place between the mountains. It lay on the path of a dry creekbed that would swell with water gushing down from the mountains during the rainy season, which transformed the landscape from a muted brown to a vibrant green. We raced through the flat beds, climbed parts of the mountains, and picked the flowers off the desert plant *harmal*. We gathered up locusts and beetles, competed to see who could throw pebbles the farthest distance, and collected bunches of *masāweek* twigs from the *arāk* tree, which we used for brushing our teeth.

Other times we would go off to play in the farmers' open fields. The villagers of Tarfa'a cultivated large farms known as *al-bilād,* which were irrigated naturally by running water from nearby springs. An abundance of delicious things were grown there: mallow, alfalfa, and banana trees thrived alongside mangoes, sycamore, limes, and *abāna* fruit, which is similar to kiwi. We played hide and seek in the alfalfa fields, climbed the high sycamore trees, and drank from the springs.

It was beautiful to live in a place without walls or ceilings or restrictions, and particularly without my mother's screaming and my father's cane. Many nights, I fell asleep wishing that I could live in Tarfa'a forever. Mecca for me meant narrow streets crowded with cars; it meant broken and dirty sidewalks; it meant the vulgar slang of the slums and the conflict, outside on the pavement and inside our apartment. My aunt was quiet and patient, always smiling. I wished she were my mother.

The Wadi Fatima of my memory will always be a magical green landscape of springs and farms, but there are no such scenes in Tarfa'a today. The springs of Wadi Fatima dried up in the late 1990s after a dam diverted their water to supply the increasingly populous city of Jeddah. The plants withered and the trees dried up. The land became desolate and sad.

On February 28, 1991, the Gulf War ended. Saudi Arabia and much of the world celebrated, but I did not. With sadness in my heart, I went back to Mecca, back to our dark apartment and my angry family.

———

If I think back to the sounds of my childhood, I hear the harsh words and escalating pitch of my parents and my siblings, intertwined with the softer thrum of purring cats and chirping birds. We had an array of sleek, silky cats who would lie around the apartment. In Islam, dogs are haram, forbidden, but not so cats. (One of our religious figures, Abu Huraira, a companion of the Prophet [PBUH], had a cat that he carried around in the sleeves of his robe.) I named all my cats for Italian soccer players: Cannavaro, Di Matteo, Baggio, etc. Our bright, trilling canaries were kept in cages. Each day my father would take the birds from the cage, wash their feathers in water, and let them fly around the house, their wings fluttering through the warm, stagnant air.

We were not the only ones who kept birds. My cousin Muhammad, one of Uncle Sa'ad's sons, kept a pigeon hut on the roof of their house. Muhammad, who was two years older than me, used to play soccer with us on that same roof, and he was the one who taught Amal and me how to play board games. With him, we played Chutes and Ladders and UNO. Once, when Aunt Aziza, his mother, called for him to help her carry some parcels, Amal and I stealthily took out one of his game boards and began to play. When Muhammad discovered us, he started to yell; we had touched his things. Always trying to avoid a beating, I ran to the roof, leaving Amal to fight alone with him. But Aunt Aziza had other ideas. She threw a slipper into cousin Muhammad's back, hard, and then proceeded to wreck the game board as well.

Sometimes, our visits to my uncle's house stretched into the night. Then my brother and I would sleep together with our cousins Amal, Muhammad, and Ahmed, strewn across the floor of one room. I remember one night when Muhammad woke me up before the others. "There's something you have to see," he said.

Silently, he led me up to the roof and showed me a pigeon egg on the verge of hatching. I watched, captivated, as a blind, featherless baby pigeon pecked its way through the shell and emerged. The tiny, thin-skinned bird trembled as Muhammad cradled it in the palm of his hand. Gently, he slipped it into my palm so I could feel its heat and its newborn hatchling skin and sense the frantic pulsing of its heart.

But then, without warning, Muhammad vanished from my life.

The first clue as to why came on a morning that began like any other fourth- or fifth-grade day in my girls' primary school. Miss Sanaa, our religious studies teacher, entered the room. Her light hair was worn twisted in a bun, as always, and she carried her preparatory book under her arm. Miss Sanaa was fair-skinned, with a round face, thick eyebrows, and a beautiful smile. She was among the few teachers who were patient with us; she didn't carry a wooden ruler and she didn't scream at us the way so many of her colleagues did. If asked, most of us would have said that she was our favorite.

As she walked to the front, the class stood, and just as we did every other day, we answered her greeting in one voice: "Peace be upon you, and God's mercy and blessings be upon you." But this morning, Miss Sanaa fixed her gaze first on another girl, Yousra, and then on me. Yousra and I possessed an insatiable appetite for questions; we asked about everything. But today, no questions were allowed. "I'm going to explain a new lesson," she said. "I do not wish any of you to ask questions either during or after the explanation, especially you two, Manal and Yousra. Keep your questions to yourselves for today."

Yousra and I quickly looked over at each other, our eyes widening. Suddenly I was even more curious than I had been before.

The lesson was titled "Menstruation and Postpartum." Miss Sanaa presented all of it in a vague way, largely beyond the grasp of our still girlish minds; my mother had told me that I was born into this world via her belly button. Miss Sanaa wrote the lesson on the blackboard and recited it aloud without expression, almost as if we weren't present at all. Listening to her speak was like hearing a new language, one made up of characters we recognized, but words whose meanings eluded us entirely. Then she wrote out the homework assignment, sat down, and buried her head in her papers until the bell rang.

Unlike in the west, the simple biology of puberty and childbirth had no place in her lesson. The biology and physical changes were lessons that I never got to learn: not at school, nor at home, nor in any of the religious brochures and pamphlets that were distributed to us everywhere we went: mosques, malls, souks, schools, even in airport terminals. But we had no doubt about what "becoming a woman" meant socially: "Have some shame," our nearly teenage selves were admonished. "You are women now!" Miss Sanaa was there to teach us our Islamic duty surrounding our time of becoming women and then later mothers, saying things such as "Don't pray or fast during the times of menstruation and postpartum! After the blood stops, you should wash yourself and resume praying." But where was this blood supposed to be coming from? Most of us still had no basic under-standing of what menstruation and postpartum were, and we carried these questions around in our heads, afraid to speak them.

I knew only one thing about this blood, and that was what Mama had told me on the day my sister and I were propositioned by our neighbor's son. If she had found blood on our underwear, we would have been ruined. "Do you mean like when a toy gets ruined, and you can't play with it anymore?" I had asked her. She silenced me with a signal from her hand.

My sister and I were forbidden from jumping down from high places, and we could not ride bikes on the roof with our brother: phys-ical activity, it seemed, produced blood. But when Mama was busy in the kitchen, I'd sneak up and join my brother anyway. At night, I checked my underwear for blood before I put it in the laundry basket.

I was thirteen years old, an intermediate school student, when the blood finally came. A group of us had been challenging each other to see who could jump down the largest number of stairs without falling; I had managed the largest number of stairs that day, and I was exceedingly happy about it. But when I returned home, I found bloodstains in my underwear. I washed them out quickly and hid the underwear so my mother wouldn't see it. Then I crept out on the apartment balcony, sat alone, and sobbed, wishing that I had listened to Mama when she had told me not to jump with the other girls. How was I going to tell her that I was ruined?

The blood did not stop. After a few days, my fear overcame my shame, and I decided to tell my horrible secret to my cousin Amal. I went to her house that weekend, took her aside, and told her what had happened. "Did the blood keep flowing," she asked me, "or was it just a few spots?"

"I found stains the next day and the day after."

She laughed. "Congratulations," she told me, "you're a woman now! This is the blood of the menstrual cycle."

I was completely confused. How could this be a happy moment when I had spent days sobbing? "Amal," I said, "please help me. Tell me what the menstrual cycle is."

Amal told me that she'd eavesdropped when her older sisters discussed their periods. Eventually she learned that women got their periods once a month. She'd found things called "sanitary towels" among her sisters' things, and taught herself how to use them when her own period came.

"You're a *woman*?" I asked her. "Why didn't you tell me? You should have explained all this instead of letting me suffer like I suffered this week!" My next thought was: How do I get these sanitary towels without telling Mama? But sanitary towels and telling my mother would be the least of my problems.

——

After I told Amal my secret, she told her older sisters. They informed me that I could no longer talk to my male cousins, let alone play with them. If one of my male cousins wanted to walk past where I was sitting, or even enter the house while I was there, I had to first be hidden out of sight. This isolation extended to Aunt Zein's house as well. Her oldest son banned his children, my friends Hammam and Hossam, from having any contact with me. We no longer raced in the yard or read our favorite books. We could no longer assemble LEGO blocks or play Atari games. Muhammad and his pigeon hut were lost to me too, and we didn't even have a chance to say goodbye. I saw him once in the hallway by accident and desperately wanted to say hi, but could not bring myself to do so. And he would not speak to me. I visited my uncle's and aunt's houses less and less. I felt isolated and alone, and I was angry and confused that people who had been as close to me as brothers had disappeared. I no longer knew what they looked like. I cannot compare the feeling to anything except the empty grief one feels after a loved one dies. I suppose it was akin to death, a severing from half of the people I had known.

Men and women were not always so strictly segregated in Saudi Arabia's homes, schools, offices, and public places. The wife of one of my older cousins did not cover her face, and she would sit with her brothers-in-law during a meal. Even a woman's need to have one designated male guardian—a father, husband, brother, uncle, or son—to provide permission for the most basic activities—including travel, particularly outside the country—is a relatively recent development in Saudi society. It was the younger generation, my cousins, who imposed this level of segregation and religiosity on their elders and set these draconian rules for their parents, rather than the other way around. I remember my aunt saying, "I'm so thankful that my kids are teaching me about Islam."

After 1979, after the siege of the Grand Mosque in Mecca, my generation was brainwashed. In school, we were taught to go home and lecture our parents about prayer and sins, most of which involved the behavior of women. Those born female in Saudi society now pass through two stages in their lives. First, as young girls, they are supervised and monitored; then, as adult women, they are controlled and judged. Their first menstrual cycle is the abrupt turning point. There is no transition into adolescence. Young women in Saudi Arabia do not experience anything like the "teenage years," that time to experiment, have adventures, and even make mistakes and learn from them. As soon as a girl reaches puberty, from the moment her breasts begin to show, she is obliged to enter a state known in Arabic as *khidr* ("numbness"). She must be outwardly devoid of emotions and feelings. In public, she must veil herself from prying eyes and avoid speaking. She must observe a long list of religious and societal taboos.

It wasn't until I was in secondary school that I learned about the ritual washing that must be performed after your period, after intercourse, and forty days after the blood stops when a woman has given birth. One of my secondary school teachers began shouting at our class: How could you not know the correct way to wash? After she was done with her scolding, she said that we must start with the right side, beginning with wetting our hair and scalp and then continuing down the body. Once the right side had been cleaned, the same process had to be performed on the left. If you do not wash properly, she told us, our prayers to God would not be accepted. I had not known. After my period had finished, I had simply taken a regular shower.

There were other daily ritual washings to be performed. Each day the mouth had to be cleaned, then the nose, then the face, and then the hands and elbows, then you wiped your hair and finally your feet. There were specific prayers to be said before washing and after, which were impossible to forget because of the stickers all around to remind us. There were stickers on the bathroom door with the prayer to be said before entering the bathroom, stickers of prayers to be said before leaving the house or the school. When you're stopped at a traffic light, that too is a time to pray. You should say *Astaghfiru Allah,* God forgive me, God forgive me, over and over, until the light changes. These were on top of our other obligations, such as reading the Koran and the five daily acts of prayer, both of which had their own set of required ablutions. And veiling.

The first time I wore a veil, I was ten years old. I had seen my favorite teacher, the religious studies teacher, Miss Sanaa, leaving school dressed completely in black, an abaya over her body, a niqab covering for her face, hiding everything, even her eyes. Her feet and hands were covered in black socks and gloves. I went home and told Mama that I wanted to wear the niqab and gloves. She was surprised, but she bought me the pieces and taught me how to wear them. My sister laughed at me, but I refused to be discouraged. Instead, I felt very grown up as I walked to school the next day, bursting with pride.

But as I made my way home in the afternoon, I discovered that the niqab was a rather difficult piece of clothing for our hot climate. It was hard to breathe through the dark fabric as it drew up against my mouth and nose. The gloves made it impossible to get a proper hold on anything. But I had to keep wearing my new covering; it would be far too embarrassing to tell Mama that I had just as quickly changed my mind.

As it happened, the end of my adventure with the niqab and gloves came a few weeks later at the hands of two other girls: my sister and my cousin Amal. One day, while the three of us were walking to my uncle's house on the next street, my sister turned toward me and in a single, swift motion pulled off my niqab. She and my cousin ran away, laughing, the niqab clutched tightly in her hand. Exposing my face in the street felt disconcerting. I felt betrayed, but it was also the perfect excuse to stop wearing the niqab. I could blame it on the two of them.

That summer, when we went to my grandfather's house in Egypt, the first thing I noticed was the women, who walked freely in the streets, wearing colorful clothes and uncovered hair. I pressed my nose against the car window, feeling more like a spectator at a Cirque du Soleil performance than a passenger driving through an ordinary Egyptian neighborhood. When we stopped at a traffic light, I looked over and saw a woman seated behind the steering wheel of a car, driving, something I had never seen in Mecca.

While we were in Egypt, my sister and I did not wear a niqab or a black abaya over our shoulders, or even a hijab over our hair as we were accustomed to doing in Saudi Arabia. We wandered about uncovered. Until we returned home.

Within a couple years, we had no choice but to take up the veil. By the early 1990s, the over-the-head abaya and full-face niqab were imposed on all female students, just as they had been on women in other areas of Saudi life. It was the most stringent form of niqab. While the traditional niqab left a slit for the eyes, we were now supposed to lower our head scarves to block out this opening entirely. It was hard to get used to it on my journey to and from school. The full face covering made me almost blind, and I stumbled every day on the steps of our building. One time when I fell, our neighbors' sons watched and laughed.

6

My Barbie Is Murdered

I know the exact day and event that transformed me at age thirteen from a moderately observant Muslim into a radical Islamist. Until that moment, my shift had been a slower, more cumulative process, a series of adaptations and accommodations. But after this particular afternoon, I became almost unrecognizable to my younger self. I became extremely observant, down to the most minor acts; I renounced nearly every small pleasure I had known as a girl; I brutally enforced my new beliefs upon my family. And I can say with certainty that this happened as a direct result of the environment I lived in, from my schooling and education to the radical preachers broadcasting on TV; the cassettes and VHS tapes of their fiery sermons; the books and leaflets that were distributed for free in common gathering places, like the souk, our local market. There was now one completely acceptable place to direct the emotions of my own teenage upheavals and frustrations: into the global Muslim political struggle and calls for an Islamic state or caliphate.

As a teenager, at least sixty percent of our time in class was spent studying religion and religious subjects—including *Tajweed,* the rules for reciting the words of the Koran; the hadiths, the sayings of the Prophet Muhammad (PBUH); the *Fiqh,* Islamic jurisprudence; and the importance of *Tawhid,* Muslim belief in the singular pre-eminence of God; and Islamic culture and history. But we were not studying a classical, historical understanding of Islam. We were studying a hybrid Salafi ideology, which decreed that Islam must be returned to its purest form, the form they believed was first practiced by the Prophet Muhammad (PBUH) and his Companions (Sahabah). This was the doctrine that Juhayman and his followers preached when they captured the Grand Mosque, the doctrine that the Saudi royal family allowed to dominate much of the kingdom in the aftermath of the siege. This Salafism requires strict adherence to the most literal interpretation of the Koran, believes in no other law but sharia, and embraces the tenets of jihad against nonbelievers.

Inside Mecca and other cities across the kingdom, sharia was on display most Fridays, when a prisoner would be led into the large square near the Grand Mosque after prayers. One of my very religious friends during secondary school told me about following a great crowd with her father and siblings until she caught sight of a blindfolded Pakistani man being led to his beheading. He was being dragged by his hands and was crying. At one point, she said, he peed himself, the stain adding to his humiliation and fear. Scared and anxious herself, she did not stay to watch his final moments; she begged her father to leave before the man's head was laid against the stone and severed with a blow from a sword.

I sometimes saw pickpockets near the Grand Mosque. When the authorities caught them, they would periodically cut off their right hands for stealing, a punishment described in the centuries-old sharia law texts, although contemporary scholars debate how literal or widespread these sanctions were. Afterward, the traumatized stump would be plunged into boiling oil to cauterize the veins and arteries and stop the bleeding. If the person was caught stealing again, he would have his right foot cut off above the ankle. Of course, there are some people in positions of power in the kingdom who have stolen billions of dollars, but their hands and ankles have never been cut off. That punishment is only for the small-time pickpockets.

Extreme Salafi beliefs reject any moderation or innovation in Islam. They condemn not only Shiites (members of the sect most common in Iran and the eastern part of Saudi Arabia) but millions of other Sunni believers as well. (Salafis are Sunni Muslims, but the overwhelming majority of Sunnis are not Salafis.) Salafis are confident that only they and they alone will survive the time of judgment. They also believe that they are the true warriors against a centuries-old conspiracy to corrupt and destroy Islam.

In the 1980s and 90s, as this form of Salafism gained traction in the Saudi kingdom, the overall state of the Muslim world played directly into the Salafi narrative of a war against Islam. The Russian wars in Afghanistan and Chechnya, the Serbian/Croatian attacks in Bosnia and Herzegovina, the massacres against the Muslim Rohingya in Myanmar, the first Palestinian uprising—these were all cited as proof of a widespread, international conspiracy to exterminate Muslims. According to our teachers and clerics, no one was at greater risk in this global struggle than women. The anti-Islamist forces were determined to deflower women, to bring them out of their houses and remove their veils.

There was no counternarrative. By that time the extreme Salafis controlled all media; books that did not conform with their ideology were banned. The fixation on declaring things forbidden (haram), which had begun with girls' education, now extended to censorship of the printed press, radio, and television. They also rejected anything new that might disrupt official communications, such as satellite channels and the Internet, and innovations like credit cards and insurance. No battle was too small. In their Friday sermons, imams denounced the infiltration of satellite dishes inside the kingdom, declaring a religious war on the dish. People who owned one were branded as traitors to the faith. "O nation of Islam, these satellite dishes are tornado-sized storms of sedition which will pluck our homes from their roots and destroy them. I swear by my God: they are a torrent of sinful desires, designed to swallow up all traces of modesty, chastity and faith," wrote Sheikh Hamad Aldahloos in one fatwa. Radicalized youth began targeting rooftop satellite dishes with rifles, and a 1990 decree from the Ministry of the Interior officially banned their use. (That decree remains in place today, despite the fact that Saudi Arabia owns the most influential satellite channels in the Arab world—MBC Group and Al Arabiya—is the headquarters for eighty-five channels, and has the second-highest satellite TV penetration in the Arab region, at ninety-seven percent.)

At the heart of Salafi ideology is a deep belief in Hell. What I remember most from my own life during this period was the all-consuming fear that I, as a Muslim, wouldn't reach the level of righteousness and devotion required to escape condemnation from the eternal hellfires.

No Saudi student could fail to hear the message. During the school day, religious sheikhs frequently visited schools to give lectures via the public address system. Because we were girls and young women, we were not permitted to lay eyes on male clerics, but attendance at these faceless lectures was mandatory. In middle and secondary school, the lectures grew more frequent and were supplemented by speeches from some of our most devout teachers after the noontime prayer in the school's mosque. It was not mandatory to attend these events, but as a curious teenager, I went.

These religious lectures were overwhelmingly designed to arouse feelings of guilt or fear in our hearts. They were vivid and mesmerizing, and they terrified us with talk of the torment of the grave. We were commanded to imagine the Day of Judgment, when we would be standing between the hands of God and, for those who fell short in performing their religious duties, the agony of the fire. Similar lines were heard in schools across the nation, such as these words from a sermon about the importance of praying on time: "Whoever neglects his prayers, God will punish to drown thirsty; even if he drinks the water of all the seas in the world, he will not quench his thirst; and

God will narrow his grave, pressing on him until his ribs no longer hold their form. God will set fire to his grave, and send to him a snake called 'The Brave and the Bald.'" The preachers would also spew horror stories about the violent, brutal deaths suffered by sinners or even simply negligent individuals. Their voices building to a crescendo, they would recount these happenings as if they were real-life events to which each preacher had been an eyewitness.

The lecture that forever changed me centered on the ritual act of washing and shrouding the dead. There are a number of death-related rites in Islam. When a Muslim dies, his or her body must be washed in a mixture of three liquids: water, camphor, and a liquid prepared from the leaves of the *sidr* tree—the same type that grew in my grandmother's courtyard back in Wadi Fatima. Then the body must be shrouded in white cloth and a prayer offered before burial.

"Death will act as your preacher today!" began the teacher who delivered the lecture, determined that the gravity of the subject should pass none of us by. The lecture was steeped in melancholy. It described the desolation of the grave and the time we spend alone there with only our deeds for company. "What have *you* done to prepare for the grave?" the teacher asked us, spitting contempt. And then: "Who will act as the body while I demonstrate the shrouding process?" One girl was singled out and moved to the front of the room. We watched, wide-eyed and frightened, overwhelmed with guilt and feelings of deficiency, as the volunteer's eyes were covered with cotton and a white shroud brought down onto her face. At once the audience and the corpse were joined together in a collective wave of hysteria. Sounds of plaintive wailing rose around us until every other sense was overwhelmed.

Then the teacher commanded each of us to seclude ourselves in a dark and quiet place when we went home, in order for us to feel the loneliness of the grave, our grave. "Remember," she said, "there will be nothing there to amuse or occupy you in that hole except the good deeds you did during your life. So ask yourself today: Are your prayers on time? Are you complying with the conditions of the religious veiling? Are you being complacent with regard to haram things like singing, wearing tight clothing, and plucking your eyebrows?" She went on to recount the rest of the long list of forbidden things and actions.

The idea of death pursued me and tore at my insides as I walked home. When I got back to the apartment, I hid myself away. I took out the cassette tape we had been given after the lecture: *Throes of Death.* The teacher had told us to play it whenever we became lazy with our acts of worship or our souls tempted us toward sin. I put the tape in the player, placed the headphones over my ears, and listened to the earth-shattering yells of a preacher: "Have you prepared for death?" Plaintive moans swirled around him as the tape wound its way forward; the image of the girl in the shroud passed through my head, and I began to cry. I promised to God that I would reform myself and be a good Muslim. I remembered what they had taught us at the school lectures: that your religion cannot be complete until you have changed the evil around you. I would have to change not only myself but also my family.

———

Growing up in a conservative, religious society had already made me *multazima,* compliant, with the central Muslim rites: prayer five times a day, fasting, reading the Koran, performing the daily religious recitations, and wearing the facial covering that we had been obligated to wear since the beginning of middle school. Basic religiosity had been imposed by my family as well, on both my father's and my mother's sides. My father's side had separated me from my male cousins. My mother's side, during one of my visits to Egypt when I was ten years old, had insisted on my participating in the ritual of five daily prayers.

But after the lecture on death, I felt that all my previous attempts at being a good Muslim were woefully insufficient. From that day forward, I embraced religious fanaticism. This story is in no way unique to me; it's the story of an entire generation brainwashed with extremist discourse and hate speech, an entire generation who grew up being imprisoned, first by the constraints of our society and its religious leaders, and then by our own actions—by our own thoughts and minds.

It is difficult to convey the number of duties and prohibited acts that we as young women had to contend with. They became exhausting and overwhelming, and ultimately suffocating. Independent thought was all but impossible. We simply followed the course set before us, afraid of stumbling, just as I had been afraid of stumbling with my face shrouded in the niqab.

Every public and most private spaces were saturated with radical books, brochures, and cassette sermons; almost all focused exclusively on death, the torture of the grave, and the hereafter. Throughout Mecca, these materials were distributed free of charge in the markets, the schools, and the mosques, and they were exchanged among family and friends. These pieces of religious propaganda were overwhelmingly intended to ensure the compliance of women.

I still have one such booklet, printed on stock paper the size of a playing card, so that it might easily be carried in a pocket or a purse. Entitled "A Gift to the Muslim Woman," its focus was the full veiling of the body, head, and face. It reads in part:

> My Muslim sister: today, you face a relentless and cunning war waged by the enemies of Islam with the purpose of reaching you and removing you from your impenetrable fortress. . . . Don't be tricked by the ideas they are promoting. One of the things that these enemies of Islam are trying to discredit and eliminate is the niqab. The facial covering is what distinguishes a free woman from an infidel woman or a slave and avoids her being confronted with the wolves that walk among us. As the scholar al-Qurtubi said: the whole of the woman—her body and her voice—is *a'ura* (sinful to put on display) and should not be revealed unless there is a need for her to do so.

One of the conditions of veiling is that it acts as a container for the entire body, without exception, and it should not be incensed or perfumed. This is demonstrated by the *hadith* which tells us that any woman who applies perfume and passes by others so they can smell her scent is an adulteress. Veiling is not imposed upon you to restrict you, but to honor you and give you dignity; by wearing the religious covering, you will preserve yourself, and protect society from the emergence of corruption and the spread of immorality. . . . My Muslim sister, keep this booklet and give it as a gift to your sisters after reading it.

Other taboos included wearing pants, styling one's hair, and even parting one's hair on the side—because doing so causes a woman to resemble the infidels. Nail polish is forbidden, because it prevents the ritual waters of ablution from performing their task. In fact, the things most frequently cited in religious lectures, which preoccupied most of our efforts and consumed most of our time, were often not only superficial but also incomprehensibly trivial, such as the prohibition against eyebrow plucking. Even though the hadith that the religious scholars used to justify this prohibition was not an actual hadith at all but rather a statement by the Prophet Muhammad's companion Abdullah ibn Masud (PBUH), the argument was still put forward that plucking a woman's eyebrows represented an interference with God's creation, and that whoever plucks her eyebrows is a cursed woman destined to be banished from God's mercy.

To comply with this decree, women's beauty salons affixed notices over their entrances declaring that eyebrow plucking was excluded from their services; many even specifically added that plucking was condemned and was a religious violation. But women with unruly eyebrows often circumvented this prohibition simply by dyeing their unwanted hairs.

As teenagers, we also heard extensive preaching on the requirement to obey one's husband. This, we were informed, would serve as one way that a woman could guarantee her entry to paradise.

Preachers stressed the necessity of women gaining their husbands' permission for everything, whether visiting family, cutting their hair, or even performing voluntary religious fasting. They emphasized the need for women's complete subordination to their husbands in all facets of life. As one Saudi sheikh said during a lecture, "If your husband has an injury filled with pus, and you lick this pus from his wound, this is still less than what he can rightfully expect."

I comforted myself with the promise that these arduous duties would pave my way to paradise. And I imagined the alternative, a hell fraught with sinful desire, which I would avoid. Each day I wore gloves and black socks, along with a niqab that completely concealed my eyes. I stopped visiting my aunt's and uncle's houses to socialize or have fun and went only out of the obligation of kinship, a very important concept in the Saudi world. Ignoring the ties of kinship and duties to one's relatives is grounds for being denied entrance to paradise. But in my newly religious eyes, not all kinship ties were the same. By the time I was in secondary school, I refused to accompany my mother on her trips to Egypt, since Egypt was a sinful country where women were not veiled, people went to the movies, and men and women mixed together. I considered it impossible to be in such a country and not to object to the sins of its people. And I never forgot to advise my mother about continuing to wear her facial covering when she traveled there.

A key component of our school curriculum was the Doctrine of Loyalty and Disavowal. The first stage of disavowal, as we were taught, is to hate and to become an enemy of the "infidels," in this case meaning anyone who is faithful to a religion or creed other than Islam, including atheists or anyone who follows another version of Islam, such as the Shiite sect. We were instructed to express our hate and enmity in a myriad of ways. We were not to smile at these infidels or greet them. We were not to reside in or travel to their countries. We were not to participate in their holidays or wish them well or attend important occasions of theirs like weddings and funerals. We were not to copy the way they dressed or talked, nor to record our history using infidel systems like the Gregorian calendar. We were not to appoint them to any positions of authority in Muslim countries. In primary school, we even had a lesson titled "The Impermissibility of Standing by One Who Turns Away from God and His Prophet," where we read these lines: "God almighty, cut off the friendly relations between Muslims and infidels. Even if a Muslim lives far away, he is your brother in religion; and as for the infidel, even if he is your brother by blood, he is your enemy in religion." We were, however, to seize any and all opportunities to invite infidels to follow the religion of Islam and pray for their guidance.

On one of my last trips to Egypt, I had already put these Salafi teachings into practice. While I was visiting my grandfather's familial house in Egypt, a neighbor named Umm Mina came by one morning. My uncle's family was living there—Umm Mina was their friend—and we all shared breakfast together. After we'd been eating for some time, my cousin offered her a plate of eggs. She refused them politely, saying, "No, thank you, I'm fasting!" For Muslims, fasting means completely abstaining from all food and drink, even water, so I was puzzled by her response. "Did the guest forget that she was fasting?" I asked my cousin later. I was shocked when she explained that their neighbor was a Coptic Christian and that, in the Coptic doctrine, fasting means only abstaining from animal products. I became furious, vehemently protesting against my cousin's willingness to receive an "infidel" in the house, let alone be friendly with her and share a meal. After that, I refused to greet Umm Mina whenever she came to the house or even sit in the same room with her. And of course, soon after I avoided traveling to Egypt altogether.

Even in Mecca, I avoided going out of the apartment, and when I did, it was only to go to school or the Grand Mosque. I was eager to go to the mosque once a week with Mama, who still fasted each Monday and Thursday without fail and then broke her fast in the Grand Mosque, where she would obtain the maximum religious gain. My reason for going was to meet Muslim girls and women from other countries like Turkey, Pakistan, and Iran; I wanted to preach Salafi ideas to women who had journeyed to Mecca for *Umrah,* a non-mandatory, lesser pilgrimage to the Holy City, which, unlike the hajj, may be performed at any time. But before I left home, I now requested my father's permission.

On the occasions when I went with Mama to the souk, the local market, I completely stopped talking with the sellers because an unmarried girl should not be heard. I also stopped reading the detective novels and science fiction novels that I had adored so much: my Agatha Christie books and the Arabic novels *The Impossible Man* and *The Future Files* were banished to the scrap heap as immoral works. I replaced them with religious books and cassette recordings of overwrought sermons filled with threats and intimidation and cries of lamentation and grief.

I had never owned cassettes of music or songs before. Music was one of the great taboos, or forbidden (haram) things, in Saudi culture; religious discourse routinely described it as "the post mail for adultery" and the "whistles of Satan." What little music I heard was accidental, usually while watching television. I largely stopped watching TV to avoid inadvertently committing that particular sin, and insisted to my parents that we lower the sound whenever any music came on. There were no remote controls. so I would get up and turn the knob myself.

The only acceptable form of "music" was religious *anasheed,* a form of a cappella chanting that occasionally included a bit of percussion to keep the words on a consistent beat. The themes centered on the tragedies Muslims faced around the world. They urged support through "jihad of the soul" and monetary donations. In the early 1990s, one of the most famous and popular of these religious chants, whose lyrics we memorized, can be translated as:

> *Kill me and tear me apart, drown me in my blood*
> *You will not live on my land, you will not fly in my sky*
> *You are filth and debauchery, you are the cause of the plague*
> *You are infidelity and treachery, your way is to conceal the light*

My healing is in killing you, you will not live serenely
You sold the Afghani people peacefully, without shedding blood
O swords of God, raise yourselves from slumber to light
Teach these grown men a lesson, banish them to nothingness
Exhaust the infidels with beatings and condemn them to wander in the desert
Raise the flags of the religion and rule with the Sharia of Heaven.

My extremism did not remove all music from our home. My father still kept his tapes of Umm Kulthum and Abdel Halim Hafez and Farid al-Atrash. My brother held on to the tapes of his favorite boy bands, the Backstreet Boys and *NSYNC. But I tried hard to dissuade my family from listening to singing, watching television, or collecting magazines with photographs, since we had been taught in school that the presence of photographs in the home would prevent the entry of angels. During this period, Islamist magazines and newspapers also appeared, distinguished from regular publications by their lack of photographs. Particular attention was paid to excluding all photographs of women. Mama, however, had a big collection of fashion magazines that one of her brothers, Uncle Ali, had brought her from Italy, and she used them to find designs for the clothes she made.

One time, when I was alone in the house, I gathered up all of my mother's magazines and all of my father's and brother's tapes that featured singers. My sister's possessions were locked up, so I couldn't reach those. Then I climbed up to the roof of our apartment building and set everything on fire. As the flames consumed the glossy pages and charred and melted the plastic covers, I thought of the gains I would make in God's eyes for destroying these evil things with my bare hands. I felt glad to be rescuing my family from sin. After that, I deliberately recorded over any new tapes that my brother bought: rather than hearing his favorite bands when he played them, he would be greeted by the voice of a cassette preacher's sermon instead. This preacher would talk about the contempt of singing and warn of God's intention to pour molten iron into the ears of anyone who listened to instruments.

After my bonfire, Mama hid all the family photograph albums

from me to prevent me from burning those as well. She considered our few pictures to be precious. It was two decades before I saw them. I stumbled upon this small treasure trove while cleaning out Mama's room after she died. And I was grateful. A significant number of Saudis reject the idea of photography for reasons of privacy, so images of relatives and friends are often rare. Many of those, like me, who later renounced their extremism, say they have never regretted anything as much as having ripped up their family photographs.

—

My constant interference in our family's everyday life was a source of ongoing tension. Extremism frequently turns its champions into angry people, driven by conflicting desires. At first, I pitied my less enlightened parents and siblings. Then I felt superior to them, poor sinners that they were. Then I lost patience with their unwillingness to see the one true path and resorted to threats, intimidation, and yelling. At night, I was tormented by thoughts of what would happen to all us of when we reached our graves.

My relationship with my brother—my best friend for so long— became very strained. The friction between us reached its peak when I searched his wallet and found pictures of beautiful and rather scantily clad Lebanese singers. I waited for my father to come home before I staged the confrontation. My waiting paid off: my father had his own firmly held religious beliefs, even if they were not always as strong as mine, and my brother was forcibly removed from our apartment for a day. I forgot about the incident, but my brother never did. He still remembers it and says, "You caused me a lot of pain during your extremist days!"

Even after I became very devout, the one thing my heart would not allow me to relinquish was the beautiful Barbie doll that I had brought back from Egypt. Perhaps it was because she was the last tangible evidence of the one happy period of my childhood, the only surviving proof of a more innocent and simpler time. Or maybe it was because of the amount of effort I went through to get her. Either way, I held on to her like a precious treasure, giving her a position of honor on my bookshelf. I clung and clung until one day a very devout friend visited me and destroyed her while I was preparing tea. I came into the room with the pot and the cups to see what remained of Barbie lying there, her lovely clothes torn, her delicate limbs snapped, and her soft, long, golden hair all chopped off. My friend's name was Mariam, and she was an American who had converted to Islam and come to Saudi for Umrah. She, like me, had been indoctrinated into the militant Salafi school of Islam, and she had refused to return to America. She was doing what Salafi decree preached, destroying that which was haram.

After my radical phase ended, I looked for a replacement Barbie doll everywhere I went. I bought several new Barbie dolls to make up for the sadness of losing my first, and I've kept them all so that someday another little girl might play with them.

It was not just dolls with beautiful faces and bodies that were forbidden, but all forms of human and animal representation. As a fatwa from Salafi scholar Muhammad ibn Uthaymeen states, "It is not permitted to take photographs of animated beings, because the Prophet (PBUH) condemned all photographers to everlasting torment: 'The most stringent punishment on the Day of Judgment will be reserved for those who depict the forms of others.' This makes clear to us that photography is a major sin, since condemnation and warning declarations of severe punishment were bestowed only upon major sins." But one of the hobbies I truly adored was drawing. I created another world for myself when I drew, a beautiful world, full of happiness.

While my handwriting was disorganized and unruly, my drawings were elaborate and perfectly proportioned. I grew to expect the same question at the beginning of each academic year: "Manal, are you sure these drawings are your own?" The teacher would present me with a blank sheet of white paper and whatever tools were available, and I'd start drawing right there in front of her to prove that I truly was the only one responsible for my creations. At the end of the school year, the teachers would take my sketchbooks to use as examples for students in the following year. Many of my drawings were displayed in elegant frames on walls in the school, which made me exceedingly proud. When I created bigger drawings, I loved nothing more than to use the walls as my canvas, and happily spent all my free periods creating colorful designs. At school, we were not allowed to draw faces and animals due to the prohibitions against representation, but at home my notebooks were filled with images of creatures and smiling people.

I was proud to win any drawing competition that I entered, both at a school level and even a national one. It just so happened that the company that I would eventually work for after graduating from college, Aramco, the Saudi national oil company, held an annual contest for children's drawings. I submitted an entry during my second year of middle school, and my *Oasis and Palm Trees* won. As a prize, they sent me an electronic drawing pad. The pad was designed to be plugged into the television so that whatever was drawn could be displayed on the screen. Our television set was very old (we still had an aerial) and there was no way for me to connect my new gadget, so I gave it as a gift to my neighbor's daughter, who loved drawing as much as I did. I happily did all of my brother's drawing homework as well. He told me once that his teacher admired his drawings and had asked him whether anyone at home was helping him. He told the teacher it was his older brother, since saying that it was his sister would have been too embarrassing.

Both my brother and my sister knew how much I loved my drawings. They also knew I wouldn't hesitate to give up and retreat in the middle of a fight if they so much as threatened to rip them up. One time my sister made good on her threat and ripped up a sketchbook whose contents I'd worked on all year. I wept and wailed as if grieving the death of a friend. Afterward, I taped all the pieces together, and I still have that sketchbook.

One of my school teachers suggested that I take a distance-learning course to develop my drawing skills. She gave me a brochure for the Master Art diploma at the Penn Foster Career School, a correspondence school in Pennsylvania. My father helped me pay the

enrollment fee, and each month I received study modules and a se-
lection of drawing tools. I found it hard to juggle my art assignments
with my compulsory schoolwork, but when I obtained my diploma at
the age of seventeen, I felt very pleased with myself.

My relationship with drawing ended abruptly not long after, following a single day in our religious studies class. I had known that
drawing animate beings was haram. But that day I learned that the
people who made such drawings would be among the most strongly
punished on the Day of Judgment. I spent a full week feeling confused, unable to sleep from recurring nightmares. I was trapped between two equally painful agonies: my feelings of sinfulness and guilt
at having breached the commands of my faith on the one hand, and
the thought of abandoning the drawings that I had worked hard on
from almost the first moment I could hold a pencil. A little part of my
soul was poured into each and every one.

After a week of relentless insomnia and guilt, I saw no other option. I climbed up to the roof of our apartment building and burned
all my drawings of living things. I stood silently and cried as I watched
my papers and notebooks burn. The conflicting sensations of comfort
and pain raged inside me like the fire leaping before my eyes.

Much later, I learned that drawing is prohibited in Islam only for
those who intend to worship the pictures in place of God. But the
militant religious discourse to which I was subjected was based on the
principle of forbidding not only that which is explicitly sinful but any
thing that *might eventually* lead one to commit a sin.

But perhaps the greatest and most lasting casualty of the entire
period of my adolescence was my relationship with my sister. In our
apartment, after many years, we eventually got a landline telephone
with two receivers. One receiver was in the guest room, which my
sister commandeered for her own room. She was forever locking the
door. The second receiver was in our main room. One day when I was
in my third year of middle school and my sister was in her last year in
secondary school, I picked up the receiver to make a phone call and
overheard her talking to a man. I stayed on the line, silently listening

to the whole phone call. I was shocked to hear my sister talking to a stranger and exchanging words like "I miss you" and planning to meet in secret. When the conversation ended, I was enraged. I kept the secret to myself until the next morning, when I told my two best friends and asked them what I should do. They listened but said nothing. I decided I would tell my mother. If I confronted Muna directly, I knew that I would receive a harsh beating at her hands.

Even before I had finished speaking, Mama was terrified. She confronted Muna, but my sister denied everything, calling me delusional and a liar. Muna later beat me severely, which made me even more determined to catch her in the act. Religion wasn't my only motivation. I also wanted revenge. Years before, when I was in primary school, Muna had found my diary, where I used to write fictional stories and imagine myself having all kinds of childish adventures. Once I wrote a love story between me and one of my second cousins. My great mistake was to use our actual names, not knowing that Muna read everything I wrote. Muna tore the story from my notebook, hid it away, and blackmailed me, telling me that she would show it to Mama and Abouya.

I was in agony, terrified of the consequences if my parents read the story. One day, my mother finally confronted me in front of my brother, who was still very young, only in second grade. Looking very disappointed, Mama asked, "Is it true that you are writing letters to that boy that you think you are in love with?" Muhammad planted himself between Mama and me, interrupted her, and said, "Manal would never do that." All the shame that I felt was now a hundred times worse.

I answered, "They are not letters, they are stories I wrote."

I will never forget the look in Muhammad's eyes as I spoke. I felt that I had lost my brother's trust. My sister never showed the actual story to Mama, instead she blackmailed me for weeks. I searched for it everywhere, in her bag, among her clothes and books. I snuck into her room using the spare key Mama kept hidden away. But I could not find my story. Once when we had a short truce, I politely asked her to give it back to me. I was still terrified that my father might see it. Muna finally agreed and went to the kitchen to grab a screwdriver. She had hidden the story in the motor box of the ceiling fan. But even though she returned the story, I never forgot the agony she had put me through.

I kept looking for proof of Muna's relationship with the boy whose voice I had heard on the phone, searching the house until one day I found a strange cassette in my mother's sewing machine. I was curious and played the tape. It contained a long message from the boy. On the recording, he called me all kinds of names, referring to me as "their enemy," saying that I was the reason they couldn't be together, calling me "the devil alive." That night I handed the cassette to Abouya. It was proof of Muna's sins, and she would now have to atone.

Abouya began to beat her. All the other times when he had beaten her, Muna would fight back and eventually he would give up. But not that night. As she begged him to stop, I stood and watched, terrified and guilt-stricken, and unable to change anything.

The cassette ended up with my cousins, who told the whole family that Muna was in love with a stranger. It was a huge scandal. Aunt Zein told me later that she stopped going to large family gatherings because it was too much to take all the questions and criticism. What made it worse was that while Muna's boyfriend was Arab, he was not Saudi. I had thought Abouya wasn't racist: all of his best friends were Egyptians, and I had never heard him belittle any nationality, unlike everyone else around me, even my mother. But there was a strict dividing line in his thinking. He could be best friends with someone from outside Saudi Arabia, eat with them, live in the same area, share ups and downs. But none of them could ever marry one of his daughters or any of the women in his family.

After this, Abouya cut off our landline and our access to the outside world. He locked us in the apartment and barred us from seeing anyone or having anyone visit us. We couldn't even go out to buy food. The only place he allowed us to go was to school and back, and only if we were accompanied by Mama or by him. My brother was locked in with us too. The next year, when Muna asked to attend medical school in Jeddah, Abouya's first reply was to beat her again.

I wish now that I could simply erase my radical teenage years from my life and repair the damage I did to my family and myself. It wasn't until many years later that I realized that in my quest for Salafi religious perfection, a precious, free-spirited period of my life had been stolen away.

7

The Forbidden Satellite Dish

hroughout secondary school I kept a diary, recording the events in my life, my thoughts and experiences. Many of the entries are predictable, but not this one, written on June 4, 1997:

There are ten days left until the secondary school exams, and I'm feeling very scared and uneasy. These are my final years of school; all the teachers think highly of me, and I don't want to let them down. The problem that's plaguing me now is these awful feelings of fear and dread. I know I'll be asked about my studies on the Day of Judgment: for whom was I studying? For whom did I stay up late all those nights, and for what purpose? And what will I say? God, forgive me for all the times I studied for myself and not for the good of Islam. Make all this studying for your benefit, and don't let the devil get close to us. I've made a pledge to myself: I'll do everything I can to become someone of significance, not for the sake of fame, but because I want to serve Muslims everywhere; I want to offer them something useful. I want to be like Necmettin Erbakan

[1926–2011], *the head of the Islamist Welfare Party in Turkey, or Ali Begovic [Alija Izetbegovic, 1925–2003], the president of Bosnia and Herzegovina. I want to visit all the countries of the Islamic world, solve their problems and repair them single-handedly. I'd hate to live my whole life without having had an impact on the course of things in our great world. I wonder, will I achieve my impossible dream? I don't think so!*

The fact that I ended my secondary school years with such ambitions was something of a miracle. My views had remained extremist and closed-minded. But, more than that, I had grown up in a society that considered teaching, in girls' schools of course, the only acceptable career choice for a woman. It was a job that would keep her as far from the sight of men as possible. Girls who wished to deviate from this path and work as a doctor or nurse for female patients were viewed with a great deal of suspicion. And this was at a time when Saudi Arabia was recruiting engineers, medical doctors, and PhDs from Egypt and other Arab countries due to a lack of qualified people among its own population. None of this, however, stopped me from nurturing my dreams.

I had two major motivations. The first was an overwhelming desire to lift my family out of poverty and improve our social standing. The second was my mother, who carried a deeply held conviction that education, academic success, and an independent career should be the entire focus of our lives; she single-handedly made education a household priority. My mother came from an educated and academically successful family. Although she did not attend school beyond the fourth grade, all but one of her siblings and their children are university graduates. Mama's dream was for me to become a doctor, but mine was to become an engineer or a nuclear physicist. Back then, it wasn't even possible for girls to study these fields, but this did nothing to dampen my enthusiasm.

The universal expectation was for girls to learn how to perform domestic duties such as cleaning, cooking, washing clothes and dishes, and raising children, in preparation for becoming a good wife. But Mama was strongly opposed to us doing any chores. She had only one domestic worker, an illegal immigrant from Nigeria, who came to help during the day; everything else she did herself. I don't recall Mama once asking my sister or me to help her with anything; in fact, she was angry if she saw us devoting time to any task other than our studies. "I don't want any reward from you, or any thanks," she used to say. "My reward will be at the end of the year when I see top grades on your school certificates. I want you to be the number one students not only in your schools, but in the whole of Mecca." If one of us got second place, we had failed our mother. None of us would receive her blessing until we were the best.

But getting top grades was difficult, particularly in the sciences. We studied sixteen different topics per semester, but had no access to laboratories and other essential materials, and thus no practical lessons. The only way to make up for this was to ask parents for help, hire a tutor, or use the already completed notebooks of an older sibling. None of these options was available to me. My parents were not educated, and they couldn't afford a private tutor. As for my sister, she took pains to destroy her notebooks at the end of every year. "Make some effort to find the answers yourself," she told me. "You don't deserve to get them by doing nothing."

But I wasn't going to let my mother down. From my fourth year of primary school through my last year of secondary school, my grades were not only the best in my class but the best in the whole school. At first I worked for my grades to please my mother. I was never rewarded with presents or money; I worked because the satisfaction of achieving was a gift in itself. I started to enjoy the respect that my academic achievements won for me from the teachers and headmistress. Their interest made me feel as if I mattered; it gave me a sense of self. And it was a great achievement for the school that one of their students was able to join the ranks of top students from all over the city.

In school, my grades won me third place in the entire region of Mecca, and in secondary school I achieved first place, with a score of 99.6 percent. The newspapers published the names of the top ten students, and I proudly checked the list to see mine above them all. My teachers told me that there was a cash prize of 5,000 riyals for the student with the top score. Immediately, I thought about everything that Mama needed and drew up a list of what I would buy: a new washing machine to replace our old, broken one; a new oven; a set of pots and dishes. If there was anything left over, I would buy my father a Rado watch, since he'd been without a watch for some time. When my uncle had complimented his old one, Abouya had taken it off his wrist and given it to him as a gift.

Honors Day arrived. The ceremony was held at the offices of the General Administration for Girls' Education. But I didn't wear graduation robes as I had dreamed of, nor did I receive a certificate of achievement, or a gift, or even the special cash prize. All I received that day was a shield bearing my name. It wasn't even inscribed with anything to show that I earned first place. The government had discontinued the award that year, and in general, girls did not receive the same type of recognition as boys. I left the ceremony feeling only crushing disappointment. I put the shield in the box with the rest of my shields and certificates, and I felt even more determined not to rely on other people for anything. I would realize my dreams myself.

However, the graduation wasn't a complete loss. Aunt Zein surprised me with a beautiful gift of engraved gold bangles, just like the ones she wore. It was the only graduation gift I received. I had to sell them later to buy clothes for university.

After a girl finished secondary school, it was customary for would-be suitors to come knocking at the family's door. My best friend, Malak, married when she was eighteen, right after we graduated, and my friend Manal married a short time later. Mama, however, was adamant that no one should broach the topic of betrothal or marriage with her. She immediately refused any and all interested parties without even consulting Abouya or us. While I was still at school, one of my teachers tried to arrange an engagement between her brother and me. I didn't even know about it until after my mother had refused, saying, "My daughters will marry after completing their education."

———

I struggled to decide what I wanted to study at university and which university I should attend. My first-choice subject, engineering, was not available to women. And female secondary school graduates received no guidance with our decisions. If you did not want to study medicine or nursing, the only other choice for girls was to become a teacher. Thus the cycle continued: you are taught by women, and then you teach women, and the women you taught will go on to teach the next generation. This was to prevent the mixing of women and men in the workplace, which was both a religious and a social taboo. But what it has led to is too many applicants for these professions and a glut of educated women who cannot find employment outside of these three fields. In 2012, the Ministry of Labor revealed that eighty-five percent of those seeking jobs were women, despite the fact that more women obtain university degrees and certificates of higher education than men.

Without a scholarship to study abroad, I had three choices for university. My first option was to enroll in Umm Al-Qura University in Mecca, ten minutes away from where I lived. It didn't provide many opportunities or a particularly qualified teaching staff, but it was known for a Salafi-inspired radicalism that would have suited me very well at that period of my life. Another choice was to study at one of the colleges of education, institutions designed to prepare women for the teaching profession. Regardless of one's major, one's course of study was dominated by religious and education-related material.

My third option was to study at King Abdulaziz University in Jeddah, an hour's drive away. It was unthinkable that I would live on or near campus; I would have to commute. King Abdulaziz University provided many more opportunities than Umm Al-Qura, but my still-radical self had serious concerns. The school was located in a liberal, progressive city. Despite its proximity to Mecca and the fact that it served as the arrival point for the majority of Muslim pilgrims, Jeddah was considered the most "open" city in Saudi Arabia. The university had a bad reputation among Meccans because it allowed girls to uncover their faces. It even allowed girls at the College of Medicine to participate in mixed education. My sister had enrolled at the university before me, and when she decided to study at the College of Medicine, she faced strong objections from my father and some of my male cousins over the mixing of the sexes. My cousins categorically told my father not to allow her to attend a "mixed" school. My father, remembering Muna's flirtations with the Arab boy, listened. This ideological combat soon turned physical; she was severely beaten by my father and imprisoned in the apartment.

Somehow Mama managed to smuggle Muna out of our building and get her to the school to take the acceptance test; I remember Muna leaving that day with a bandage over one of her eyes. She passed the test, earning top marks. Still, my sister needed my father's consent before she was able to enter the school. To this day, I don't know how Mama persuaded my father to sign the permission papers. (Females in Saudi Arabia still cannot enroll anywhere without having permission from their assigned male guardian.) But she did.

I submitted my registration papers at the University of Umm Al-Qura, but they were so dismissive and disparaging, shouting insults and herding the female students from place to place like hapless sheep, that I decided to enroll in the College of Education instead. It wasn't possible to major in physics there, so I chose the English department, although I wasn't very happy with my decision. For her part, Mama was very disappointed that I had chosen the College of Education: "I want you to be a doctor, like your sister," she said.

"But Mama," I replied, "the Faculty of Medicine is mixed—and anyway, I hate the sight of blood. I can't imagine myself ever being a doctor. What I really want is to study physics." Mama cried. "Twelve years of top grades, and all that effort wasted for you to go to the College of Education?" she asked.

The combination of Mama's tears and my own lack of conviction about the English department made it impossible to remain stubborn. The only choice left was King Abdulaziz University in Jeddah. My concern now was how to approach my father. How would I tell him I'd changed my mind again? To my surprise, he agreed without protest. Unlike with my sister, none of our relatives told him not to let me go. I withdrew my registration from the College of Education and headed for Jeddah with my father.

By then the period to register for any university was over and the doors were closed. My sister helped me to be placed on the "wait list." Eager to make sure that I could get off the list if a spot opened up, my sister and I spoke on a daily basis with the dean of admissions and registration. After a week of asking at the office and a week of going up to the university gates, only to be denied entry, I began to lose hope. Would a whole year of my life be wasted?

Then, unexpectedly, the dean invited me to an interview. I thought that she would use the interview to decide if I merited one of the vacant spots. To my surprise, when I got there I discovered that she wanted to tell me in person that I had been accepted. "We'd be honored for a student with an academic record like yours to join our university," she said.

Though her words certainly made me happy, I had no idea what an impact that they would ultimately have. Those words opened the door to a new stage in my life, a door that would lead to a way out of the narrow confines of the first eighteen years of my existence. Despite all the differences and problems between my sister and me, I discovered that there was one thing that united us: the importance we placed on education and on excelling in our studies, no matter how hard we had to struggle to do so.

———

At King Abdulaziz, the girls' university buildings were completely set apart from the boys' buildings. We even had a separate gate, where we had to show a university ID in order to go in and out. This meant that for the first time in my life I had a card with my name and picture.

At that time, official, government-issued ID cards were available only to Saudi males. They received them upon turning fifteen, whereas women remained dependent on men their whole lives. The names of females were only added, without pictures, to a card known as the "Family ID."

We were taught by male professors, though we never saw them face-to-face. Everything was done via closed-circuit television; we saw and heard the professors, who were sitting in a classroom in a separate building lecturing the male students, but they couldn't see or hear us, so we were denied any chance to participate. As if that wasn't enough of a disadvantage, the CCTV often crashed, and then we would simply miss the lecture. If we wanted to ask the professor a question, the only way to do so was by telephone, which was supervised by a female assistant who sat through the lecture with us to maintain discipline and record our attendance. Only the medical students escaped these constraints: the buildings belonging to the College of Medicine and Pharmacy were separate from ours, and it was permissible for female students to attend lectures given by the male doctors.

The excessive measures undertaken to separate boys and girls meant that we existed in two entirely different worlds. This unnatural separation caused problems that would never be found in a less rigid society. Human beings have lived primarily in mixed communities since the beginning of time, since God created Adam and made Eve to be his companion. God made the coexistence of males and females the basis for the continuation of the human race; He made it so that one is not complete without the other. But my religious observance prevented me from talking to any men at all, even the seller from whom I bought my clothes. I would whisper to my mother what I wanted and she would speak on my behalf. In this way, we respected the fact that my voice was sinful to put on display, because it would seduce the seller, unlike my mother's voice, which belonged to an old, married woman. It didn't bother me that my mother called me by my brother's name, Muhammad, when we were in the street, for even my name was considered *a'ura* (sinful) when uttered in front of men.

At university, however, I heard stories about telephone relationships, made possible by mobile phones. Boys and girls had many clandestine ways to share numbers. A boy might walk past a girl in the marketplace and drop a piece of paper with his number into her bag. If he had a sister who knew the girl, he might ask his sister for the girl's number or even steal it from his sister's mobile phone. More indiscriminate boys wrote their numbers in women's public toilets or flashed them on pieces of paper held up to car windows when a girl passed. Sometimes the numbers were exchanged as text messages. We even have a specific word for these practices: *targeem*, or numbering.

More daring than the phone calls, I heard occasional stories of dates, where boys and girls met each other outside the university's walls. These relationships could never be openly discussed; they were conducted with utmost secrecy and discretion. A young man could talk on the phone with a girl for months without even knowing what she looked like.

I couldn't believe this was happening in Saudi Arabia. If a girl in Mecca was found to be conducting a romantic relationship—even if it consisted only of phone calls and messages—she would face severe beatings from the men in her family, not to mention very likely risk a lifelong confinement inside her home.

There was no worry that I would ever speak to a young man in public or private, let alone accept a phone call or a message from him. I might have been at university, but I still very much railed against "Western values." I forcefully defended the constraints imposed upon Saudi women with the reasoning that these constraints were protecting our society from decay and preserving virtue. I didn't dare request permission from my father to go out of the house for anything other than to attend school or visit the Grand Mosque; I already knew that he would say no, and for the most part without giving his reasons. I also didn't mind that things were like this: he had the right to do that, I reasoned, because he knew my own best interests better than I did. If I ever did dare to ask permission for a trip or to attend a weekend activity on the university campus, I knew that I'd face anger and reproach. Even after I'd relinquished most of my radical ideas, I was still reluctant to leave the house or do anything without asking him first. It was important to me to have my parents' blessing. I tried to please my father in any way I could, but there was always some aspect of what I did that made him dissatisfied. Both of us ended up sad: I was unhappy trying to make him happy, and nothing I did seemed to make him happy anyway.

My father lived his life according to a very strict code. Among his most-repeated sayings and rules, "Don't borrow money from anyone so that you owe them a favor. Don't spend the night in someone else's place, because you might see aspects of their character that you dislike. Don't accept recompense from anyone, even if they are in a position to pay you; all recompense comes from God."

Although the last time he had hit me was in the third year of secondary school, my fear of him remained the dominant factor in our relationship. It was hard to love him fully when a constant unease governed our dealings with each other, but I did love him in spite of everything. I knew he'd been deprived of his own father before he was even born, and that at a young age he'd left his mother to transport pilgrims between Mecca and Jeddah. I appreciated that he never spent nights outside the house and that we never once woke up in the morning without finding our school money waiting for us. Our family relied on my father's work as a taxi driver to put food on the table each night, so he worked even when he was sick. He never took a day off. His work was arduous, and he didn't return home until after midnight, but for seven years straight, he woke my sister and me at six in the morning to drive us to our university in another city. For five of those years, he was waiting outside the gates to bring me home at two in the afternoon. Then he would return by six in the evening to pick up my sister. Calculating the distance between Mecca and Jeddah, he endured five years of spending six or seven hours of his day on the road—in addition to his taxi driving—just so we could get to and from university on time.

At the beginning of each semester, our teachers asked us to buy books and lecture pamphlets from the university bookshop. The bookshop was located beyond the girls' campus, so we couldn't go there ourselves. While my classmates sent their drivers with a shopping list, Abouya was the one who went there for me. He might have to wait two or three hours to get a copy because of the thick, frenzied crowds at the university bookshop, and each time he refused to allow me to pay for the cost of the books from the monthly stipend the university gave me, no matter how expensive they were.

I came from a very poor neighborhood in Mecca, and an even poorer family. Although I had traveled to Egypt, I couldn't really conceive of the fact that there was an entirely different Saudi world only an hour away. When I went to study in Jeddah, it was a huge social leap, and one for which I wasn't prepared. I heard girls talking about clothing brands, and I saw my classmates with luxury bags, expensive watches, and designer sunglasses. I listened to stories about summer trips to Geneva and London, and I saw drivers in luxury cars waiting for the students outside the university gates. The other students bestowed looks of superiority or pity on those who were less well off, and I felt those looks wherever I went.

My father's taxi was a Toyota Corolla, and like all the taxis in Mecca, it was painted bright yellow. Abouya had bought it secondhand. The air conditioner didn't work, which was quite an inconvenience given that we lived in one of the hottest regions of the world, where daytime temperatures commonly exceed 40 degrees centigrade (104 degrees Fahrenheit). Each afternoon, when I left the university, I took special care so that none of my classmates would see me getting into the distinctive yellow car. I didn't want to hear their hurtful comments. But it also hurt me knowing that I was ashamed for my classmates to see my father.

Money had always been an issue for my family, but once I got to university, things got a little easier. The monthly financial allowance from the school (1,000 riyals for male and female students in the scientific departments, and 800 riyals for those in the arts departments) was a huge help when it came to buying things I needed for

my studies, even clothes. I worked in the women's sports club to sup-
plement my stipend, earning an hourly wage of ten riyals ($2.60), and
I could earn up to 500 riyals per month. Despite my long hiatus from
drawing, I was still a good artist, and I would also create drawings and
paintings to sell to my classmates, usually for 35 riyals, but sometimes
for as much as 70. On one occasion, I received a request to work on a
mural that was two by three meters. I spent a full month completing
it, and was paid 1,500 riyals, the most I'd been paid for anything in my
life. I used the money to buy a new, remote-controlled television and
a VHS player. Abouya still has them.

My financial independence liberated me. Having money enabled
me to make decisions and follow them through. Not only did I no longer constantly consult my father, I did some things without him even
knowing: fear of physical violence had been replaced by a fear of dis-
appointing him. Now, for the first time in my life, I had the freedom
to choose the color of my clothes and shoes, my hairstyle, even where
I went (inside the campus). These choices, although simple, gave me
the feeling that I had some say over my life. I had been conferred a degree of responsibility, I could trust myself. These were feelings that I
had always been deprived of, though I hadn't noticed the deprivation.
I had thought that being under the control of a male guardian was the
normal way to live. How could I have known otherwise?

Though we were permitted to do many things in the university,
wearing pants remained a taboo. They were allowed only in the sports
club, and even then they had to be loose and worn with a long T-shirt
to cover the derriere. I found out about the university sports club from
my sister. Although women's sports are banned under the Saudi code,
King Abdulaziz is the exception. It is the only government school in
the country that allows girls to play sports. I had always loved sports,
and I registered at the sports club in my first week. Though I'd been
kept from playing sports after I reached puberty—no more soccer
with my cousins or riding bikes or running races—my passion remained alive. If I didn't have a lecture to attend, I would spend my
time in the sports club. All of my close friends at the university were

also members of the sports club, and I participated in every activity available: basketball, volleyball, badminton, table tennis, karate, cycling, running, billiards, and foosball. I kept my sporting activities a secret from my family, because in their view they were socially and religiously forbidden. Sports was the first taboo that I broke, and I didn't feel an ounce of guilt. I was happy to be making up for those lost years. But I was also careful to make sure that my sports never affected my academic achievements: I remained a top student throughout all my university years, never once breaking my covenant with Mama.

Because of the separation of the sexes in Saudi society, a female subculture known in Arabic as *boyāt* (*boya* in the singular) began to thrive. The expression *boya* is made by taking the English word *boy* and adding an *a* sound, used in Arabic to feminize a word. It referred to women who were tomboys. There was also an entire subculture of feminized men.

At my university, there were a considerable number of boyat. They wore men's hairstyles, men's shirts and even men's fragrance. Each boya had a close female friend with whom she'd walk hand in hand and from whom she was rarely apart. Some of them went to the sports club. My classmates and I often met in our free time to work on projects or homework, and I remember their reactions when I suggested meeting at the club. "I'm afraid of what the sports club will do to my reputation," they'd say. "I don't trust that place."

The aspersions cast on these female friendships took their toll on one of my own friends. Rana was also from Mecca, and we studied together in the College of Science, though we were in different departments. We both adored basketball, and we always played on the same team—we understood each other perfectly. We wore the same clothes, read the same novels and books, and later on listened to the same music. It was a treasured friendship, and her company helped me feel less sad about the childhood friends I missed: Manal, Malak, Jawahir, and my female cousins, Amal and Hanan.

One day, a member of the sports club threw a veiled comment

in my direction. Her barb implied that because Rana and I spent so much of our day together, we must be lovers and lesbians. It was only a throwaway comment, but it hurt and humiliated me deeply. Homosexuality is explicitly forbidden under strict sharia, and the punishment for homosexuality is death. Stoning and other forms of execution are still carried out today against gays and lesbians in some Muslim countries. I stopped talking to Rana completely, and I didn't explain why. I liked her very much, but I couldn't allow anyone to call her morals or mine into question, even if just in passing. What other people thought was very important to me in that period of my life. I stayed away from Rana until we graduated and never explained the reason. Years later, when I'd stopped worrying about what people expected of me or what they were saying, I told her that I owed her an explanation. I visited her and we talked as if we'd never been apart. She forgave me, and we resumed our friendship. She's someone I turn to when things are darkest. I'm still saddened to think that such meaningless words and opinions controlled my happiness, my unhappiness, and even my choice of friends for so many years.

The friends I met at the sports club came from all parts of the university. Another of my friends was a girl named Sara, who was born in Jeddah and had lived there all her life. We studied together in the College of Science, and we coordinated our schedules to be able to meet in the sports club and play basketball. One day, as I waited at the university gates for my father, I saw Sara leaving the campus and was surprised to see that she didn't cover her face. I was astonished and disappointed at the same time. How was it that Sara could expose her face like this to the outside world? How could God accept her prayers when she was unveiled? Sara wasn't one of the girls who used makeup, but she had a natural, radiant beauty that could easily capture a man's interest.

I found myself facing a huge dilemma. Sara was among the nicest of all my friends. She welcomed me with a wide smile whenever she saw me, and she always performed her prayers on time. At the end of the month she collected money from the girls at the sports club to tip the cleaning lady, Aunt Aisha. One time, when Sara and I hadn't seen each other for a while, she welcomed me with a warm hug. I wasn't used to receiving such gestures from anyone. In my family, the only time I had been hugged was when my aunt consoled me after the death of my grandmother.

Despite Sara's kindness, I didn't know how I could possibly continue our friendship after seeing her expose her face. I tried to stay away from her: she was disobeying God, I told myself, and she deserved His wrath. Sara tried to ask me why I was avoiding her, and I made endless excuses instead of telling the truth. This was the first real test of my radical beliefs. I remembered what we had been taught: that we should base our love and friendship for another person solely on her level of piety. But Sara made this hard to do. I decided to continue our friendship in the hope that someday I'd be able to sway her beliefs, but that someday never came. Sara didn't change. I did.

——

The first Saudi television channel began broadcasting Arabic-speaking programs in 1964, and the second, an English-speaking channel, debuted in 1983. There were no others, and this lack of choice led us to refer jokingly to the two channels as Compulsion 1 and Compulsion 2. Still, they were not entirely useless. I owe the beginnings of my English education to Compulsion 2, which included the program *Sesame Street* in its schedule.

Then the haram satellite dishes arrived. Though only a few satellite channels were available inside the kingdom, all owned by other Arab governments, the differences between the types of programs they showed and the ones shown on our two channels were easily noticeable. Conservative religious shows dominated the Saudi channels' lineup. Our news broadcasts were largely preoccupied with banal updates on the royal family: "His Highness received a guest, His Highness waved goodbye to a visitor, His Highness has traveled." Despite the bans on the sale of satellite dishes and receivers, there was a black market for these contraband goods. Although this made the dishes and receivers astronomically expensive, it didn't stop people in cities like Jeddah from installing them on their roofs. I would listen to my university friends talk about the Arabic-dubbed serial dramas from Mexico—one called *Guadalupe* was particularly popular. They would talk about the news channel Al Jazeera, too, and how it was a different type of news broadcast. This caught my interest. But in more conservative Mecca, it remained a social taboo to have satellite channels; friends and family might even shun you. I knew that my father, who had been swayed by the religious rhetoric warning of the dangers of the dish, would flatly refuse to have one in the house.

But I also noticed that our neighbors in our apartment building in Mecca had their own dish on the building's roof, so I asked them to help me get another dish for our apartment and implored them to keep it quiet. I spent part of my government-sponsored university allowance to pay for our dish—which was ironic, considering the dish was banned by the government. I placed the receiver on top of the video player, and I was careful to cover everything with an embroidered cloth cover so Abouya wouldn't see it. Then I made sure to delete all the channels showing music videos, so that none of us would accidentally stray into sin.

Mama was very happy to have the Egyptian satellite channel. When Abouya was out, we gathered around the television to watch old Egyptian films, amazed to be seeing them in Saudi Arabia. For a long time, we kept our secret from my father. But one day, while waiting for us in the car outside the building, he noticed a thick black wire running down from the roof and ending inside our balcony. "Is this the wire from a dish?" he asked me.

What was there to say? What could possibly excuse our deception?

"We'll settle this when you get back from university," he told me.

I spent that day's classes dreading the coming altercation, but, shockingly, he never broached the subject with any of us ever again. I felt comfort in the fact that he knew, and that we knew he knew, and that there was now an unspoken understanding that none of us would ever mention it. Gradually, Abouya began to follow the Al Jazeera broadcasts just as we did, and the dish became an open part of our household. It was our electronic window to the outside world.

——

I didn't realize it then, but the satellite dish was a slippery slope. Even though I had deleted the music video channels, I could not escape the haram sounds of music. In April 1999, I wrote in my diary: "The final match of the inter-faculty basketball league ended in the victory of the team from the Faculty of Home Economics, led by captain Rania K., over the team from the Faculty of Medicine, led by captain Tara F., and the score was 30–44. My team, from the College of Science, took third place. I tried to sit outside the club when music was being played for the break in the middle of the match, but I had to go in when they were giving out the medals."

The first song I ever purposefully listened to started as an accident. One day I walked into the living room as my brother was listening to the Backstreet Boys. I stopped, struck by the beauty of the words and the music. But I was too embarrassed to tell him that I wanted to stay and listen. I waited until he left the house and then put the headphones over my ears and pressed Play on the tape recorder.

Show me the meaning of being lonely . . .
There's something missing in my heart

To my ears, the music flowing through the headphones was the dreamiest, most beautiful thing that I had ever heard. I could not understand how something so beautiful could be the work of the devil. The lyrics struck a chord with me; I felt truly lonely in my closed-off world of rigid beliefs, and I too felt there was something missing in my heart. Yet I remained torn: I loved the music, but I felt guilty whenever

I listened to it. As the Backstreet Boys sang about loneliness, I imagined the pain of molten iron flowing into my ear, because that was what the clerics had preached would happen. Whenever this guilt became too much to bear I would renounce music for a while. But then my brother would buy a new tape, and I would listen to it on the sly.

To live your life with such constant guilt is torment. But that wasn't the only feeling I experienced. Inside my mind, there was a growing sense of contradiction between what I heard in sermons and what I saw all around me. Despite the prevailing rhetoric that condemned music ever more aggressively, both of the public television channels opened their programs with the national anthem, and their shows were accompanied by music. There was a store that sold musical cassettes near our building. Photography was labeled as haram, but there was a photography shop near our building. A picture of the king was printed on all the banknotes, and his picture hung everywhere, on the streets and inside buildings. It was haram for men and women to socialize and shake hands, but the television showed clips in which men from the government welcomed mixed official delegations from other countries, and the Saudi men chatted and shook hands with the women.

I had three choices. My first option was to commit the sins of listening to music and watching television in spite of my religious convictions, which would mean ignoring my feelings of guilt and accepting these contradictions. But this would make me a sinner, something I knew I could not live with. My second choice was to reject everything I had been taught about music and television, but this too would have big consequences: outright rejecting the tenets of my faith would place me in the same category as those who had been excommunicated from Islam, even if I continued to pray, fast, and read the Koran. The third option was to look for an acceptable way out of my dilemma. But how would I know where to look for the answer when I couldn't tell anyone what I truly felt?

———

My plan had always been to study physics. After three terms of general study, I enrolled in the physics department, only to discover that it was very small and unpopular; there were six other students and me. I hadn't come this far in my education to study something no one cared about. One of the largest and most popular departments in the university was computer science, and it was also the hardest to join. Fifteen hundred girls had taken the departmental admissions test, competing for two hundred available spaces. I asked to switch my enrollment to computer science: my academic record was good enough that the university said I did not need to sit for the admissions test. By the time I graduated, only sixty of the original two hundred girls remained in my cohort, because computer science was more rigorous than most of the other scientific departments.

I bought my first computer with a loan from my uncle and my grown-up cousin Miss Fayza. Initially, I only used it to complete my homework. But that changed with the introduction of the Internet. We were supposed to use email to submit our homework and to communicate with our professors, so it was essential for me to have working Internet at home. The obstacle was convincing my father. He had come home one Friday after weekly prayers and the imam's sermon talking about a new evil, the Internet, and we heard him repeat the same rhetoric about it that had been previously used to vilify the satellite dishes.

My father even handed me a cassette tape with a sermon describing the dangers of the Internet. The evil of the Internet, proclaimed the tape, is that it helps girls and boys to date and exchange messages without being watched or held accountable by anyone. Chatting on Messenger was to be avoided at all costs. The Internet also provided an open door for ideas and beliefs that would pollute our pure, extreme Salafi doctrine. I promised myself that if I managed to get access to the Internet, I wouldn't use these chat rooms or read anything that would affect my beliefs. (The government has had a similar reaction to other widespread technological innovations. When cell phones with cameras first appeared, they were banned in Saudi. I had to smuggle an early Nokia camera cell phone into the country from Bahrain in 2004. There was a large black market for these banned phones, with smugglers hiding them inside car bumpers or car door frames, while customs officials and police used ultrasound devices to ferret them out.)

To subscribe to the Internet you had to have a landline, but Abouya had disconnected our home telephone line after the incident with Muna and the Arab boy. In order to get a new landline, the telecommunications company required proof of the apartment's rental contract. This made the situation more complex than I'd anticipated, so I asked my mother for help. I explained that I needed the Internet to do my homework, and that I'd take care of all the expenses from my university allowance. Mama got hold of a fake rental contract from a local real estate office for a small fee. We applied for a landline: once again, we had no choice but to keep this secret from my father.

At first, with the cassette sermon fresh in my mind, my willpower was strong. I resisted visiting chat rooms and websites that railed against Salafi ideology. Instead I spent my time doing homework or strengthening my faith by reading postings on the pro-Salafi sites. But I couldn't resist following political analysis and world news, and as I explored, click by click, I stumbled on a number of sites opposing the Saudi regime. And, though these sites were later blocked and censored, I always found a way around the obstacles.

I began reading articles and postings that criticized extremist Salafi ideology. I read opinions on the niqab, on singing, on drawing animate beings, and also on loyalty and disavowal. My whole life, I'd known only one perspective on these subjects, and as far as I'd been concerned, it was the right one. Now I felt increasingly troubled by everything I read. Gradually, I realized that the ideas I had embraced and defended blindly all my life represented a singular, and highly radical, point of view. I began to question everything. I began posting in forums, discussing these radical ideas and rejecting them. I started drawing again, and I stopped judging Sara for revealing her face. Nothing did more to change my ideas and convictions than the advent of the Internet and, later, social media. When social media began to flourish during the Arab Spring of 2011, I found myself in possession of a voice—a miraculous thing in a country where women are almost never heard.

But a decade before that came September 11. That was the date of the complete transformation in my beliefs, the start of my rebellion against the teaching of hatred and hostility toward non-Muslims. It was an event that divided Saudi society into two sections—those who were shocked and those whose contempt of the West, particularly of America, was heightened. Hatred for Americans was prevalent in Saudi Arabia for many reasons. A central factor was the presence of US military bases, which had been used during the First and Second Gulf Wars. Other factors included the strong bias against Israel in the Palestinian conflict with Israel; the sanctions against Iraq, which were seen as a form of siege and starvation; and America's support for dictatorial regimes in the Arab world. But on that day, we were glued to the television screen, watching the replays of the buildings falling.

We had grown used to watching bloodshed, massacres, and destruction in Muslim countries like Afghanistan, Bosnia, Chechnya, and Iraq; now, for the first time, we were seeing the same thing in America. As I watched thick plumes of smoke rise into the sky and saw the Twin Towers burn, my feelings were a mixture of shock and deep sorrow. The scene that etched itself in my memory more firmly than any other was seeing victims jumping from the upper floors of the World Trade Center. "This is madness," I said to myself, in tears. "Neither mind nor conscience can accept what we are seeing here." When I went to sleep that night, I prayed to God that Muslims had no role in the tragedy.

I woke to news that the attack had been carried out by Al Qaeda, which was led by a Saudi, Osama bin Laden, and soon after, that fifteen of the nineteen hijackers were from Saudi Arabia. The heroes of yesterday's Afghan War were the same monsters who had perpetrated this attack. It was a shock, and it changed my convictions about what jihad for the sake of God really meant. I could not believe that God would demand the killing of innocent people. The atrocities of September 11 were followed by a series of terrorist attacks inside Saudi Arabia, in which hundreds of civilians and military personnel lost their lives. The name *Al Qaeda* popped up every time.

I was done with Salafism.

———

I entered my own period of mourning that fall. On October 25, my aunt Zein died. She had devoted years of her life to caring for her mother, my grandmother Sitti Alwa (God rest their both souls) after she developed dementia. She would wash her mother, clean the urine and waste away from her body, and change her clothes, just as one would do for an infant. She did this even though Sitti Alwa would insult her and rant and rave at her, and even throw her out of the house. My aunt was patient and dutiful to the end. "Lord, let me die a quiet death," she used to call out in prayer. "Let me cause no trouble to anyone." God answered her prayer; she left this world peacefully, in a diabetic coma, without giving anyone a chance to bid her farewell. I loved my aunt very much, and spent days crying because I hadn't been able to see her before she died. I saw only her body, lying on the ground, a colorful pink head scarf with red flowers and green leaves surrounding her peaceful face. A golden stud adorned her beautiful nose, and her gold bangles had been placed in her soft, caring hands. It was as if she were sleeping. But this was a sleep from which she'd never open her eyes, no matter how much I wished to see them and to hug her one last time.

On June 27, 2000, Sheikh Hamoud bin Aqla al Shuebi pronounced the following fatwa: "To grant a woman an identity card bearing her picture is an abomination which is not permitted by sharia law. It will result in great religious, moral and social evils." But a little more than one year later, in November 2001, the Saudi interior minister, Prince Nayef bin Abdulaziz, decreed that Saudi women twenty-two years or older would be able to obtain personal identification cards with the written consent of their guardian. Newspapers reported that the purpose of the new ruling was to help women "perform their activities with ease" and to prevent fraud and identity theft. But others claimed that the real reason was security; in a number of cases, would-be terrorists had been arrested wearing women's clothing. Whatever the reason, the issuing of an ID card was now possible, although optional.

Not long after the decree, I asked my father to take me to the Office of Civil Affairs in Mecca. I didn't tell him why. When we arrived, I tried to make it a happy surprise: "Abouya, did you know that I can now get an official identity card? They issued the decision this week, and I'm here to submit my application."

My father looked at me, his expression a mixture of outrage and disbelief. What he had heard me saying was this: "I want independence from you, and I don't need you after today. My picture will be on the identity card, and men will see it." I know that's what he heard because those were the accusations he flung at me, word for word, in response to my request.

I insisted that he was my father and that I would never abandon him or stop being obedient to him. I explained how the card would be very important for me after I graduated, when I needed to prove my identity in the workplace and elsewhere. I reminded him how many times we had been stopped at checkpoints between Mecca and Jeddah, how he'd been interrogated to make sure that we were his daughters, and how we'd been able to do nothing but take out our university ID cards as proof.

My father wasn't moved. He shook his head and pointed for me to go by myself. I knew that I wouldn't be able to apply for the ID card without his signature, but I went to the registry office anyway and sat there waiting, holding back my tears. I took an application form and the guardian consent form and returned to the car chastened. Abouya looked at me and said sarcastically, "Where's the card?" It was a clear statement that he was still the master of my fate. I didn't know what to do. I couldn't just fake the guardian consent form as Mama and I had done for the apartment rental contract; to do such a thing with government papers would be fraud.

The identity card remained my obsession. I became cold with my father, and took every opportunity to remind him of what I wanted. In turn, his hurtful responses often drove me to tears. "You want to be a man?" he would ask. Or, "That's it? You don't want to depend on me anymore?" But I never tired of approaching him, consent form in hand, to repeat my request.

Finally, after several weeks, he surrendered. We went to the Office of Civil Affairs together and applied for my ID card. The serial number on the card was 1091, meaning that only 1,090 Saudi women had received their cards in the weeks before me. I tucked the card in my wallet and carried it with pride: for the first time ever, I had something to prove my identity. The most important thing of all was the picture. I looked miserable, but I didn't care: it showed my face, my eyes, nose, and mouth, with nothing blurred or concealed or veiled. It was the day my homeland acknowledged me as a Saudi citizen. But more than that, it was a symbol of my newfound courage to assert myself. I had changed and perhaps, in some small way, so had my father.

8

Employed and Homeless

Growing up, we never had pocket money. If my brother or sister or I wanted something, we would save a riyal or two from our school breakfast money each day. I remember I wanted a magnetic board with English letters because I really wanted to learn English. The board cost 50 riyals. I saved for weeks to buy that board. No one was rich at the government schools we attended, but there weren't many girls poorer than us. One of my friends had an allowance of 500 riyals for clothes. I didn't have any clothing allowance. My father gave my mother 50 riyals a year for our clothes, so she would buy material and sew Muna and me our two dresses each year.

The only time we were allowed to buy anything was at the start of school, when we went to the stationery store for books and school supplies. Abouya would also buy me a coloring book. The rest of the year, though, I was afraid to ask him for anything. He beat all of us for no reason, so I certainly didn't want to give him an excuse.

Abouya was very generous when people came to visit. Whenever Uncle Ali came from Libya, he bought great quantities of food and gifts. But we lived in an old apartment with secondhand furniture and had no toys except what my mother scraped together or what we saved for ourselves out of our breakfast money. One time, when I desperately wanted to buy some things for my Egyptian Barbie, I asked my mother if I could sell some of the gold jewelry that my Libyan uncle had brought me. Mama said yes, so I sold some of my rings and necklaces, and then she took me to the toy store. I bought a kitchen set and a bedroom set for Barbie.

Mama sometimes told us that our father made good money. For years, he worked for a gas station. But he didn't bring his money home, and he wouldn't put it in a bank. He "banked" nearly all of his earnings with his boss. He only took enough money to pay the rent, the grocery bill, the electricity bill, and a little bit extra beyond that. We lived in a horrible apartment while my father's salary lived with his boss.

When I was in middle school, my father was fired. He went to see his boss with the receipts for years of salary to collect his money. He brought a big black suitcase to put the cash in. But all the boss did was kick him out of the office. Abouya yelled at him, saying that he would go to the Grand Mosque and pray that God punished him. And the boss basically said, sure, go ahead and ask God to punish me. Abouya came home with nothing. Everyone was angry. We had dreamed of moving to a house that we owned, but now the money was gone. We partly blamed Abouya for his blind trust in his employer.

Abouya changed a lot after this incident; he lost his trust in people. He managed to sell a piece of land in Jeddah that he had gotten from the government. (The government used to give land to citizens to build their own homes; he was going to use the savings from his salary to build a home on that land.) He bought a pre-owned taxi with the proceeds. Then he went back to his first job, driving pilgrims to Mecca.

All of this made me determined to find a good job.

My quest to find a job began as I approached my fourth year of university. Teaching wasn't an option. Only boys' secondary schools taught information technology, and even if girls could study computer science, I didn't want to return to the same dismal government girls' schools that I had endured all those years. Since my major was a new one, I couldn't get a master's or doctorate; the university didn't have the necessary academic staff.

The longer I hunted for a job, the gloomier my prospects seemed. One day Maram, one of my classmates, dashed my hopes of finding employment anywhere. "The best you can aim for is to work as an instructor in one of the training institutes," she told me. The job she was talking about didn't even require a diploma, and the money wouldn't be enough to afford any of the things I wanted. "You'd be lucky to get 4,000 riyals," she said.

Just as she'd helped me earlier to enter the university, my sister came to my rescue again. During the summer before my senior year, she helped me get an internship at the university hospital, where she was doing her final year of medical training. My sister didn't believe in the niqab: she wore it only outside the hospital. My parents never tried to force it on her, perhaps because they knew she'd never accept it.

In the past, Muna and I had clashed over the niqab as well. But the day I entered university hospital for my interview, I decided that I, too, would uncover my face. I'd never revealed my face to men before—I'd never even contemplated it—so I had no idea how it would make me feel.

Outside on the street, I lifted my niqab and placed it in my handbag. The first thing I sensed was the air on my skin as I walked. I felt it touch my cheeks, my forehead, and all the other parts of my face for the first time since I was still a girl. Breathing felt different, too: the barrier was gone, and I finally inhaled freely. It was like opening a long-closed window into a dark room. That was the moment I rediscovered my face.

At the hospital, I walked uneasily through the corridors, toward the office of Dr. Abdelbari, the hospital's head of information technology, who would be conducting my interview. I kept my head down; I felt completely naked whenever a man walked by, and I quickened my step to disappear from his sight.

Dr. Abdelbari welcomed me as I entered his office. "Peace be upon you, too," he said, and held out his hand. I looked down. I'd never shaken hands with a man in my life, and I couldn't bring myself to do it now. I apologized profusely, and thanked God that no one else was watching. I was certain I had ruined my chances of getting the summer internship. I sank into the chair opposite his desk and studied the piles of papers.

Dr. Abdelbari was a man in his late fifties, originally from Pakistan. He was slim with white hair and a warm voice. He was wearing a white *thobe*, the long robe traditionally worn by Saudi men, but without a shemagh, the white-and-red-checked head covering. He was surprised that I spoke English, which I needed to know for the internship. The government schools where I had studied were known for teaching nothing more than the basic rules of the language. I told him that I'd taught myself, because I loved learning languages.

"We'll give you a monthly remuneration of a thousand riyals if you prove yourself," he told me.

It was a very small amount given the long working hours, but getting the experience made up for the low wage. I woke up at six every day to arrive at the office by eight, and when I finished my work at five in the afternoon, I had an hourlong journey back to Mecca ahead of me. I was very surprised that the workplace was mixed. The department gave me a desk in one of the offices, and I shared the space with another intern, a girl named Sue from Kenya. The team with whom we worked was comprised of three male employees and one woman. None of them was from Saudi Arabia, which made me feel somewhat more at ease. It was the first time I'd dealt with men other than my father and brother, and I was overcome with curiosity. I was like a twentysomething Alice in Wonderland, having fallen down my own peculiar rabbit hole.

I became enthralled by any man who spoke even a few words to me, including the reception clerk. I'd obsess over one man and then a week later become infatuated with another. I noted every detail—the way they talked, their clothes, the style of their facial hair, their hands, their walk—but I never showed my feelings; I was careful to maintain a cold and uninterested air, all the while terrified that my eyes would somehow give me away. Summer ended, and the IT department didn't give me the financial reward it had promised. But they did give me my very first certificate of experience and, perhaps most important of all, my first experience of a normal work environment, with no separation between women and men.

Uncovering my face when I was anywhere outside with Abouya and Mama—or in any public place in Mecca, for that matter— remained unthinkable; it would never be deemed acceptable in our environment and social circles. My cousin Amal never saw the face of her other grandmother, who belonged to a Bedouin tribe and never took off her covering, even in the presence of her family. The first time my father saw my face uncovered in public wouldn't be until some years after I had moved far away to the Eastern Province. Even then, he was very upset with me. More than once he ordered me to put my niqab back on. I told him I would, but I didn't. With time, my parents got used to seeing me without it.

Today, my friends who grew up as I did, wearing the niqab, are divided into two groups. One group insists, like me, on wearing only the hijab when at home in Saudi Arabia. (All females in Saudi Arabia, even non-Muslims, are forced to wear the abaya cloak whenever they leave the house.) The other group has kept the niqab, whether because of the social pressure or because of their husbands' commands or because they believe in it. But none of my friends who wear the niqab on a day-to-day basis wear it outside Saudi Arabia. They wear either the hijab or no form of head covering at all.

The phenomenon of Saudi women deveiling in transit is so well known that I remember a Tunisian work colleague making jokes about it. "When Tunisian women get on the airplane to leave the country," he would say, "they put the hijab on, and when the Saudi women board, they take it off!" Part of the reason for this lies with the law, secular and religious: Tunisian state law used to prohibit the wearing of the hijab, while Saudi religious law imposes it. My retort was simple: "This is what happens when the state intervenes in a person's private life; it creates two separate personas. It compels you either to lead two separate lives, or to violate what's imposed on you when the state isn't looking."

The propaganda declaring that the niqab is what separates Muslim women from the infidel complicates the debate. As I grew older, I came to believe that it is a very ugly thing to describe women with uncovered faces as infidels. One time, I was on a flight between the Saudi cities of Dammam and Jeddah. A girl about ten years old was sitting next to me. I was chatting with her because she wasn't sitting with her family. "Are you an infidel?" she suddenly asked me.

"Why do you think I'm an infidel?" I asked.

"Because you don't cover your face," she replied.

Despite my black abaya and hijab, she doubted that I was a Muslim.

———

During that same summer before my last year of university, a man my age, Sultan, approached my family to inquire about marriage. He was a cousin from my father's side. Though my sister and I had escaped being married at eighteen so that we could complete our education, girls like me were not free from the constraints of social norms. As we prepared to graduate, we were expected to welcome the knocks of suitors at the door.

I was strongly opposed to the "supermarket method" of selecting a bride, a process where neither the prospective bride nor groom has much of a say in the end result. The potential groom's mother comes to visit the girl first; if the girl wins her approval, she goes home and describes the girl to her son. The prospective groom then comes with his father to meet the girl's father. During this meeting, the groom also gets to see the girl briefly. This supervised encounter is known as a *shoufa,* and it's the only permissible way for boy and a girl to lay eyes on each other without being married.

The day came for Sultan's mother to pay my mother a visit. I was very upset at the thought of her seeing our modest house, and the only clothes I owned that were appropriate were my university clothes. Since our father did not allow us to go out except to visit my family and the only family member left was my uncle—my grandmother and aunt having passed away—I had no formal dress clothes, no colorful long skirts or elegant blouses. My friend Jihan offered to lend me some of her clothes for the day. I was very embarrassed; I'd never worn anyone else's clothes before.

When Sultan's mother arrived, I served her coffee and juice. It is customary in Saudi culture for the suitor's mother to be able to briefly look upon the intended girl. But there should be no conversation between them, and the girl should never be the one to open the door and welcome her prospective mother-in-law into the house. I stood in front of Sultan's mother with clothes that didn't belong to me and a mind that was elsewhere. I was only going through the motions.

Though I wished that she'd hate me, find me ugly, and dismiss any possibility of an engagement, she contacted Mama again to set a date for Sultan and his father to visit with my father. If my feelings had been mixed before, now every fiber of my being resisted. When my college friends brought in pictures of their engagements or marriages for us to look at, I would think that something like that might be nice for me. But whenever I was alone and thought about excelling in my studies and my work, dreaming of a job that would lift my family out of poverty, I could not imagine being married. Slowly, I began to consider the real reason for my aversion to marriage, and memories of the barber Abdulaleem and my bloodstained yellow *jalabiya* came flooding back. I told my parents that I was no longer interested in completing the rituals of engagement.

"Give me one reason for your refusal!" my father demanded.

For once in my life, I spoke the truth. "The day of my circumcision disfigured me horrifically," I replied. "I don't think I'll ever be able to get married, and I don't think I'll ever be able to forgive you."

In those few sentences, I was finally able to voice the blame, help-lessness, and frustration that I'd held within me since I was eight years old. I wanted to wound my father, even as I closed my eyes and pre-pared for the slap that I was sure would come. But there was nothing. Abouya simply turned and exited the room. He never raised the sub-ject of marriage with me again.

━━━

In 2002, as I prepared to graduate with first-class honors and a high grade-point average, I still hadn't found a job. The prospect of sit-ting at home after five years of hard work was devastating. One of my classmates, Marwa, who was from the Eastern Province, mentioned that Aramco, the giant Saudi oil company, ran a summer internship program. "They award a monthly remuneration of 4,000 riyals to the interns," she said. I hadn't even known until then that women could join Aramco; the Aramco office in Jeddah employed only men.

I was desperate to get a spot. "Will you help me apply?" I asked.

She said she would.

I gave her all of the necessary paperwork and waited.

When she called, her first words were, "Manal, pack your bag." Then she told me that we were going to be colleagues that summer.

My father had to sign a consent form for me to do the intern-ship, but this was one form he was happy to sign. It was a dream for any Saudi to work at Aramco. "It's an honor to belong there," he said proudly.

For the first time in my life, I'd be completely alone as well.

I still keep my plane ticket from Jeddah to the eastern city of Dammam in my box of precious things: it reminds me of my journey from a troubled, angry home in a poor, miserable neighborhood to a world that was the opposite of almost everything that I had known. I was assigned to work in Aramco's Expatriate Recruitment Unit. The department's driver, known as Uncle Ali, met me at the airport. As our car pulled through the gates of the Aramco residential compound, I had the biggest shock of my life. I stared out the car window like a new arrival in a foreign land; nothing about my surroundings resembled the Saudi Arabia I knew. I saw clean, organized streets, with trees, lush public gardens, and water fountains. I saw American-style wooden houses, their large windows free of the protective iron bars soldered onto most Saudi residential buildings. Instead of high walls around the houses, there were beautiful gardens. We passed a woman behind the wheel of a car, wearing sunglasses, her hair uncovered. Fascinated, I fixed my gaze on her and craned my neck around to get a better view. There were women walking in the street without abayas; some of them were even running or riding bicycles. "Are you sure we're still in Saudi?" I asked Uncle Ali. Looking into the rearview mirror, I could see him smile.

In the housing office, I received a key to my shared house, Number 622 on Sixth Street of Aramco Dhahran Camp. I'd be living with Rima and Dina, two dental students, and Alia, a computer science student like me. I headed to my new home and carried my small bag over the threshold. The house was built in the American style, just like the ones I'd seen in the movies. There was a backyard, an open kitchen, and large windows for sunlight to stream through. Everything was tidy, awaiting our arrival.

Neither the dishwasher nor the fully automatic washing machine was what I liked best about the house—though both were fantastic luxuries. My favorite thing of all were the two faucet taps—one for cold water and one for hot. Though this was fairly common in Saudi Arabia, it was something I'd never had at home. Our apartment building was very old, and when the building's external water tank emptied, usually within three days of its monthly filling, we survived the rest of the month without running water. We kept a small water tank inside our apartment and a larger one on the balcony, and each day, we measured out the minimum amount of water we needed for bathing or for brushing our teeth. Muna and I had complained constantly to our father, but nothing changed.

That summer I developed an obsession with bathing; morning and night, I would soak in the bathtub for hours. For the first time ever, my bathwater flowed from the taps on demand, and I was determined to enjoy it.

I began my duties as a trainee in the employment office, working under a man named Abdulhadi. He was young and animated. Everything about him was quick: his speech, his steps, how he moved his hands. It was hard to understand half of what he said, but he was cheerful and I loved working with him. Abdulhadi assigned me a number of tasks, many of them completely new to me, and one by one I learned to carry them out. This won me respect and appreciation, especially from the department administrator. At the end of the month I received my first paycheck. I bought Rado watches for Mama and Abouya. Mama wore her gold watch with a circle of tiny diamond chips around the face until she died; Abouya still wears his each day.

As the end of the summer approached, the administrator told me there was a vacancy in the department. "Why don't you submit an application?" he asked. But Abdulhadi had already suggested my classmate Marwa for the position. So he set about trying to find another vacancy for me. One morning he told me that a new division for information security had been established in the Information Technology Business Line. They were hiring recent graduates. If I wanted to go for an interview, there was a good chance I would get a place. The division was a lot more relevant to my field of study: the Employment Office had limited opportunities for someone with a computer science background.

I had two interviews. Although my competitors were all graduates of American universities, I was offered a position. "They gave you an official post?" Abdulhadi asked me afterward. "I thought they'd only hire you on a contractual basis. You're very lucky." I didn't understand the difference at the time—all that mattered to me was the job—but later I learned that I had indeed been very lucky. Contract employees

were only hired for one year at a time; your services might be terminated at any point, and you didn't have the right to medical insurance
or various other privileges the official employees enjoyed. Because of
this, an official post with Aramco was very hard to come by. When
I signed the contract, I couldn't believe the starting salary—8,000 riyals, with an extra 400 added due to my graduating with honors. This
was double what my classmate Maram (who'd told me my best hope
was to become an instructor in a training institute) had predicted.

There was, however, one clause in the contract that had been
crossed out in blue pen: "At the employee's desire, the company will
provide them with a residence in the dedicated staff compound in the
location of their work." I asked why it had been erased. "I'm sorry," she
told me, "Saudi women aren't allowed to live there."

"Is it permitted for Saudi men?" I asked.

Yes, she replied. Saudi males could live there, along with men and
women of other nationalities.

"But I'm an intern," I said, "and I was given a house there. Why
not now, since I'm going to be a full-time employee?"

"After this year," she said, "the company will no longer provide
accommodation for female interns either."

No one was ever able to explain why. There were rumors the ban
had been ordered by the Ministry of the Interior. But, if so, why did
they not ban women from driving, ban the consumption of alcohol,
end mixed work environments, close the movie theaters, and require
women to wear an abaya? Others said that it was the result of bad
behavior by a Saudi woman, who had been forced to leave. Whatever
the reason, the consequences were more serious than I could have
imagined. The Ministry of the Interior prohibited Saudi women from
living in a hotel or furnished apartment without her guardian or a
mahram. The rules also prevented landlords from leasing to women;
the lease agreement had to be in the name of a man, even if it was a
woman who would pay the rent.

As I signed the employment contract, I briefly wondered if I was
making a mistake. I had a way out of Mecca, but how would I find a

place to live? I didn't mention my housing worries to my father for fear that he'd refuse to sign my papers; I still needed a guardian consent form.

When I called my mother to tell her, our conversation was formal and bittersweet. "Congratulations, Daughter," she offered, somewhat sadly.

"It's good news, Mama!" I reassured her. "We're not going to live in poverty and need anymore; we'll lead a new life, a better one, I promise. You won't need your sewing machine after today."

"But you'll be far away from me."

"I'll visit you, Mama. It's only two hours on the airplane."

Despite everything, I was certain I'd miss my father and mother very much. But I couldn't for one moment pretend that I'd miss our neighborhood. Nor would I miss our problems, our unhappiness, or the constant interference in my private life. These were the things I'd already been trying to escape.

After talking to Mama, I called my old classmate Maram. "Please congratulate me," I said, "I signed a contract with Aramco, and my salary is twice what you predicted I would earn. Isn't it good news?" I was shocked by her cold response.

"Aramco, and you'll work with men! You'll never marry, Manal—not now, not ever."

After that, I didn't call Maram again.

The summer internship program ended, and I was forced to return to Mecca until the employment papers were complete. Earlier in the summer, the landlord of my parents' apartment building had decided to tear down the building to construct new, furnished apartments to house pilgrims traveling to Mecca, and my family had been evicted. I was shocked when I saw where they had moved. If I had thought that our previous apartment was old and miserable, it was nothing compared to this one. I phoned the Aramco employment office every week to find out when I'd be able to return. The longer I stayed in Mecca, the more suffocated I felt, and I prayed to God that it wouldn't be long. To pass the time, I spun dreams about the future: I would use my first two paychecks to move my family to a new apartment, in a new neighborhood. I couldn't wait.

Before I could do any of this, however, I had to find my own place to live. Otherwise, I would be employed but homeless. After two long months, at the beginning of October 2002, Aramco said the paperwork was ready. All that was needed was for my father to sign the guardian consent form. Then I would be given a plane ticket to the Eastern Province.

———

On the morning of Wednesday, October 9, 2002, my parents saw me off at the Jeddah airport, and I promised them that I would live up to their expectations. In my head were a thousand questions—not least of which was where I would spend the night when I arrived; in my wallet, I had just 500 riyals. When I worked in Aramco's Expatriate Recruitment Unit, we had a very specific protocol for how we welcomed our new foreign employees. We would meet them at the airport, show them where they would be working, and then give them a complete tour of the compound, so they would be oriented and feel at home. "Here's the bank," we would say, "here are the supermarket and laundry facilities; here are the post office and the barber, and here are the cinema and the restaurant." Finally we'd stop at the housing office, where they would receive a key to their house, equipped with everything they could possibly need: new towels, shampoo, toothbrushes, dish and laundry soap, and enough food for a week. I was looking forward to receiving the same kind of treatment when I arrived; after twenty-three years as a woman in Saudi Arabia, I should have known better.

I landed at Dammam airport and collected my small bag. Everything I owned—clothes, shoes, all my possessions except for a few books—fit into one small suitcase. There was no one there to meet me, not Uncle Ali or anyone else. I took one of the airport taxis and asked for a receipt to give to the employment office in Dhahran. There was nobody to greet me there, either. I felt lost. The only thing I could think of was to head to Abdulhadi's office. He'd been so helpful to me during the summer; perhaps he could be again.

He greeted me warmly. "I don't know where to go from here," I explained. "I don't even know where I'm supposed to work."

"Don't worry, Manal," he reassured me. He asked Uncle Ali to drive me to my department and told me to call if I needed anything.

"Actually, I don't even know where I'll be staying tonight," I confessed. "Aramco won't provide me with housing."

He told me that my department was obligated to provide a hotel room if I needed one, but he wasn't sure how it would be done, since women weren't permitted to rent a room without a mahram or guardian. Thanking him for his advice, I headed to my new office with the driver.

When I reached the area belonging to my department, it looked deserted. It was isolated from the rest of the Aramco complex, and the collection of single-story, prefabricated buildings was not very inviting. Their cheerless sandy color did nothing to help. But at least I had arrived. Gathering myself, I entered building 3133 and asked for the Information Protection Division. I already knew two men in the division. The division planner, a man in his forties, was the head of the Planning Group. He escorted me to the office belonging to the head of the Compliance Assessment Group. This man was to be my new boss. My boss was probably in his early thirties. He wore a light beard and Western-style pants and a shirt; something about his mouth reminded me of Don Vito Corleone in *The Godfather*. The division planner, on the other hand, wore traditional men's robes and a shemagh. Both of them had been part of the team that interviewed me. As he welcomed me, my new boss said, "I had to persuade the rest of the group heads to let you work with us." I felt very happy that more than one group had wanted to hire me, and a little of my uncertainty faded away.

The division planner gave me a tour. "Here's your office," he said, pointing to a cubicle. It contained a beige aluminum table with a laminate wooden surface and an office chair with wheels.

Where was everything else? I wondered to myself. How could I protect any information from here? Only later I was given a desktop computer with an Internet connection and a phone.

We passed by the workshop, a small room with a number of servers. Inside sat two men, close to my age, both engrossed in the screen of a laptop. "Amro is your colleague from the Compliance Assessment group," the division planner told me, "and Khalid is an information security consultant, visiting from America."

My ears pricked up when I heard his title. "What are you doing?" I asked, the first in a torrent of questions.

"We're carrying out a penetration test," the men told me. The new terminology was like hieroglyphics to me.

The tour continued; here a male colleague, here another male colleague, and in the next room yet another. When we'd finished, I asked the division planner if he had left out anyone in the division. "No, Manal," he told me. "I'm quite sure we haven't missed anyone."

"So there are no girls here apart from me?"

"No, there aren't."

That was how things were and how things remained for the ten years I worked at Aramco. Not a single woman other than me was appointed to the Information Protection Division as a professional technical employee, except for one female contract employee who worked with us for one year. We had another full-time female employee who joined us in 2008, but she had a degree in English literature and did not work on any technical projects.

I mentioned to the division planner that I didn't have a place to stay that night. "I don't know what to do," I said. He made a number of phone calls before informing me that he had booked me a room at the Dhahran International Hotel, ten minutes from the office.

"I've booked a room in my name and at the division's expense," he told me. "As an unaccompanied female, they won't let you book a room there yourself. Try not to draw anyone's attention when you're going in and out. If anyone realizes you're there alone, you'll have big problems with the religious police."

I thanked him profusely; but now, I had a second dilemma: "How will I get to work tomorrow?"

He gave me the number of a taxi firm and told me that the division would pay my fare for the first week. "You have a week to find your own accommodation and vacate the room," he added.

Although there was a five-star sign over the hotel's entrance, my room was dirty and the furniture worn. But I was too relieved to care. I called Mama to reassure her. "Don't worry, Mama," I told her, when she asked about where I was staying. "They gave me a house inside the Aramco compound, and I'll use the Aramco bus to get to work. I'm just fine, and tell Abouya the same."

I wanted to cry to my mother, "I'm all alone, Mama. I'm in a hotel room in a strange city, I'm completely broke, and I don't know what I'm going to do." But I knew I couldn't. Mama and Abouya would demand that I come back home.

I sat on the bed and removed my earphones. The silence made every stray sound seemed larger and louder. My room connected to the neighboring room via a locked door, and when night fell, I heard voices beyond the door, a man and a woman. At least I have neighbors, I thought. But when they began to have sex, my peace of mind turned quickly to panic. I was terrified by the sounds I heard. I'd never seen sex in a film and I'd never heard people having it.

I turned on the television. As the woman's voice became louder and louder, I kept raising the volume to try to drown her out. Finally, with the audio blaring as high as it would go, I broke down in tears and sobbed like a little child.

The next day, I asked the front desk for a room without a connecting door, and I called one of my former classmates. I described what had happened in the hotel and she told me that she could help. She had an uncle who lived nearby. She called him, and then called me back to say that she had given him my number. "He said that he can rent a furnished apartment for you—he's married and has a family ID. He'll be waiting for you in front of the hotel tomorrow morning."

Tomorrow was Thursday, then the first of Saudi Arabia's two weekend days. (It's now Friday and Saturday.)

The uncle pulled up outside the hotel in a black Mercedes. I'd never ridden alone with a man before, aside from Uncle Ali (the Aramco driver) and a few anonymous taxi drivers. I opened the door hesitantly and climbed into the backseat. "Am I the driver now?" he asked. "Ride with me in the front." I felt my face grow hot. I threw my black scarf over my face, reluctantly moved into the front seat, and pressed myself as close to the door as possible.

"How are you, Uncle?" I asked. In Saudi culture, it's customary to refer to older people as uncle and aunt as a mark of respect, hence Uncle Ali—we don't call anyone by their first names unless they're the same age as we are or younger.

This uncle wore dark glasses. "I prefer that you use my name," he responded.

I told him I was looking for a furnished apartment, but instead of looking for a place, he started driving me around Khobar City. "Here's Al-Rashid Mall, here is Khobar Corniche, and the corniche restaurants." We spent hours going around in his car, but I felt as if I could say nothing.

As we waited for a traffic light to turn, he asked, "Do you intend to cover your face the whole way?"

I ignored his question and asked, "Can we please go and look for an apartment now?" But we didn't visit a single place. I was trapped in that car. My hands trembled. I pretended to call my parents on my cell phone. Eventually, the uncle pulled into the parking lot for a grocery store and asked if I wanted a drink. My heart was pounding and I couldn't speak, I simply shook my head no. I wanted to open the door and run, but I wasn't even sure where we were. I knew no one.

When he got back in, he was carrying a drink I'd never seen before. "This is called Power Horse. It lets you run like a horse all night long."

Suddenly I was terrified. "I'm calling your niece now," I said, feeling my body shake beneath my abaya. "Please take me back to the hotel."

That apparently was enough. "Okay, okay," he replied. "But do me a favor, and don't tell her that we didn't look."

This time, I did dial my classmate for real. I told her, "Yes, I'm with your uncle now. We're on our way back to the hotel."

I spent my second night in the Eastern Province in tears, just as I'd spent my first. The uncle called and messaged me relentlessly afterward, but I ignored every call and text.

On Saturday, our next work day, I asked Abdulhadi to help me. He promised to find me somewhere to live in the next few days. The week passed very slowly. When I paid attention to the work, I was interested, but my mind was constantly preoccupied with a very different question: where was I going to live? Finally, Abdulhadi called me. "I've found you a residential compound in Khobar," he told me. "They have a collection of prefabricated buildings and they've agreed to lease one to you."

Residential compounds are like islands, completely cut off from Saudi society. They permit their residents to do all the things that are forbidden in Saudi culture; for this reason, Saudi citizens are usually not allowed to live in them. The compounds' residents are normally Europeans and Americans; their companies cover their rent, which is typically around four or five times the cost of a regular apartment. I told him that I didn't have any money to pay up front. "Can I pay for this month when I receive my salary?" I asked. Abdulhadi promised to lend me the full amount, with the understanding that I'd pay him back once I got my housing allowance.

He gave me the address of the compound and I took a taxi there. My future home was part of a collection of temporary units still in need of the most basic things like windows, doors, and furniture. "We're in the process of finishing them," the compound manager promised me. "They'll be open by the end of the week." When the end of the week arrived and I could leave work for the day, I gathered up my things from the hotel room and headed to the compound. The temporary houses were still not ready; in fact, nothing had changed since my first visit. No furniture, no windows, and not a door in sight.

My knees grew weak and the world started to spin before me. I dialed the division planner's number and prayed to God that he would answer—he didn't have to, since it was after official working hours. Relief surged through me when he picked up. "I'm here on the street with my bag," I told him. "My housing was supposed to be ready today, but it didn't happen. Can you call the hotel again? I'm forever grateful . . . I promise I'll find somewhere to live within a few days."

I called Abdulhadi every day the following week, but he no longer answered his phone. I'd either become a nuisance, or he'd changed his mind about lending me rent money. The division planner had no advice; he just told me emphatically that I had to leave the hotel at the end of the week. I talked to the division head, the man who oversaw our division, but he had nothing to say. I was lonely, desperate, and angry. At that moment, I truly understood what it meant to be a Saudi woman. It meant being confronted with every possible kind of obstacle and discrimination. It meant being told that if you want to race with men, you'd have to do it with your hands and legs cut off. I started to wish I had been born somewhere—anywhere—else.

There seemed to be no other option except to back down, admit defeat, call my father, and request to return to the gloomy apartment in Mecca. That night, I slept without crying. My tears had dried up.

———

Something made me remember meeting another full-time Aramco employee named Lamia earlier during my summer internship. She was also Saudi, a little older, from Jeddah, and she had complained to me that she'd been living in a room in Steineke Hall, a hotel-like residence in the Aramco compound, for six months. Several times, the staff had notified her that she had to vacate her room and find a place to live, but she had never been able to find anywhere else in the city. I went to Steineke Hall and talked to the receptionist. Lamia was still living there. I sat down to wait for her in the lobby. When Lamia arrived, she recognized me immediately. She told me she'd received a warning from her department and had to move out at the end of the week.

"My father's coming from Jeddah to find me a home," she said. "You're welcome to share with me, if you like. We can split the rent and bills."

I threw my arms around her, on the verge of tears. "Oh, God, thank you," I cried. "I swear, He has sent you from heaven. I didn't know where to go or what I was going to do." That night, for the first time since I had arrived, I truly slept.

We found an apartment, and Lamia's father signed a pledge permitting his "daughters" to live by themselves and guaranteeing their proper behavior—although each night we left a pair of men's shoes along with our own outside the apartment door (it is Saudi custom to remove one's shoes) so that our neighbors would think we had a proper male chaperone living with us. The lease agreement was in Lamia's father's name, though we were the ones who paid the rent.

But while the apartment solved our most serious problem, it created a new one: how would we get to work? We couldn't drive, and Saudi Arabia had no public transportation. We discovered that the Aramco bus, which transported employees from Khobar City to the company's offices each day, passed our building at 6:15 every morning. Seeing that it picked up a fellow employee on the same street, we went down at 6:00 a.m. to wait for it. We should have known that as Saudi women, it could never be that simple.

As we climbed up the steps of the bus, the Filipino driver gestured for us to stop. "Madam, where are you going?" he asked.

Lamia and I exchanged looks. "Apparently we're getting on the bus!" we replied.

"Sorry, you can't," came his answer.

"Why? We're both Aramco employees."

"Women aren't allowed to take the employees' bus, it's only for men."

"Well, are there any buses for women?" we asked.

"No, madam, sorry!" he replied. "You must get off."

———

I hadn't known it when I applied to the company, but Aramco had a long history of discrimination, starting with Saudi nationals. In the

1950s, there were repeated strikes and demonstrations. Saudi employees both demanded better working conditions, including a forty-hour workweek, and protested against having so many Americans and so much American control at Aramco. The Saudi authorities were by turns conciliatory and repressive; they ultimately sought to identify the workers behind the protests and remove them. While they did grant labor reforms, they also undertook a campaign of arrests and torture to crush the strikes.

By the time I arrived, Aramco had been entirely Saudi-owned for more than two decades, but it still had discriminatory practices in place. Women were the ones most affected, Saudi and non-Saudi females alike. A non-Saudi woman had to be unmarried to be hired by Aramco, regardless of her age. After I was allowed to live in Aramco housing, I had an Indian neighbor in her fifties. She had been married for thirty years, but although she lived with her husband, she was forced to conceal her marriage and state that she was single in order to keep her job. Female employees of any nationality were prohibited from using the Aramco employees' bus that transported workers between the cities and the compound—they could only use the recreational buses that traveled to the mall or to another Aramco residential compound. And although women were permitted to drive inside the residential compounds, they weren't allowed to use Aramco cars, or to register for driving lessons offered by the company, or even to be present as observers at the company's safe driving and defensive driving training sessions.

The restrictions on Saudi-born women were even greater. Before being hired, a Saudi woman had to submit to a blood test to ensure that she was not pregnant. Pregnant women could not start work. A classmate of mine from university was about to be hired to work in the Information Protection Division as a full-time employee, but she failed the medical exam when her blood test revealed that she was expecting. For years, Saudi women employed at Aramco could not apply for the homeownership loan offered to male Saudi employees, they could not receive a housing allowance, nor could they apply for a scholarship program for foreign study abroad. When I worked there, Aramco offered women only six weeks' maternity leave, and it still does not provide day-care facilities for employees' children, though Saudi labor codes require a company nursery if there are more than fifty female employees in one city or more than ten children. Women are also not permitted to take jobs in the oil fields or refineries; they are restricted to office work.

At the end of October, 2002, the month Lamia and I moved into our new apartment, Lamia, our colleague Afaf, and I wrote a letter of protest to Aramco's management demanding our right to live in the compound. Though I didn't recognize it at the time, this was my first taste of activism. Eight and a half years later, I would be driving a car through the streets of Khobar.

9

Love and the Falafel Man

As Lamia and I were starting our new lives in our Khobar apartment, my sister was graduating from medical school and beginning a job at the university hospital. Muna moved my parents and our brother from Mecca to a nicer neighborhood in Jeddah, paying the rent for the first six months. The two of us agreed to share the payments after that. My parents insisted on transferring their secondhand furniture from the old apartment to the new one, but I was determined that nothing from our old life would move with us; I wanted to cast off those miserable memories. I bought everything for their new home, from the furniture and appliances to the spoons and dishes in the kitchen. I bought mobile phones for my parents and my brother so we could keep in touch easily, and began giving small allowances to Mama and Muhammad.

After all this was done, I had no money left to buy furniture for my own room. Night after night, I slept on the floor; for the first six months, I lived out of the suitcase I had traveled with. The happiness that my family's new, comfortable life had brought them—with water that flowed from the taps all month long and a clean and tidy neighborhood—was more than enough to keep me going.

I finally told my parents the truth about Aramco's terrible housing rules and introduced them to Lamia and to her family, so they would feel reassured about how the situation had been resolved. Happily, my parents accepted the idea of my living in the city. "So long as you're living with your older colleague, and so long as we know her family in Jeddah, you have our blessing," they said. When, finally, I had some money left over for me, I bought something very special for our Khobar apartment, one of the things I had loved most about the house in the Aramco compound: a fully automatic washing machine. I bought it alone. When I first started living in the Eastern Province, I returned to asking my father's permission for everything, and he would get very angry if I failed to do so. But gradually I stopped asking and made my life mine.

Getting around was our biggest challenge. Lamia and I were using private drivers, taxis—anything that was available to us—and it was draining a good deal of our salaries. Eventually, Lamia suggested that we buy a cheap car and look for a private driver. The cheapest make available at that time was a KIA. We started asking the taxi drivers who ferried us around if they knew anyone who would work for a monthly salary, although, as women, we couldn't employ a driver under our own names. (Happily, the state code was changed in 2014, enabling female employees to now recruit their own drivers. And the rise of Uber and other app-based vendors has completely changed the transportation landscape, although Saudis still lack public transport and pedestrian walkways.)

One of these taxi drivers helped us find Mumtaz, a young Pakistani man in his early twenties, but there was a problem—he didn't know how to drive. We promised Mumtaz that we would get him driving lessons and pay for a driver's license, along with a monthly salary of 1,200 riyals and 200 riyals more for his food and living costs. Mumtaz didn't speak Arabic or English, so to communicate with him, I dusted off the little Urdu I remembered from my extremist days going to the Grand Mosque.

Mumtaz didn't much care for hygiene, and we were always complaining about his smell. Lamia decided to buy him toiletries—soap, shampoo, and deodorant—and request that he use them every day. Once we'd solved the problems of the language barrier and the smell, the next issue was that Mumtaz knew nothing about the layout of Khobar, nor its traffic rules. Lamia and I studied a map of the city streets so we could direct him from the backseat, which resulted in more than a few close calls. I asked Aftab, a Pakistani colleague in my department, to explain the traffic rules to Mumtaz. We had enough burdens without his traffic violations as well.

But there was still the problem of how Mumtaz behaved if he drove either of us anywhere alone. He would adjust the rearview mirror, look up, and observe our every move. Once he made a comment about my eyes and how I looked. I couldn't muster a response, but I knew Lamia would take care of it; she was older than me and far more willing to tick him off. Sure enough, she reprimanded him harshly, and he never dared to comment on my appearance again.

My work was challenging, especially after our group leader selected me to manage my first project. I was terrified I'd fail. I had never managed anything before, and the fact that I was both a graduate of a public university *and* the only woman in our division put even more pressure on me to prove myself. Until then, I had always thought that my English was good, so I was shocked to find myself struggling with reports and emails. Neither my university nor Aramco had trained me in the technical terms I needed to know for work. Even more challenging, English was the official language spoken at Aramco, so I needed it for every meeting as well as for reports and emails. Then Lamia told me about the Aramco English Learning Center. I could study in the morning, she said, and return to my office after the lunch break. After taking the placement exam, I was put in the advanced section, which required students to attend half-day classes for six months. But my boss flatly refused to let me leave the office, telling me that I had to improve my English myself.

Fortunately, I didn't have to do everything on my own.

One of my colleagues, Amro, gave me considerable support and encouragement. Whenever I had questions, he would answer them willingly, no matter how silly they were. I often sat in the group meetings with no idea what was being said. I wrote down scores of new words so that I could look them up later, rather than asking for their meanings and appearing stupid. I mentioned to Amro how frustrated I felt after having been a top student. He smiled. "Work is different than study," he said. "We all started from scratch; we had to be patient and persistent to acquire the knowledge we have today. Don't be in too much of a rush; one day you'll be the specialist in your field. You'll be the one we all turn to with questions."

Every bit as challenging as the actual work were the personal relationships around the office. I was still uneasy about—even fearful of—mixing with Saudi men. The only two male colleagues I didn't deliberately avoid during break times were Albert, from South Africa, and John, from New Zealand, and even then, one of my male Saudi colleagues would ask me, "What do you hope to gain by associating with these infidels?" after he watched us drinking coffee together. Outside of working hours, I had no friends and socialized with no one, apart from Lamia and another colleague, Alia, whom I had met during the summer internship. There was a very sensible reason for this. Everything I was doing—living and working far away from my family, without a male relative to monitor me—was socially unacceptable for a Saudi girl.

My parents went to great lengths just to keep my job at Aramco a secret from my own family; if anyone found out, Mama and Abouya would face severe disapproval or worse. Whenever anyone asked Mama about my work, she told them that I was a teacher in one of the Aramco schools in the Eastern Province and that I was living in the company accommodation for female employees. But even then, there was constant questioning: "How can you permit her to live there alone, even if it's in the company housing?" My parents found themselves under so much pressure that they eventually resorted to additional lies: "We're taking turns traveling to the Eastern Province, to stay with her and supervise her," they said.

I, too, felt the pressure from family, acquaintances, and even perfect strangers, so I simply kept to myself. That way, I didn't have to lie or hide the truth; doing so made me feel as if I were somehow living in sin. On one of my trips between Jeddah and the Eastern Province, I was interrogated by a woman sitting next to me on the plane. "You are from Jeddah and you work in Aramco and you live alone?" came her accusing tones. "How can your family permit you to do this? Don't you fear for your reputation?" Every time I traveled after that, I made sure to bring headphones and a book.

Each day at lunch, I boarded the shuttle bus to the dining hall—unlike the Aramco city bus, female employees could ride the shuttle bus inside the compound—to eat with two women who were working as contract employees. I didn't know at the time that they were from the Shiite community, but neither I nor anyone around me (or so I thought) cared about the Sunni/Shiite sectarian divisions anyway. One day, however, I bumped into an older male colleague in the mixed dining hall, and he answered my smile with a sullen face.

After lunch, he stopped by my office. "Aren't you scared what will happen to your reputation from eating lunch in the dining hall?" he asked.

"Excuse me?" I answered. "What does my reputation have to do with the dining hall? Am I supposed to starve?"

"Well, it's well known that girls who eat in the dining hall go there to look for relationships with men."

I sent an email to the division planner, Amro, and my group leader to ask them if it was considered taboo for female employees to eat lunch in the dining hall. I didn't get a direct response, which made me uncomfortable. I decided from then on I'd get a cold sandwich from the Coffee Man, a small shop in our office building, and make dinner my only proper meal, eaten largely alone when I got back to the apartment.

At one point I also decided to stop wearing my abaya in the office. I made sure my outfits were formal and modest, and I still covered my hair. Within a couple of days, the same colleague who had complained about my coffee break habits was at my door, voicing his disapproval. I went back to wearing the abaya and soon found an unsigned letter on my desk thanking me for adhering to a modest dress code. The letter only made me feel more resentful.

I had been under the illusion that my male colleagues were open-minded, since we worked in a mixed environment, but I soon discovered that was far from the case. My Saudi colleagues never introduced me to their wives; I didn't even know their names. By chance, I met one wife in a training session at Aramco's Department of Adult Education (these sessions took place outside working hours, and family members of Aramco employees were allowed to attend). My colleague's wife told him about our meeting, and he was deeply distressed. "Please," he begged, standing before me in my office, "don't tell her that we're working in the same group. Don't mention anything about me in front of her!" I was very surprised. This man was quiet and calm; he was one of the men who treated me very respectfully. But he was terrified that his wife had discovered he was working with a woman. If a man in the office spoke to his wife on the phone, he never addressed her by her first name but instead as the mother of his oldest child, "Umm Muhammad" or "Umm Abdullah," just as my mother used to call me by my brother's name when were in the marketplace. And the men were always eager to end the calls as quickly as possible. Almost daily, I wondered what these men thought of me, the only woman working among them.

The Information Protection Division was brand new when I joined; it had been set up after a computer virus had attacked Aramco's network infrastructure. In our second year, our administrator decided that each of us should take a series of specialized information security training courses. After completing the three courses, employees would be awarded a title. Information Security Consultant III would be awarded after the first stage, followed by Information Security

Consultant II for the second stage, and Information Security Consultant I for the third. It was obligatory for all the employees in our division to attend.

I arrived at the start of one workweek to find everyone gone. They were all in Khobar attending the first training course. I was rushing off to find a driver to take me there when the division head explained that I couldn't go. "It is not permitted for women to attend."

I filed an official complaint with all my supervisors. Aramco's response was that the Saudi Ministry of the Interior did not permit women to be present alongside men for training courses held outside the compound. Only an official waiver granted by the Governor's House (known as the Imara and responsible for the administration of the Eastern Province) and then approved by the Ministry of the Interior could allow me to attend. Aramco had decided against delaying training for the division's male employees to wait for permission for me that might or might not be granted.

It was difficult not to feel as if every rule had been invented to ensure that I would fail.

I requested that we petition the Governor's House to let me attend the training course, but my request was ignored. Then I asked my group leader if I could travel outside Saudi Arabia to attend the same courses, but the answer was no. The only way for me to complete the training was to borrow books from my colleagues and study them myself. And that was what I did. I passed the first three tests on my own, and I was awarded the same certificates as my colleagues. But there was one more test to pass before I could earn my first title.

The fourth test focused on the topic of ethical hacking. Although I had spent my first year at Aramco working with a team of ethical hackers, books alone were not enough: both the training course and the exam assumed that the student had access to a specialized computer lab. The first time I took the test, I failed. It was the first time I'd ever failed anything. I went to the administrator's office and explained my situation. I showed him the cost of attending the same course abroad and the dates it was being offered. My direct boss was very annoyed with my decision to go over his head, but my diminishing patience had made the decision for me.

The division ultimately decided that it would be cheaper for a training coach to teach me in private at an Aramco office than to send me abroad. It was my responsibility, they told me, to find an appropriate location for the one-week course; if I couldn't find a spot, the trainer would not come. I booked a meeting room, and I got hold of a portable projector for the trainer to use during the sessions. I was the sole attendee, which made it the most useful training course I had ever attended. I passed the test and received my first title: I, Manal al-Sharif, could now call myself an Information Security Consultant III.

It was 2004; I had spent only two years with the company, and in that short period, I'd already faced many obstacles. But I was determined to beat them, one by one.

———

The Information Protection Division was not the only department housed in our sand-colored building. One day I was walking down a neighboring hallway when, glancing at the signs outside the doors, I saw a woman's name, Hanan. I stopped and introduced myself, telling her how happy I was to see another woman. It was a Wednesday, and on Wednesdays her department shared breakfast with a third department on the other side of the building, in an area I'd never visited before. "Why don't you come along?" she asked. "There are other women that will join us."

At the breakfast, the men and women ate in two separate places, which surprised me, because there was no segregation of men and women anywhere else inside Aramco. But I was very happy to meet other female employees. Two were my age, although I was the only one who worked in a technical field. I sat in the office of a girl named Reem, and we got to know each other. Then, quite unexpectedly, everything changed.

A young man around my age entered Reem's office, carrying a tray of hot falafel. Reem offered me some food, and we continued our conversation, but the man stayed where he was. He had sleepy, almond-shaped eyes and long, dark eyelashes. In that moment, that was everything I noticed and all that I could remember.

For a second, I shifted my gaze in his direction, and I saw his eyes watching me. I felt the blood rushing to my face and butterflies in my stomach. Reem was still talking, and I looked back at her, though I couldn't follow anything she was saying. After a while, a colleague called and the nameless man left the office.

Though I was working in a division composed entirely of men, I'd never felt anything like this for any of them. When I had worked in the hospital, I would have fleeting crushes that lasted for a week and then promptly disappeared. This was different. But there wasn't to be another breakfast for some time: we had entered the month of Ramadan, where everyone fasts from one hour before sunrise to sunset.

I knew nothing of this young man, but I thought of him constantly. There was no way, however, for me to learn anything more. I didn't dare enter the other department without a reason. I had always found the month of Ramadan to be among the most beautiful times of the year and the fastest to pass, but this Ramadan lagged and idled.

At the end of each day during the thirty days of Ramadan, when you break your fast, you may ask God to grant you one wish, and that wish will be granted by God. Thirty wishes for thirty days. During that Ramadan, I used my wishes on just one thing. "Your call each day," my childhood friend Manal later reminded me, "was, 'O God, make the falafel guy mine!' How silly you are," she added, "to wish to marry a man when you don't even know his name."

After Ramadan, I gingerly approached my female colleagues to ask about the Wednesday breakfast. Reem assured me it was resuming and said I was welcome. When I saw the falafel man again, I was sure he could hear my heart pounding. After only a few Wednesdays, I recognized his distinctive French cologne.

I gradually found more friends. One of my female classmates from King Abdulaziz University joined my project as a contract employee. She was very religious and wore the niqab, but her intelligence and ambition had made her want to join Aramco regardless. This girl, Reem, Dalia (another female colleague), and I ate lunch together every day. I made sure to go to Reem's office at lunchtime in the hopes of seeing the falafel man before he left the office to eat with his male colleagues. He, meanwhile, had started walking by my cubicle after lunch on the days that I did not walk into Reem's section or missed seeing him. My male colleagues' inquiring glances made very clear what were they thinking. But his visits, although they made me feel awkward, gave me some hope that our feelings were mutual.

I still didn't know anything about his personal life, so it came as quite a shock to me when out of the blue several months later Reem produced a picture of a young child. "Look, Manal," she told me, "this is his son."

I felt suddenly sick. Saudi men don't generally wear wedding rings, so it's impossible to know their marital status unless they mention it. "Reem," I gasped, "really, I had no idea before now that he was married."

Reem laughed. She and the falafel man, whom I'll call K., had planned the photo as a prank; he was not married, but now my feelings had been laid bare.

Sometime later, Reem and I ate lunch alone, and she raised the topic of K. without invitation. "K. says he is from a very conservative family, and that he would never marry a girl who works in Aramco."

I felt foolish. For a year, I had entertained all kinds of hopes about our future together, hopes predicated on nothing more than the glances K. had scattered in my direction. Occasionally, he would speak to me, but he had never said anything about his feelings. I silently scolded myself for even opening myself up to the criticisms that Saudi society visits on women who work among men, convinced that my beliefs about K.'s intentions toward me were nothing more than fantasies.

That morning I had brought in a small plant that I planned to give to K.; it was similar to a plant of mine he had admired the last time he had passed my cubicle. After lunch, I walked quickly to his office, plant in hand. My words were like a stream of bullets: "Don't worry," I said, "it wasn't your fault, it was mine. It was my fault for falling in love with a man who holds this view of women. Thank you for disclosing your true feelings to Reem; thank you for saving me a lot of hardship and for finally putting an end to my confusion! And thank you again for all the words that deceived me. Please, take this plant to remember me, and try to learn that not *all* women fit the image you have in your mind!" I slammed the plant down on his desk and left before he could catch sight of my tears. Only once I had gone did I realize what I had said. Love? I was mortified.

After work, I went back to my apartment in Khobar. I threw my abaya on the sofa in the living room and collapsed on its cushions. How could I have been so stupid? How could I forget that I was a Saudi woman, that my society shows no mercy toward girls who uncover their faces and work with men? A man could live his life as he wished. If he decided to get married, his past would never return to haunt him. He was free to have relationships outside of marriage, too, and he would never have judgments slung at him simply because he worked with women. I felt as if I was burning up, remembering every look K. and I had exchanged. Lamia couldn't understand what had come over me, and brought me water and medicine. I spent the night on our green sofa, delirious; going to work the next day was out of the question.

The next day, at five minutes after five in the afternoon, an hour after work at Aramco had ended for the day, my phone rang. I didn't recognize the number. The caller's speech was sporadic, timid, rushed: "I'm calling to see if you're okay. . . . You didn't pass by the girls today during the lunch hour, so I went to your office to check on you . . . they said you were sick. . . . May God keep you safe, Manal."

"How did you get my number?" I asked.

"From my friends at the telecom company," he replied.

The call was over. But he sent me two texts.

I read the messages a hundred times. But I kept my feelings a secret.

At work, our relationship continued as it was before: glances from afar and cursory exchanges in the hallways. But now I looked forward to leaving the office each day, because that was when I'd receive a phone call and have a furtive, heart-racing conversation, conducted just out of earshot of any others. With the help of cell towers and text messages, we grew more and more drawn to each other. Finally, I agreed to meet face-to-face. Still, I was hesitant; I feared that people would see us together, or that the religious police would arrest us and cause a great scandal. So we agreed to meet an hour before sunset on Najmah Beach in Ras Tanura, a part of another Aramco compound about an hour's drive away and the location of the Arabian Gulf's largest refinery. I boarded the Aramco bus that traveled between Dhahran and Ras Tanura. Women were allowed to use it, since it traveled from one Aramco compound to another. (Aramco has compounds all over the country, in every city where it has major operations.)

I arrived first, wondering as I stood there what he would think of me. Would he see me as a cheap girl who had consented to speak to him on the phone and now to meet him face-to-face? I took off my sandals and walked barefoot on the white sand, heading for the remote part of the beach where the refinery stood. The flame from one of its chimneys was shooting up into the sky, seeming to consume the air around it. It seemed an appropriate metaphor. A great number of Saudi love stories end not in marriage but in heartbreak. Most men will not trust a woman who permits him to speak with her alone before their engagement. But I was completely enamored with K. I had ignored Mama's many warnings; I had shrugged off any sense of betraying my father.

For the first time since I had been a little girl, I lifted my scarf from my hair and draped it over my shoulder. The salty sea breeze touched my face and scalp. I sat on the beach alone and waited. Then a text arrived: "I'm here, I'll see you in minutes."

I still had time to back out; I could hide between the houses overlooking the beach and explain this day away as nothing more than a delusion. How had I, a proper Muslim girl, agreed to meet alone with this strange man, with my face showing and my hair uncovered? But it was as if I'd grown roots, deep ones that stretched down into the wet sand. I drew my knees toward my chest with both hands, took a long breath, and gazed at the waves, hoping their repetitive motion might soothe me.

I saw him first as a silhouette, then I smelled his cologne, and finally he dropped down to sit near me, appearing even shyer than I was. We didn't talk: he simply reached out and nestled my palm in his. It was the first time my hand had touched a man's. I left it there. We sat in a silence broken only by the waves crashing before us. I decided that day that he would be my husband.

The following months passed in much the same way. We exchanged calls, texts, and quick, superficial conversations at the office, never progressing further; his conservative background and my religious one would not allow it. But things were not as perfect as I'd imagined. The divide between our two ways of thinking became more evident every time we talked. He was strongly opposed to women working at Aramco and uncovering their faces, not from a religious perspective but from a cultural one. If I were in Malaysia, where women walk about with their faces uncovered, K. would not object to me being uncovered. But he was adamant I follow the most conservative practices inside the kingdom. Saudi society judges you on your adherence to tradition; the requirement that women fully cover their bodies is based more on this than on religious precepts. Facial veiling isn't a specific requirement for Muslim women in the Koran, which describes women accompanying the Prophet Muhammad (PBUH) into battle.

Our arguments were frequent and they often ended in my asking how it could be considered acceptable for him to work in Aramco, but not acceptable for a woman. His response was always "I am a man, and nothing brings shame to a man." My mind urged me to leave him, but my heart would invariably win. I tried to convince myself that if he asked me to marry him, I could put the niqab back on and quit Aramco. But I wanted to work—and my parents depended on me financially. We could not find a way to agree.

I was also consumed by religious guilt. I had broken the prohibitions against having contact with a man outside of my family. I had done wrong, I believed. My inner turmoil was made worse by the gossip spread by the girls who worked in K.'s department. Once I told one of my female lunch companions, "You know, the gossip of the girls in the other department has become so painful that I've decided not to be around them anymore."

Her response stung: "Make sure your enemy has nothing to hold against you, Manal."

"What do you mean?" I asked her. "What do they have?"

"I swear to God, you are very well aware of what you are doing," she replied. "I don't need to explain any more than that."

There was another case of infatuation in K.'s department. One of my lunch companions, Dalia, didn't return the affections of an older colleague, but he pursued her anyway. She complained frequently of his harassment, but that didn't stop gossip about her from spreading. Someone told her that I was behind it: they claimed that I was calling her honor into question in order to draw attention away from K. and me.

I was sitting at my desk, writing a report, when Dalia stormed in. "Who are you to talk about me," she screamed, "you slut, you lowlife, you bitch! Look at yourself and K. first before you throw your dirt at other people." Then she spat in my face.

It was horrible. I had never gotten into a public fight; even in primary school, my sister had been disgusted by my refusal to fight back. I didn't even know how to return an insult. I finally understood why my sister had complained to Mama about her not letting us play with the street children. I realized the value of becoming hardened to these words and learning how to defend ourselves.

I told K. what these other women had said. I was caught in an untenable situation: gossip about K., the fallout over my decision to briefly stop wearing the abaya, my drinking coffee with foreign male colleagues, my family facing pressure because I was living alone. I asked K. whether he would approach my father to ask for my hand in marriage but we could not get beyond the subject of Aramco and the niqab. Dalia's words ("You bitch!") and the contemptuous looks I received from my old university classmate every morning were eating away at me inside. There wasn't a single person I trusted except my friend Malak, back in Mecca. But she couldn't help; she was just as confused as me.

Things continued in this vein until Mama came to visit. At the end of her stay, I accompanied her to the Aramco airport. (Aramco has its own airport and aircraft, which the employees and their families can use.) She called me the next day.

"The officer responsible for issuing boarding passes admired you very much," she informed me excitedly. "He asked me about you after you left. He took my number and his mother called me today to inquire about you and him getting engaged."

I had long objected to the manner in which these proposals were made, but this one was different: it offered a way out from my daily torment, and that was all that mattered now. "Yes," I told Mama, "I give my consent."

She was very happy, and I miserable. I sent a text to K. informing him that our relationship was over: "Someone has asked for my hand in marriage, and I have given my initial consent." I didn't get any response, and I knew it was the end.

The next day my mother received a call from a Saudi mother. When she called to tell me, I assumed that the shoufa meeting with the airport employee's mother had been arranged. But it had been K.'s mother on the other end of the line. "We wish to pay a visit to you and your husband in Jeddah," she had told Mama.

I told my mother to forget about the first suitor. The date was set, and I booked a ticket to Jeddah to be there for K.'s family's visit.

After all the sharp-tongued gossip, I was eager for the other girls to learn of my engagement. I put aside thoughts of the arguments about the niqab, about my resignation from Aramco, about everything else.

I entered the office the next day with my head held high, and told one of my lunch companions, "K. approached me officially about our engagement."

"Are you sure?" she asked. "I don't find the two of you at all compatible. And he's very arrogant."

I didn't give her opinion much weight; I didn't give any opinion much weight. What mattered to me was that the gossip would stop. I hoped that the news would reach Reem and Dalia, and sure enough it did. Reem offered her congratulations to K., and next thing I knew he was calling to berate me. In the midst of screamed insults, I understood one thing: that if the news of our engagement reached any more of his work colleagues, everything would be over.

"Do not *ever* think that you can ever be my wife while you're working here," he told me. "On the day we get married, you will resign from Aramco, and until that day, the subject of our engagement is to remain a secret. I am ashamed that my future wife is revealing her face and working with men."

On the day of our engagement meeting, he was still angry and we weren't talking. Mama met his mother and K. met Abouya and my brother.

For the first time, my father offered calm advice. "My daughter," he said gently, "I don't think he is a good fit for us. He thinks very highly of himself, what with him being an only son. You will become very weary with him."

But my father had no idea how weary I already was. "Abouya," I wanted to tell him, "I am willing to have a man trample my dignity if it silences the girls who are slandering my reputation every day." But, as always, I didn't say a thing.

I was also deeply troubled by guilt. I thought I would never be cleansed of my sin unless K. became my husband.

The marriage ceremony was scheduled, but nothing else was resolved. On the good days, I loved him passionately; on the bad ones, I hated him. We screamed and hurled insults and hung up on each other. But there was no going back now. I could not back out of the wedding. In preparation for our life together, I even had surgery to repair some of the damage caused by my childhood female circumcision.

On the day of our wedding, K. wasn't speaking to me again. I can't remember why. The problems flowed together like drops of water until they became indistinguishable from one another; all that remained was the fast-moving river that formed in their wake. Even my father's cousins were unhappy; tribal rules dictated that our family's girls not marry outside the Ashraf tribe. But the wedding was proceeding.

My father had decided that the marriage contract ceremony would be held at the Grand Mosque in Mecca, with my uncle serving as one of the witnesses. I did not attend my own ceremony. I was sitting in a beauty salon in Jeddah, getting ready for the celebratory dinner afterward. I didn't stand in front of the sheikh, and wasn't asked whether I accepted K. as my husband. My answers were of no consequence anyway; the men returned from Mecca with the wedding contract just the same.

"Now you are my wife" were his first words to me after the ceremony. "I won't allow you to uncover your face after today."

We had reached a temporary accommodation over my continuing to work: it would be permitted after our ceremony, for the signing of the marriage contract, on April 1, but had to stop once we held our official wedding party on August 26—in Saudi culture, these are two different events and not always held at the same time. In other countries, this period between the marriage contract and the wedding party would be equivalent to an engagement, but in Saudi, a girl may not speak to her fiancé without having her official marriage documents completed and signed. K. knew that I was supporting my family financially. I still paid half the rent of the apartment in Jeddah and all the related bills, still gave Mama and my brother an allowance each month. I had borrowed from the bank twice—first to buy a used car for my brother, and later to buy a new taxi for my father, to replace his run-down old one. I was still paying back these loans. But K.

quickly became disconsolate over my continued employment. He was determined: it was either my job or him.

I was desperate to keep both, so I proposed concessions, one after the other, but whenever I offered a concession in return for his changing his mind about Aramco, he flung back another demand. We never reached a compromise, and it seemed we never would.

After the ceremony, I took some time off for vacation, during which K. reminded me daily that I should wear the niqab or consider our relationship finished. I had been wearing the black abaya in the workplace, but I had covered my hair with a colored shawl in place of a black veil. I had thought long and hard and was finally persuaded that it was okay for a Muslim woman to show her face. K., however, was ashamed for his wife to reveal her face in front of other men. I bought a niqab, barely believing that I was going to wear it again. How would I make presentations? How would I participate in meetings? How would I keep my colleagues' respect? One day showing my face, the next appearing in a niqab. Perhaps it was a blessing that I was moving to a new department for a temporary assignment.

Just as K. demanded, I returned to work after our April 1 marriage ceremony with the black niqab over my face. The news spread quickly to my old department, and I received emails from some of my old colleagues: "Congratulations, Manal, on having chosen the right path." How odd it is that we judge a woman by her clothes and the place she eats lunch and the subjects she talks about with her colleagues on her coffee break, yet we don't judge a man if he doesn't grow his beard or if he works with women or speaks to them. Why do Saudi women allow subjugation to a man and adhere to men's rules and conditions? Why did I?

The niqab had a bizarre effect on me; without intending to, I became more and more introverted. I should have been competing with my workmates when we delivered presentations, but I found myself holding back. I no longer fearlessly entered into debates: such behavior didn't seem to fit with my new attire. Because no one at work could see my facial expressions, I would even carry a card with a happy face on one side and a sad face on another, so I could display my feelings. Otherwise, the niqab numbed me.

K.'s dominion over my life continued. It seemed that he wanted to change everything about me. "Don't walk quickly like a man does, don't talk in a loud voice, don't talk to your workmates about anything except work. You will not make the next business trip on your own. Your brother will accompany you." Sure enough, my brother was forced to leave university for a full week to accompany me on a business trip to Hanover, Germany; he was twenty-one years old, still considered a minor under Saudi law and needing Abouya's permission to get a passport, but his job was to supervise me. Married life was supposed to be joyous, but I was very unhappy. My misery increased when we set the date for our official wedding, and with it, the date of my resignation.

One day, K. passed by my office at lunchtime to see me talking with a man from the office next door. That was when we hit rock bottom. The subject of the conversation was perfectly ordinary—a film I had seen with K. over the weekend in Bahrain—and it was conducted from behind the niqab, but it was not related to work, and that meant it was strictly prohibited. I was only aware of K.'s presence when I saw his shadow leaving. My heart sank, and I timidly proceeded to his office.

"Out of my office, slut!" he screamed, his words like a physical blow. He raved as if he had caught me in an act of great betrayal. Worse, his colleagues in the adjoining offices could hear everything.

I tried to talk to him after work; I sent a text message to apologize. His reply was stinging.

I thought we were finished, but I persisted, and he finally deigned to visit me. "If your intention is to divorce me," I said, "then divorce me and release me." And he said the words "You are divorced." Under Islamic law, uttering those words is all that is required for a man to divorce his wife.

I wanted my torment to end. I taunted him by making the sounds of *zaghareet,* a call we traditionally make during times of celebration. "Please leave the apartment," I told him. "I don't want to see you ever again."

But then, next day, when I began to gather up his gifts—I wanted him out of my life completely—the yearning for him began to return. I called another friend, Alia, whose first engagement had ended in separation: I knew that she'd be the most understanding of all my friends.

"Alia, I don't want to be weak," I said. "I want to forget him, I don't want to call him and beg him to come back to me, like I have done every other time. I still love him, but it's a dangerous love, the sort of love that makes you hate your life and hate yourself."

Alia took me to Khobar Corniche. As we walked along, I remembered, here was where we once sat; here we saw a flock of migrating flamingos, resting; here we ate popcorn . . . everything reminded me of him. I gave Alia my mobile phone; I didn't want to give in and call him.

After a week, my tears and my longing began to subside. I busied myself with my work and decided that I would remove the niqab when I returned to my division at the end of the assignment. I would pass by every man who sent an email congratulating me on my choice, and greet him so that he saw my face.

Then I received an email from K. It was a letter of apology, his first ever. He wrote to me of how he had been reckless, of how he still loved me and could not live without me. He wanted us back together, he said, and he would have no other wife in the world but me. I deleted his message without replying. I was not going back to him.

Next, I received a call from his older sister, a religious woman who was a professor at the university. Up until now, K. and I hadn't disclosed our problems; they had escalated in private and ended in private, without a single person knowing. This had given a false impression to everyone—including my family—that we were happy. On the phone, K.'s sister listened quietly to my side of the story.

She advocated patience. "If a woman marries a man, it is her duty to change her personality and her life to align with his," she told me. She told me of how I was at fault for speaking to men about things that did not concern work: "A man's jealousy must not be underestimated."

Her words transported me back to the religious lectures of my school-days, to when we had sat on the hard ground of the school courtyard as we listened to the sheikhs, with no carpets for cushioning. The sun would blaze down upon us, until our clothes were almost too hot to touch. K.'s sister quoted from the hadiths, the sayings of Prophet Muhammad (PBUH), which compel women to obey their husbands, and reminded me that my entry to paradise was inextricably linked to K.'s satisfaction with me.

I felt extremely guilty, but I told her that my mind was made up. "I'm waiting for my papers," I said. "Please ask him not to delay them." I hung up, convinced that I could never atone for my sins.

One day, after returning home from work, my landline rang with a call from an unknown number. It was K. He begged me to look out of the window. His car was parked in front of our building. "Why are you here?" I asked.

"I'm coming up to your apartment now," he said. "Please open the door."

"Why should I open the door for you? When will you understand that it's over? I cannot continue like this. To be alone and happy is better for me than to be with someone and miserable."

I heard him crying on the other end of the line. "I still love you madly," he said weakly. "I can't imagine my life without you."

I felt myself wavering. Behind all the do's and don'ts and domination, was there really a heart tender enough to cry? There was nothing but my silence and the sound of his tears.

I put on my abaya, went down to the car, and got into the passenger seat beside him. As I watched his tears, all I wanted was to wipe them away. Instead, I took his hand and squeezed it tightly between mine.

I went back to him once more, full of hope that this incident would be enough to change everything.

The wedding party took place, and we returned from the honeymoon. I went back to my old office, and I didn't wear the niqab, though I was under oath to put it on the moment I left the building.

My problems at work were resolved. But no one knew what happened when our door closed each night.

After the wedding, I had to get used to leading a double life. I hid that I worked in Aramco from his extended family and friends, and I wore the niqab when I was with him so that his acquaintances wouldn't see my face. To silence a few gossiping mouths, I had sacrificed everything.

Our marriage was a continuation of the same tiresome fights of our courtship. All that changed were the insults I was subjected to. Whereas his slurs had previously been directed at me alone, now they extended to my family. I learned to respond to the insults against me and even to forgive them, but what he said about my family was impossible to forgive or forget. He knew exactly how deeply he hurt me. He scoffed at me because my mother was Libyan and my father was a taxi driver. He told me repeatedly of the concessions he had made in becoming associated with me, a girl of lower social standing than himself. (It was only much later that one of my friends said in surprise, "But Manal, your tribe is one of the most highly respected in all of Saudi Arabia. It was he who improved his social standing by marrying you.")

Sometimes I would challenge him. "Have you ever once tried asking without yelling to see the result?" I would say. "Whenever you ask something from me by commanding or prohibiting, I feel less and less well disposed toward you and I become more and more stubborn."

His response was always the same: "My friends always tell me that you are Hejazi [referring to the region where I'm from, the Hejaz, literally the 'barrier' region], and if I don't treat a Hejazi woman in a degrading way, then *she* will take advantage of *me*."

His older religious sister was forever reminding me that I was the woman and he the man, and that it was my duty to tolerate everything for the sake of obedience and comfort and his satisfaction. His satisfaction was God's satisfaction, she would remind me, and his wrath God's wrath.

The only thing that made life easier was that after our wedding celebration, I moved to his family house, where we lived with his mother and sisters. I loved them very much, and they loved me. His mother had the tenderness and affection of my late aunt Zein. She never interfered, but I knew she was upset. I asked her to pray to God that our souls would be calmed. I still loved her son. And I was pregnant.

At dawn on October 30, 2005, our son Abdalla (Aboudi, I called him) was born in Jeddah. K. named him after his father, who had passed away years ago. I had not planned to give birth in Jeddah, on the other side of the country, but on October 29, nine months pregnant, I left our house in Dammam after another big fight. I had a small belly and so I managed to be allowed to board a plane. I gave birth the next morning.

I was scared, knowing that I was giving birth to a baby who would have to endure unhappy parents, to hear shouting and screaming as his first words. I even wondered if I could love this baby in the midst of so much pain. I berated myself for listening to my husband's demands that we have a baby at the start of our marriage. "All my friends who are married had their babies in their first year of marriage, you make me feel like a failure," he would scream at me. But when the nurses laid Aboudi's tiny body down on my belly, he looked at me with his puffy eyes, matted hair, and wrinkled skin as if he knew that I was his mother. At that moment, I fell in love. His life was what mattered most to me from that day on.

It was the twenty-seventh day of the holy month of Ramadan, the busiest time of the year to find any flights to Jeddah. When my mother gave my in-laws the happy news, they couldn't find a flight to come to see the baby. My husband, who could now call himself Abu Abdalla (father of Abdalla), drove eighteen hours from Dammam to Jeddah to see his son. Hearing that he was driving all that way was enough to make me forget the fight we had had.

When Aboudi was born, I hoped things would change, that our

relationship would mature, that the baby would unite our hearts. But that did not happen. Instead, once more the pressure mounted on me to leave my job.

One day, about two years later, as my husband unleashed a string of curses upon my father and mother, I decided that he would also taste the bitterness of an insult to his family. I began to heap slurs on his parents. It was the first time since the beginning of our marriage that I had responded to these sorts of insults in kind.

I don't recall the details of what happened next; I only know that I was severely beaten in front of my child. Aboudi was almost two, and both he and I were screaming in horror. It was not the first time I'd been beaten by my husband, but it was the first time Aboudi had watched it. I begged my husband not to hit me in front of our son: "Hit me in our room," I cried. "I don't want Aboudi to see this." I remembered the time I watched my father hitting Mama in front of us, and continuing to hit her despite our pleas. I had cried hysterically as I watched her being beaten.

In that moment, I knew one thing: I could not allow my husband to hurt me in front of my son.

———

It can be difficult for people living outside of Saudi to understand why so many in our culture, women in particular, submit, stay, and suffer this kind of physical violence. But the price of resisting can be even higher. As I grew up in Mecca, there was another family on our block whose daughter wanted to attend college. Her father was enraged at the thought of her leaving home to study. They beat this girl so severely that she ran away. The family could not find her. Days passed, and they were forced to contact the police. But this seventeen-year-old girl had gone to the police first. She had filed a complaint against her father. The complaint was ignored, but the girl refused to leave the police station and return home. There were no shelters for abused women, so the only option was for the police to lock this girl in a juvenile correctional facility—a prison for women under age eighteen.

Weeks later, her aunt intervened and took the girl into her house to live. I later heard that this girl did go to school and made it out of the country to study, although she was disavowed by Saudi authorities because she was living and studying abroad without a permissible mahram.

I cannot in any way call her "lucky," but many female victims of abuse have limited skills and education and have even fewer options. There are stories of women who are starved, stabbed, burned, kicked out of their houses, and even locked in psychiatric institutions by male family members. Some are the victims of "honor killings," murdered by fathers, brothers, or uncles simply because they are suspected of having a relationship with a man and thus bringing shame to the family. When I hear these stories and meet some of these women, I wonder in my heart how so many can claim that they are only following the rules of our religion. What has happened to the two fundamental principles of being a Muslim—living in peace and showing compassion?

———

It was summer. I asked my brother, who was now also working at Aramco, to accompany me on a trip to Europe. My husband wouldn't let me take Aboudi with me, but I was willing to compromise on anything so long as I could get away from the house. I wanted to think, alone.

When I returned, I told him, "I want a divorce." It was ironic that I was the one to say it after all the times he'd used the word to threaten me.

He refused. He ignored me, then insulted me, then beat me. Finally, he requested my father's intervention. Abouya didn't understand my request for a divorce; I had told no one in our family about the problems in our marriage, and my father had rarely visited. But now I explained everything to him in detail. He was very upset, but he remained strongly opposed to a divorce. He said, "You are the one who chose him, and you gave birth to his child. For the sake of this child, you should be patient."

Abouya returned to Jeddah, believing he had set me straight, but I had made up my mind. I realized that K. had fought to keep me only three times during our entire history together, and each of these times was when I had decided to leave him: once during our romance, once during our engagement, and once during our marriage. When Aboudi was still a baby, K. had even kicked me out of the house. I'd taken Aboudi with me, but of course I couldn't find anyone who would rent us a place to live. My brother was forced to rent a furnished apartment for us under my father's name, using a copy of our family ID card. It was humiliating; I couldn't stand the looks the employees in the building's reception area gave me. Each time I passed, their eyes said, "Look, a lone woman with her child." I soon returned to K.'s house, apologized, and begged him not to throw me out again. I didn't have any other place to live.

Then, in late 2006, Aramco permitted women to live in its internal compound.

———

It happened in October 2007, on the twenty-seventh night of Ramadan, the holiest month for Muslims and the greatest night of the year. Aboudi had been born on this same night two Ramadans before. There was no one at home; everyone except Aboudi and me had gone to the special *Taraweeh* prayer. I gathered my things and Aboudi's in two suitcases and left the house forever.

The divorce was even faster than the marriage. Several days later, I was attending a special summit hosted by Aramco to discuss the computing technology needed to support the new King Abdullah University of Science and Technology (KAUST). There were two hundred people in the audience, and the speakers were experts and chief technology officers from big companies like Yahoo!, Microsoft, and Amazon. I was representing the female IT professionals working at Aramco. I decided to forgo my abaya for the first time in years.

I was listening to the speakers when I got a text from my husband.

"Manal, you are divorced," it read. "Your papers are in the court of Khobar." I was divorced in my absence, just as I had been married.

Although I wanted this divorce, when I read that message I felt as though part of my soul had been extinguished. My eyes filled with tears and I left my seat. Standing outside, I called my best friend, Manal. When she answered, the only sounds she heard were my sobs. "I wanted this, but why does it hurt this much?" I choked out into the phone.

"Because the Prophet Muhammad, Peace Be Upon Him, said divorce is the woman breaker," Manal replied. She started crying with me.

But I could not stay outside. I had to go back in and act as if nothing had happened. I dried my eyes and returned to my seat.

When lunchtime arrived, one of the organizers approached me and asked if I was Manal al-Sharif. She told me that I would be at a table with Mr. Abdullah Jum'ah, the CEO of Aramco. I didn't believe her until I saw the CEO sitting there with a group of top Saudi IT executives.

I told our CEO what an honor it was to be seated next to him. "Manal, the honor is all mine," he answered, holding out the hummus plate. "Hummus?"

I was astonished at how humble and easygoing he was. For the entire lunch, I chatted with Aramco's CEO, and also with the Saudi leader responsible for the country's ICT infrastructure and regulations, and with the technology adviser to the US president. I wondered if this was a sign that I was right to choose a promising career rather than a failing marriage.

10

Live Free or Die

$\mathcal{I}$ grew up afraid to fall asleep. My mind simmered with genie tales and stories of Al Si'elua, the witch who would come and eat you if you ventured out beyond the confines of your home. My grandmother was full of such stories, stories of women eating children and witches who would kidnap you or cut off a leg or an arm. She told us these stories before we fell asleep, so they were the last images to pass through our minds as we closed our eyes.

During the daytime, it was the genies we feared, although we were too scared to utter the word *genie,* and so we would say "Bismillah" instead. (*Bismillah* means "in God's name." We say it before starting anything, from a meal to a project. Saying "Bismillah" will cause any genie coming your way to vanish.) As children, we were told that genies would possess you if you failed to say your prayers before performing any of a host of daily tasks: using the bathroom, looking in the mirror, getting dressed or undressed. Forgetting to pray before changing clothes meant that angels might see your aura. We needed to pray before we ate, before we started a new class in school, a new job, or a new day. There were prayers for starting a trip, even a prayer for taking an airplane or getting into a car. All these prayers were designed to protect us from the genies, who were as real to us as our own families. The genies lived in their own genie cities, had their own tribes, and had names, wives, and children. Where angels are made of light, genies are made of fire, and humans of mud, or so we are told in the Koran.

Many women, including young women, believe that they are possessed by genies. Some even pay money to have the bad genies removed from their bodies, and countless others worry about being given the evil eye and thus having their blessings destroyed. I have close friends who did not share the news that they were getting married, that they were pregnant, or that they were building a new home until after the fact, out of fear of being cursed with the evil eye. I have learned never to say, "Oh, you have a beautiful child" to certain friends, because if anything ever happened to the child, I would immediately be blamed for having given it the evil eye. Women become conditioned to say only the bad things, to complain about their lives, for fear of otherwise inviting the evil eye, and create rituals and obsessions to avoid it. For example, after you have spent the day at someone's home, your hostess might drink the last dregs of your coffee from your cup, believing that it will offer protection in case you have coveted anything while you were there. A bad grade on an exam, a food stain on an expensive leather purse—anything at all—can be blamed on someone else's evil eye.

My mother believed. When we got our hair cut, she would insist on taking the clippings with her so that no one could bewitch them. If she thought my sister or I had been given the evil eye, she would take us to a man in Mecca who sold water designed to drive off evil spirits. Some women even think it is necessary to spit this water on the afflicted to drive away the genies. Even very personal items, such as women's menstrual pads, have to be disposed of in a special way—and never in someone's home—so that no one could use them to perform black magic.

As I grew older, I stopped believing in genies possessing us and in the evil eye. But I am sure there were more than a few women who saw me, a newly single mother, and believed I had been struck by the worst of the evil eye. When I crossed the threshold into my tiny company studio room in the Aramco singles' building, there was no familiar prayer that I could utter as a divorced Saudi woman living alone.

My own family didn't know I was alone. My father had already been to visit me and had forbidden me from divorcing. My twenty-four-year-old brother had told me, "We don't have girls who get divorced." My mother was in Egypt when the divorce happened; she did not know for a year. The only people I told were two men who worked at Aramco: one because he had to sign my housing papers, and the other because I could not move without a man's help.

The axiomatic thing about Saudi society is that while there are a seemingly infinite number of rules, it is also possible for people in authority to go outside those rules, and, if not break them, at least bend them quite a bit. So it was that in 2007, when I left my husband, I moved into a small studio living space, only a few hundred square feet, inside the Aramco compound under a provision known as "out of policy." This section of the compound provided housing for single Saudi female employees whose families lived more than eighty kilometers (about fifty miles) away and who had no children. I was not yet single and I had a toddler, but I had told a member of Aramco's housing department that I was getting divorced and I had nowhere to live. Within a week, I had been assigned to a unit, living among female nurses and clerks. If Aboudi made too much noise, or if anyone complained, I would be removed and be without a home. Each time I drove into the housing cluster, I passed a sign that read: "No pets allowed, No men allowed, No children allowed."

A few months later, I appealed for a larger living space. My request was denied. Then one day I was at a small lunch with a senior executive, and I thought, Why not ask him? I made my request, and I was granted a town house. But I hadn't realized there was a difference between single townhomes and family housing, so I was merely transferred into a bachelors' area with slightly more space. There was only one bedroom for Aboudi and me to share: if my neighbors complained, I could still be kicked out.

The year of my divorce, I was assigned three new hires as my mentees. And I also told one of them, a recent university graduate, that I was divorced. I needed a man to help me get furniture and with other basics, such as opening a bank account. Like almost all Saudi woman, I could not leave my awful marriage without the help of a man—and my own family would not help me. My mentee and I remained good friends until he got married. Then, perhaps at the insistence of his wife or just the culture at large, he stopped speaking to me. Such are the ways of women and men.

Otherwise, I kept my divorce secret. I did not tell my coworkers or my boss. But the upheaval showed in other ways. I had a hard time concentrating on projects. For the first time, my performance review at work was dreadful. And I cut my hair.

I had worn my hair long for years. My ex-husband in particular did not like even shoulder-length hair, he wanted me to stop cutting it entirely. Whenever I got a haircut, he would fly into a rage and scream insults at me for touching my hair. Without a husband, there was no one to tell me how short I could or could not wear my hair. I cut it very short, as short as a boy's. It was a symbolic act; I could not tell people I was free of my marriage, but at least I could be free of my hair.

———

After I left our house, my now ex-husband refused to speak to me, and we communicated only through his sister. We had agreed to share our time with Aboudi; he would be with me during the weekdays and with his dad on the weekends. I did not know until much later that I could have asked to have my son some weekends, since I was not free during the week. Instead, Aboudi went to his grandmother's each weekend and I stayed home alone.

Saudi custody rules are murky at best and often depend on whatever individual agreements are reached between the two parents and, sometimes, their families and the judge. In 2007, when I got divorced, the policy was for children to reside largely with the mother until they turned seven. At age seven, a girl would then be taken to her father's house to live. A boy, however, would be asked if he wished to remain with his mother; the choice was his. Once he became a teenager, that boy would often become his mother's male guardian. He would have the final say over whether she could work or go out, or must stay in. If a woman remarries, she immediately loses all custody of her children. If they are young, they must be sent to her mother to live or, if her mother is unable to care for them, to her sisters—the oldest first, and if she can't, then the second-oldest—rather like an elaborate plan of royal succession. A man, however, can remarry at will or even take a second wife, with no impact on his claim to his children. I have friends who wish very much to leave their marriages but cannot, because they know that they will lose their children.

I was determined not to become a second wife. I could not imagine giving up Aboudi. My own family did not have a tradition of taking second wives, but the practice is still strong in Saudi society, particularly in the middle of the country. When women reach the end of their childbearing years, the man goes and finds someone younger. For years, Saudi men also used to bring women back from Syria, Morocco, or Egypt to be second wives. The father of one of my childhood best friends had two wives, who lived on different floors of the same apartment building. Another of my childhood friends became a second wife herself. And one of my other friends, who was married with three children, discovered by accident that her husband had taken a second wife, a woman with whom he worked at Aramco. My friend left her husband for a while and returned to her family home, but eventually she went back. Many women do not know or do not speak about the existence of second wives.

After my divorce, I had some suitors propose, all of whom wanted to make me a second wife. I was insulted to be approached for that, but men assumed I would say yes. After you are divorced in Saudi Arabia, it is very difficult to get a second chance.

But I didn't live in Saudi Arabia—I lived in a world more like something from a Hollywood movie set.

When the American company Standard Oil began exploring for oil in Saudi Arabia in 1932, there was nothing but desert and sand. So they built their own compound to live in. Over the years, the compound became a green oasis, sitting up high on a hill, overlooking the Eastern Province; most days, there is a clear view all the way to the Bahrain causeway. There are grassy parks, lakes and ponds, and walking trails. Some fifteen thousand people live behind the compound's high walls and security gates. Anyone who visits needs special permission to enter.

Behind those walls, women can drive, even if they don't have a driver's license—because most Saudi women, even many who have lived abroad, do not have driver's licenses. Women do not need to wear the abaya; religious police do not patrol the streets. The compound was originally only for Americans, but by 1980, the Saudi government had bought all the shares of Aramco, and the company is now Saudi owned. More than eighty percent of the employees working at Aramco are Saudis, but they are paid less than their American colleagues and receive fewer benefits. Of all the sixty-six nationalities working for Aramco, Americans are treated the best.

In 2006, the former president of Aramco, Abdullah Jum'ah (the man I would be seated next to at lunch on the day of my divorce), changed the policy forbidding all Saudi women from living in the compound. Although I doubt single mothers were what the company had in mind when it specified that only single Saudi women could live there, the compound was one of the best things that happened to me in Saudi Arabia.

The units were small, but I did not mind. The compound had everything, even a hospital, although Aboudi could not use it because he was technically not considered a resident of the compound. He was registered under his father's Aramco badge number, and my ex-husband still lived in Dammam. I had no birth certificate, no identity card, no passport, no piece of paper to prove that Aboudi was my son. Several years later, I could not register him for school because I had no way to show that he was my child. No Saudi mother can register her child for school if the father is unwilling to provide the necessary documents, so some children go uneducated.

What I did have was a car. I had originally bought it to be used by a driver, but I couldn't house the driver on the compound. People in family housing could have a room for their drivers, but that wasn't possible in bachelor housing. But I didn't want the car to go to waste. Since women could drive inside the compound without a license, I asked my brother to teach me. He gave me an hourlong crash course in starting and stopping and traveling down the road. The longest I would have to drive was only about twenty minutes. Most of the roads were easy to navigate, although sometimes the speed limit did rise to about eighty kilometers (fifty miles) per hour.

Now, I could drive from my home to my office. On the way, I would drop Aboudi at a compound preschool. The first one he attended was just inside someone's house; they had converted the garage into nursery space and hired Filipino maids to take care of the kids. Each morning, I would wake before dawn and dress Aboudi as he was still sleeping. I would pack my work bag as well as Aboudi's bag and his snacks, and on cold mornings, I would go down to start my car and turn on the heater, because I didn't want him riding in the chilly air. A few times, I tried to carry my work bag, my laptop case, Aboudi's bags, and Aboudi all in one trip, but it was impossible. Instead I would go up and down, through the heavy fire doors, to start the car and then to load it, and then last to get Aboudi. At lunchtime, I would leave my office and drive to the nursery to eat with him. When I left work at four, I would pick him up on my way home.

Unlike most Saudi families, who have so many kids there are not enough seats for all of them in one car, which leaves smaller children sitting on the laps of their siblings, I had only Aboudi. I could always buckle him in a child seat with a seat belt. When Aboudi was old enough, I enrolled him in a more formal preschool that was run by an American, Miss Janet, who was married to an American Aramco employee. All the teachers were Americans and there were American kids enrolled there as well. The classes were mixed, boys and girls. Even in Saudi private schools, there are no mixed classes and female teachers are not allowed to teach boys, except perhaps for one year of preschool.

Living in the compound, Aboudi and I tasted an American expatriate life. There were two huge swimming pools nearby, so I signed Aboudi up for swimming lessons and tried to learn myself. Swimming is a sport that has always been forbidden to Saudi women and girls. Even in college, there was no swimming pool, only a court for basketball and volleyball. But Aboudi and I could swim and we could walk on the jogging path. Aboudi would ride his little bicycle or his scooter. Next to my small town house was a park, and I could take my son there to play. With him, I became another child. I rode with him on the swings, went down the slide with him in my lap, and then we would run around, climb up the stairs, and do it all over again. I could sit down on the warm ground and dig with him in the sand. I could watch him play with little girls. None of it was forbidden. Growing up, I had known none of these things. Outside the compound, women, even non-Saudi women, cannot swim, or ride the swings, or go down the slide, or play soccer with their sons.

We celebrated holidays like Halloween, where we dressed up in costumes and went trick-or-treating. We had barbecues and potluck dinners. I was surrounded by people of so many nationalities: American, Scottish, Indian, Filipino, Malaysian. After all my years living amid two volatile families, to see all these people living together in peace was beautiful.

But I never went to the expatriate parties, the ones with drinking and dancing. Saudi men would go and drink a lot, but if a Saudi woman were to attend, everyone would be gossiping about her the next day, "That Saudi girl was there, she mingled with the men, and they were drinking." It would become a stain that you could not wash off. I would only go to small gatherings held by my close friends, a cookout or something like that. Even if those were mixed, men and women, it was considered okay, because I already knew everyone who was there.

And yet still I lived a very different life from many Saudi women in the compound. Those who were married and lived in family housing would often cover up in their abayas and would not leave the house. There were men whose wives I never saw, men who never spoke about their wives, who never uttered their names. But I knew the wives of my non-Saudi friends. I would be invited to their homes and they would come to my place. We would all cook together. For most Saudis, life was different. They were still following tradition.

———

Everything about the compound was convenient. We had a supermarket, open twenty-four hours a day, seven days a week, and we had many American-style establishments, like beauty salons and car shops. We had a beautiful eighteen-hole golf course with a nice restaurant, and baseball and soccer fields. Aboudi played both. I would take him to his games and sit there and cheer for him; I just loved it. There was even a theater that would show films and host dance performances, concerts, and musicals. Once I stepped outside the compound, I became aware of how silent the Saudi world is. There's no music, even at the mall, no other sounds filtering through the background. There were no movies or performances. There was only street noise: tires on the roadway, brakes, engines, the scattered honking of horns. As he grew older, I took Aboudi to many performances, hoping that he would come to love singing and music as I did.

Scattered around the compound were restaurants and cafés,

without partitions to separate men and women. Outside the compound, men and women have to sit in different, walled-off sections, and restaurants and cafés have to close at prayer time. But none of those rules applied inside Aramco. Once he had learned to sit in his seat and eat with utensils, I would take Aboudi many nights to the Dhahran dining hall. For twelve riyals, about $3.00, we could have a five-course meal. Families could sit together, men and women, in the dining halls and at the parks. It was a normal life, which made it truly another world.

But Aboudi would not be able to go to school in the compound. The official reason was that the school didn't teach Arabic, but I didn't believe that. The school was an American school, with mixed classes, and mixed education was one taboo the Saudis government would not let its citizens break.

At night, Aboudi and I would return to our home. We would pass through the wooden gate into the tiny yard, and then through the door to the house. The floor was covered in white tile and I had a white, L-shaped sofa in the living room. Our kitchen opened right onto the living room, American-style. Upstairs, off our bedroom, was a small balcony. Sometimes, Aboudi and I would sit out on the balcony, look up, and count the stars. He would give each of them names. He would say this star is Reemah, the name of one of his cousins, and that star is Leenah. Sometimes I would ask him which star is Mommy, and he would say, "Mommy is the yellow star with the laptop and the purse." We kept looking for the yellow star with the purse, but we could never quite find it. Of all the spaces in my little town house, I loved that balcony the most.

But in January 2009, I found myself sitting under a different constellation of stars, a very long way from Aboudi and from my home.

———

Aramco has an extensive professional exchange program. If you are accepted, you go to work for another company in another country

for a year or more in order to gain experience and technical exper-
tise that you could not learn at Aramco. The company pays the employee's salary and more or less all expenses, so he or she is working
for the foreign company for free. But it isn't a traditional exchange
program, because no one from the foreign company arrives to work
at Aramco in return. I applied for the program and interviewed in
2008 to work at IBM in data management and cybersecurity. Then
the global financial crisis hit. IBM had no openings. But EMC^2, a
data storage company based in New England, did. In January 2009,
I boarded a plane to Logan International Airport, bound ultimately
for Nashua, New Hampshire. And I was alone. My ex-husband had
forbidden me from taking Aboudi with me. We would be apart for
twelve months, communicating only over Skype. Professionally, it
was an incredible experience. Personally, it was a disaster to be separated from my son.

I arrived on January 17 to snowflakes falling. I had never seen
real snow, only the man-made frozen water at Ski Dubai. I was met by
two Aramco colleagues, a husband and wife, who were already working at EMC^2. They helped me with everything, including finding an
apartment, buying and assembling furniture, and getting directions
for where to go. Apart from missing Aboudi desperately, it was the
easiest move I had ever made. I did not need a man to sign my lease
agreement. I did not need a man to accompany me to the Social Security office. I could do everything completely on my own. It was so
"normal."

Right away I wanted to get a driver's license, but my one hour
of instruction with my brother was not enough for the state of New
Hampshire. The motor vehicle office insisted that I spend two months
in a driver's education program, studying in the classroom and then
training on the road. For seven weeks, I left work in the afternoon at
4:00 and went to driving school from five to seven. I studied with a
bunch of kids: our teacher was a Muslim, an American who had married a Malaysian woman and had converted. It was funny to think of
a Muslim man teaching a Saudi woman to drive in the cold of New

Hampshire. I failed the first written test because I didn't know miles and feet (as in how many miles per hour you could drive or how many feet to park away from the curb or stop from a school bus): I only knew kilometers and meters. But when I retook the same test ten days later, I passed.

I was not scared of the road test when the time came, except for one question: Where are you from? I had been told that if anyone knew I was from Saudi Arabia, I would be given a hard time. Of course, when I got in the car with a large, bald American man, the first question he asked me was, "Where are you from?"

I felt panicked, terrified even. My palms started to sweat and I kept wiping them on my pants. I couldn't hold the steering wheel.

Finally, the examiner said, "You've wiped your hands on your pants five times already. What is going on?"

I glanced over and blurted out, "People told me that if I had to say where I was from, I would have a really hard time. I'm really terrified that I'll fail." The examiner made no reply.

I failed the reverse parking section at the end, but he passed me anyway. (I passed what many consider the harder part, parallel parking. My friends often give me the wheel if they need to parallel park their cars.) I waited two weeks and my first driver's license came in the mail, granted by the state of New Hampshire. It was set to expire on the day my visa ended. I felt like I had been cheated for all my hard work. It was like in the children's story "Cinderella," where at midnight the beautiful golden coach turns back into a pumpkin. Later, I learned that I could apply for a driver's license in Massachusetts and that license would be issued for five years, so before I left the States, I got a Massachusetts license, and that was the license I carried with me back home in Saudi Arabia.

My first few months in the United States were very lonely. I found people in New Hampshire to be careful and conservative, reserved, and not that interested in making new friends. Most of the people I met assumed that with my dark hair, dark eyes, and olive skin, I was Hispanic; a few immediately started speaking to me in Spanish. At first I told people I was from "SA," but I quickly learned most thought that meant I was South African. Even if I said that I was from Saudi Arabia, I usually received a blank stare. If I explained that it was in the Middle East, people would respond by saying, "Israel?" If I said it was a country in the Arabian Peninsula or said that we have the world's largest oil reserves or even started talking about camels, they still wouldn't comprehend. But then if I said one name, Osama bin Laden, I got an "oh" of recognition. Some would add, "That's a horrible country. You should not go back."

Slowly I made some friends. Marcus, an American originally from Argentina, taught me about cross-country skiing, gave me a Red Sox sweatshirt, took me to coed soccer games, and showed me Boston; Kenta, whose parents were Japanese, would eat lunch with me at work; and a big guy from Alabama, David, taught me photography and took me for a ride on his Harley. My friend Randy would send me back my emails with all kinds of marks to correct my English, and taught me everything I know about baseball. And I found that once I got to know people, they became real friends, friends you would have for life.

Driving helped. Once I had my license, I could drive to Boston. Aramco paid for my rental car for my entire stay in New Hampshire. It was no small irony to think that Saudi Arabia's largest company was openly paying for a Saudi woman to drive abroad. I signed up for a couple of social Meetups and there I met an African American Muslim girl, Muslimah, who had moved to Boston from Chicago. She no longer practiced Islam, but she had been raised as a Muslim. She introduced me to theater, musicals, orchestras, jazz performances, swing dance, and stand-up comedy. We saw productions of the musical *Cats* for $15 a ticket in Manchester, New Hampshire. We went skiing, and when I turned thirty, she and I went skydiving together. I used every long weekend to travel to places like Niagara Falls with my friend from Alabama and my neighbor from Honduras and her two children.

I enjoyed the weather. I had not seen rain for three years before I arrived in New Hampshire, and the first time it rained, I was so excited. When Saudis see rain, our first impulse is to run outside. I jumped up and down in the office, yelling, "It's raining, let's go outside." My coworkers looked at me as if I were crazy. In Saudi Arabia, we pray for God to send us the rain as a great mercy. In New Hampshire, people wished for the rain to go away. I never stopped loving each rainy day.

But I had so many things to learn. One of the first Meetup events I went to was at a restaurant. There were hooks for jackets by the front door and Muslimah left her coat on one. I did the same, but in the pockets I left my phone, my wallet, my money, and my keys. I came back to find my phone and my money gone—thankfully, the thief had left my keys and my driver's license.

The first play Muslimah and I went to was *Spring Awakening,* in which two men kiss. I could not believe what I was seeing. I almost fainted watching it onstage in front of me, because in Islam, of course, homosexuality is forbidden, and even punishable by death. Muslimah turned to me, laughing, and said, "I enjoy watching your face more than watching the actors."

For the first time, I saw people reading in public. They would sit with a book under the trees, in subways, in cafés, in waiting rooms, on the bus. I was mesmerized. I started carrying a book with me everywhere I went. I found the public library in Nashua and signed up for a library card, which I still have. I borrowed many books; it was the first time I had ever been in a public library.

Slowly, I became Americanized. I dressed up for St. Patrick's Day, shocked to discover that even though the Saudi flag is green, I had nothing green in my closet. I learned that when I took out my credit card after a meal, I should say "Let's split it," or else I would end up paying the whole check. I quickly learned that ordering one meal in a restaurant would provide enough leftovers for a whole week. As a Saudi flying in the US, I also learned what a "random check" means at the airport. I learned that men kiss women on one cheek in greeting, but women do not kiss each other like that, basically the extreme opposite of home.

I also learned many things that I never expected. All my young friends in Boston, in their late twenties and early thirties, were overwhelmed with college debt. They were very educated, but at what price? Even those who had what could be considered good jobs often worked second jobs as waiters and waitresses to try to pay off their enormous student loans. I had friends who waited for free microwaves to be posted on Craigslist because they couldn't afford to buy new ones. That shocked me. They lived with roommates and would circle around the city for an hour looking for a parking space on the street, rather than pay to park in a garage. I never thought about paying for parking. If we went to a restaurant, they looked at all the prices on the menu before they ordered. I realized that this debt would rule their lives for years, while in Saudi Arabia, I had been paid $300 a month just to study at my university.

Everything was expensive. I could not believe that a friend of mine, who was between jobs, had to pay $800 for a visit to the hospital emergency room after he cut his finger. I could not believe that it was impossible to buy only high-speed Internet access without cable. (I hated watching American television: there were so many ads.) You can't, the cable man told me, it only comes as a package. I could not believe that I had to pay for garbage collection—to pay for the ability to throw something away. And I was very puzzled by the taxes. In Saudi Arabia, we don't have taxes, but my friends who lived in Boston paid as much as thirty percent of the money they earned in taxes. New Hampshire, at least, had no state income tax. But sales tax surprised me too; the price of what I wanted to buy was never the same at the register as what was marked on the ticket or the shelf. All of these things did not make sense.

Since it was 2009, less than a year after the housing market crash, the economy was really hurting. People were losing their jobs and their homes. Steve, the guy who came to fix my computer, was laid off the very next day. I came into the office and he was gone. That night, I went home and turned on the news. CNN was breathlessly reporting on Tiger Woods's mistresses. It was like that night after night. When I watched CNN in the States, I would think, is this really the news? It seemed more like gossip. The real problems were completely neglected, and people were kept in the dark. CNN International is entirely different. There I would learn what was actually happening in the world.

But there were other things that truly opened my mind. I read about Rosa Parks, the black woman who refused to move to the back of the bus. She had lived for a while on Maxwell Air Force Base in Montgomery, Alabama. Because it was a federal military instillation, it did not permit racial segregation, and Rosa Parks could ride on an integrated trolley. As I read this, I thought about Saudi women and the Aramco compound. Aramco was like Maxwell, a place where outside restrictions did not apply. Of course, when Rosa Parks left, she would want to ride in the front of the bus, just like everyone else. I saw so many parallels between what I'd experienced in Saudi Arabia and the American civil rights movement. Saudi women and African Americans were both victims of segregation, unable to have any say in the most basic aspects of their lives.

When I came to the United States, I was against gays, against Jews, against many other things. Living there forced me to rethink many of my opinions; it opened up my mind. I had conversations with people who likely would never have been permitted to visit Saudi Arabia, people I otherwise would never have met. I had one friend, Naomi, whom I met through dance parties. We really enjoyed each other's company. Once, when we were sitting in a restaurant, I saw two very obviously Jewish people walking out the door. As a joke, I said, "Those people are Jewish. We know each other from the nose," because both Arabs and Jews are known to have prominent noses.

She looked at me and said, "Yeah, that's right, you and I, we are cousins."

And I said, "Who is 'we'?"

And she said, "Us, the Jews."

I could not believe it. I had no idea that she was Jewish. And if I had known she was Jewish at the start, I never would have talked to her. Because I had been taught that all Jews are our enemies.

But the true culture shock occurred not when I landed in America, but much later, after I had returned home.

11

Driving while Female

*I*n the United States, I stopped covering my head with a hijab. Before that, in public, at work, or out with friends, I wore my hijab. Sometimes they were brightly colored or white, rather than the traditional black, but I still wore them. My hair was hidden, my face encased in cloth. But in private, things were different: I wore it; I stopped wearing it. I put it back on; I took it off.

When I returned to Saudi Arabia, I decided I would keep my hijab on for work. But outside of the office, I would leave my head free and uncovered. (I later learned that many of my Saudi girlfriends outside Aramco were doing the same thing in secret in their homes.) The last to know was my brother: I didn't want my parents to find out, because it would cause them tremendous embarrassment and very deep grief.

One day, when my brother and his wife were visiting me at the Aramco compound, I decided to go out with them without my hijab. I wore very modest clothes: a long, flowing blouse with long sleeves and very loose pants. But my brother was still horrified. He told his wife that he would tell me to put the hijab back on. But his wife took my side. "Manal is an adult," she told him. "You cannot control your sister." In truth, as my mahram living closest to me, he could control me in many ways. But, with his wife's prodding, he grudgingly gave up.

It was liberating. I could get in the cool blue water of the pool with Aboudi and dunk my head, toss my hair behind me, and feel the rush of bubbles stream out of my mouth as I exhaled in the watery silence. At night, when the breeze blew, I could feel the air lifting and ruffling the strands of my hair. When I turned, I could feel the hairs plastered against my skin.

Far more than my head covering had changed. When I returned to Saudi Arabia, so many of the old rules, the rules I had once slavishly followed, no longer seemed to make sense. For years, I had blamed Aramco for the restrictions and the discrimination I endured, but now I saw that what I was chafing against was Saudi society itself. Every restrictive rule existed simply for my "protection": this was the message that had been hardwired into my brain. But that circuit had been broken while I lived abroad. I was no longer so fearful of what people would think or what judgments would be passed. My colleagues said that the way I dressed, the way I thought, and the way I talked were all "totally different." And it was true. I had never been exposed to the language of women's rights or feminism. But even without the vocabulary, I discovered the concepts. There is an old Arabic proverb that translates to "If you have a right, you had better be determined." Inside the walls of the Aramco compound, I found my determination.

In 2010, not long after I returned, I started a Facebook group called Saudi Female Employees of Aramco. It was risky and it was completely underground. To complain about anything at Aramco, or indeed anywhere inside Saudi Arabia, carried the risk of punishment. But slowly we started writing our demands. We wanted day care nurseries for babies in the workplace and to be allowed access to the company cars. We were all employees, but we were not allowed to use the company cars, unlike the men. I took our demands to Aramco's labor committee: an organization purely for show, without any power. The only thing it did was listen to complaints, but at least this was a way to vent.

I also cofounded the first photography club in Dhahran; we called it Aurora. I had learned photography in the United States from my friend David. Back at home, I got together a group at Aramco. We took nature photographs, made portraits, and did event photography, printing our images and mostly giving them away. We met almost daily, usually in my town house. I didn't know it yet, but this and the Saudi Female Employees of Aramco group were to become essential to my decision to get behind the wheel of a car.

There was one more thing: on December 17, 2010, a twenty-six-year-old Tunisian fruit seller named Mohamed Bouazizi set himself on fire outside of a provincial government building. He had gone there to complain after the local police had confiscated his measuring scales when Bouazizi had refused to pay them a bribe. There were reports that a policewoman slapped him and in-sulted his deceased father. But the authorities denied his request to enter the building and complain. In that moment, in frustration and despair, he became a human conflagration. That incident and the mass protests that followed launched the Arab Spring, a wave of unrest that tore across the Middle East. From Tunisia it spread to Libya and to Egypt, the nation I knew from my childhood visits, where citizens flooded Tahrir Square to challenge years of dictato-rial rule.

Like millions of others around the Arab world, I was riveted. I followed the news, I followed the Facebook posts. I saw raw cell phone photos and videos of demonstrators occupying major streets and squares in their capitals, demanding that their oppressive gov-ernments give up power. Seeing their faces, hearing their voices, and reading their eloquent statements, I felt connected to these people. It seemed like change might be possible. It seemed like change might be possible even for us.

In the midst of this upheaval, in April 2011, I found myself in Khobar City, leaving a doctor's appointment at dusk, with no driver to take me home. I could stand on the corner or I could walk to Al-Rashid Mall, where there would be taxis waiting. I began to walk. Men who passed me rolled down their windows, shouting curses and calling me a "whore" or a "prostitute." And then came the man in the white Corolla. The driver did not simply insult me and roar off, he followed me. I turned away from the main route, and he followed. As I passed a pile of construction materials, I bent down and felt a rock. Clutching it in my hand, I hurled it toward his half-open window. The rock fell short as his tires screeched and he sped off.

I could feel the adrenaline surge through my veins. I walked a few steps and then began to cry, the salty tears mixing with my salty sweat. I ran to the mall, and with my uncovered, tear-stained face found a taxi and told the driver to take me to the Aramco compound. Once inside the safety of the car, I held my face in my hands and wept. But by the time we entered the compound, my eyes were dry. At my town house, my own car waited, cool, silent, and parked. I had spent hours learning to drive, I had a valid license. I probably had better road skills than many of the male taxi and private drivers.

As I opened my door and stepped inside, I did not hate men in their cars who had seen fit to harass me. I hated the rules that caged me inside my compound, that kept women tethered to the whim of our guardians, that kept us shut inside our homes more effectively than any lock.

The next day at work, I told one of my male coworkers what had happened on the dusky streets. "I am so tired of this," I said. "How long must we suffer this humiliation?" It seemed almost a rhetorical question.

My colleague looked at me. He was a Saudi, so I expected only perhaps a bit of sympathy, maybe some advice. Instead, he shocked me by saying, "Manal, I know it is unfair. But, you know, it really isn't illegal for women to drive."

At first I thought he was mocking me, but then I realized he was serious. "What do you mean, it isn't *really* illegal?"

"Manal, technically, there is no rule saying that women cannot drive. Nothing in the traffic code actually states that it is illegal for women to drive. It's just the custom. You'll see, I'll show you." He left my office and a few minutes later, he sent me a link to the Saudi traffic code. In his email message, he said, "Read page 50, part V, act 36: Driver's License requirements."

That night, I fed my son dinner and put him to bed, and I sat down at my computer. I read the entire traffic code. At first I felt nothing but anger. Then, slowly, I began to reread each word, aloud. I went through each line of the code. There was not one reference to the gender of the driver. Pages 117 to 121 listed all possible traffic violations and offenses. None of them included "driving while female." Nothing, *absolutely nothing,* in the official Saudi traffic code indicated it was illegal for women to drive.

Now I was truly angry. I wanted to call someone, to tell someone, *but whom*? Instead, I went back to my computer and started typing. I searched three simple words—*Saudi, women,* and *driving.*

———

The first formal protest of the ban on women driving occurred in 1990 during the run-up to the Gulf War, about four months after Iraq invaded Kuwait. All through that autumn, American soldiers had been arriving in Saudi Arabia, by the tens of thousands, to prepare for Operation Desert Shield, the invasion that would drive Saddam Hussein's forces back to Baghdad.

On November 6, 1990, as Saudi Arabia simmered with unease, forty-seven women defied the ban on driving. For thirty minutes, they lined up their cars in a convoy and drove around the capital city, Riyadh, until the religious police caught up with them and all forty-seven were arrested. Their goal had been to demonstrate to Saudi society that while they were women, they were competent enough to sit behind the wheel of a car.

I had heard about these women when I was eleven years old. They were depicted as sexually loose, un-Islamic, pro-Western women who danced in the streets with the American soldiers without any regard for covering their hair with hijabs. I remembered asking questions about these women, but the adults around me didn't want to discuss them. Eventually, people began to forget. In my twenties, when I thought about these women, it was only scorn I felt. Having absorbed the government's version of the story, I believed that they and their protest and the trouble they had caused were why my generation was not allowed to drive. And in fact the cultural taboo against driving was strengthened because of their protest. Their act of dissent had in a sense proven true the dire warnings about what would happen should women drive. But there is another side to the story.

For these forty-seven women, known as the "women drivers," those thirty minutes have stalked them for the rest of their lives. Immediately following the incident, all the women and their husbands were banned from foreign travel for a year. Those who held government jobs were fired. And they became targets of religious condemnation: in Friday sermons at mosques around the country, their names were read aloud, and they were denounced as immoral vixens, boldly seeking to destroy Saudi society. The late journalist and photographer Saleh Al-Azzaz, who documented this protest, was arrested, jailed, and tortured.

For the women, additional harassment and humiliation followed. In 2008, one told an American National Public Radio (NPR) interviewer that it was impossible to be promoted. No matter how good a job she did, she would forever be that "woman driver."

But that protest had happened a long time ago; I was barely a schoolgirl then. The world was changing, and I believed Saudi Arabia also was ready to change. So, I decided that for my next birthday, I would do the unthinkable. I would get behind the wheel of a car, outside the Aramco compound, and dare to drive.

Inside Saudi Arabia, there had never been complete unanimity on the subject of women and driving. The Saudi royal family and government officials have argued that Saudi society, not the government, should decide whether it is right for women to drive. After the 1990 protest, the Ministry of the Interior did issue a statement (although not a specific traffic rule) that "driving while female was illegal and subject to a fine." (The Ministry of the Interior is also not a legislative entity, and a driving ban should technically be issued by a legislative body.) That statement was based on the religious fatwa issued by Grand Mufti Bin Baz immediately after the November 6 protest, in which he called these women morally corrupt and underscored that it was haram for women to drive. But online I found other "grand Islamic scholars," colleagues of Bin Baz, who questioned the decision to issue a fatwa against driving. One scholar, Al Albani, even suggested that in Muhammad's (PBUH) time women could ride a donkey, so why not a car? Cars provided more protection for women.

I was not the only Saudi woman growing desperate to drive. Only days after my humiliating walk along the side of the road, a friend invited me to join a Facebook event called "We are driving May 17th." The event was being organized by a young woman named Bahiya. I discovered that I knew her aunt. I accepted the invitation immediately and asked if I could be added as an administrator. Facebook was the chief means of organizing the near daily protests in Egypt and was playing a role in Tunisia and Libya as well. All of us had seen how a Facebook event and post could pick a date and issue a call for action. I wanted this to be a big event, well beyond forty-seven female drivers.

When I told one of my friends about the event, his response was, "Manal, that's only about a month away. It's too soon. Change the date." So we did. We pushed it out to June 17, which happened by accident to be a Friday—most of the Arab Spring gatherings had been on Fridays as well. The friend also advised me to get on Twitter. Up until now, I had been focused on Facebook. It was how I had made and kept up with American friends. But Facebook is not big in Saudi Arabia—only about one-third of Facebook accounts in Saudi Arabia

belong to women, and most women cannot post using their own photos or use their real names online. If it is forbidden to show your face
in public on a sidewalk, how can you show it in an electronic gathering place? In 2011, Twitter was the preferred form of social media for
Saudis. Saudi Arabia had more than 5 million Twitter accounts and
about 2.4 million active Twitter users, defined as people who log in at
least once a month. Twitter was the way to get our message out, my
friend explained. So I learned to use Twitter.

I registered my account under the handle @Women2Drive, uploaded a photo that one of our supporters had designed, and in the
profile bio, I wrote, "We call on all Saudi women to drive on June 17."

Within days, @Women2Drive had thousands of followers.

The movement quickly took on a life of its own. At night, once
Aboudi was in bed, I posted items on Facebook. I tried my hand at
writing press releases and getting blog posts. I wrote petitions for signatures and designed a logo. The enthusiasm was powerful. People
were visiting our Facebook event page and retweeting our tweets.
Within a week, people were coming to my house, asking if they could
help.

Initially, I was encouraged that a good number of the men I knew—
granted, a small circle, and entirely inside Aramco—supported the
campaign. They saw it not as threatening but as liberating for all Saudis. Even my brother, the same brother who had been so horrified
when I removed my hijab, supported me. He worked as a petroleum
geoscientist, which required him to spend up to three weeks at a time
out in the oil fields, far away from his wife and their newborn. They
did not live inside the Aramco compound and he could not afford a
driver, which meant that his wife was trapped at home until he returned. I remember him telling me that it broke his heart each time he
left home, knowing his wife and son were helpless. They often stayed
with me at the compound so that I could help them get around.

"When I come back from work," my brother once told me, "I am
very tired, all I want to do is rest, but at that moment, I have to take
my wife all over the place." He often had to make up excuses to leave

work early so that he could drive his wife somewhere. The system left him and my sister-in-law entirely dependent. Each was without basic freedom. I also often needed my brother to drive me outside the walls of the compound. So he was "on call" for two women.

"I'm with you," he told me. "Go ahead."

I had convinced him. Now I had only another 7 million Saudi men to go.

———

Almost as soon as we started posting to Facebook, men and even some women responded with harsh criticism. They railed that we "would destroy Saudi society" and "destroy Saudi family life." Women driving "would lead to corruption and moral decay." The entire campaign was subjected to fierce scrutiny. People asked constantly who we were—at this point, none of us were posting using our real names and our real photos—who was supporting us, whether the driving itself was legal, where the event was going to be held. Most ominous of all, they assumed that we were calling for public demonstrations. This was unsettling because public demonstrations are illegal in Saudi Arabia and the punishments for conducting them severe. A peaceful sit-down protest can result in a sentence of lashes, jailtime, and being banned from foreign travel. To make sure that we could not be called a "protest," I wanted women to drive by themselves, not in groups, and to record themselves alone in their cars.

Huddled one night in my town house, we decided that the best response to the criticism was to post a video on YouTube, answering all these questions and mistaken assumptions one by one. Though we had clearly stated on Facebook and in press releases what our goals were and what actions we planned to take, no one in Saudi Arabia seemed to understand.

But criticisms were not the only comments I received. Some of the responses contained words of concern, even fear. One friend who knew that I was involved emailed me directly, "Manal, you're crazy. You'll get in serious trouble if you go through with this. Think of the danger you'll put yourself in, the danger to your son, your whole family." Although I understood her worry, I felt that the campaign's urgency and timeliness outweighed the dangers. Still, it was hard not to feel rattled by the comments, particularly those left by men on our Facebook event page. Over and over, they equated the Women2Drive campaign with women who were loose, sexually compromised, and of weak, immoral character. The comments were menacing, saying very directly that our campaign was designed to corrupt young girls and that we were "betraying Islam."

Other men let us know how they'd use their *iqal*, the thick black cord men wrapped around their heads. The iqal is an old custom. Originally needed to hold men's headdresses in place when the wind blew, now the black cord is largely decorative—although some men use it to hit their wives and their kids. I've never felt the sting of the iqal, but I've heard that the knotted rope is very painful. A Facebook page called "By Iqal" was founded to call on men to beat any women drivers they saw.

Despite this ugly resistance, I kept the image of the Arab Spring in my mind. Some of the girls backing our movement even put up a rival Facebook page stating that if any man beat a female driver, the woman would hit him back with her shoe. (Showing the soles of your shoes is regarded as particularly insulting in the Arab world.) I personally hate violence, but I felt that the message of this page was *We are not afraid. We are determined.* Again and again, when I reached out to others, I felt their personal support more strongly than I felt the doubts and hatred of strangers.

So I took the next step. I made an informational video for Women2Drive, in which I publicly revealed my identity. Unlike the other girls, I was divorced and self-supporting. I could take the risk. I remember the morning exactly. Each day I worked from seven in the morning until four in the afternoon. Then I would take care of Aboudi until I put him in bed at eight o'clock. Once he was in bed, I would work on Women2Drive, staying up until three or four in the morning. I never slept more than two or three hours a night. On the day I recorded the video, I got up at 5:00 a.m. Looking into the laptop camera, I explained what the June 17 campaign was about and exactly what would happen that day. I was careful not to call it a protest. I concentrated on speaking calmly and smiling continuously. I did not wear the full abaya; I made no effort to hide my face. I ended the video by reminding viewers, "We are your sisters, your mothers, your daughters. We expect your support, and now we're giving you the chance to show it."

My final words were this: "The whole story: that we will just drive."

I posted the video to YouTube, and within days it had had more than 120,000 views. Using my real name—including my last name, my tribal name—and showing my face gave the recording legitimacy and drew more attention to the campaign, and it also made me the public face of Women2Drive. Threatening comments directed at me began pouring in over social media. The posters wanted to dissect my appearance and speculate on whether I was a Sunni or a Shiite Muslim. If I were Shiite, that immediately made me suspect as a possible Iranian agent. Some commentators pasted a monkey's face or a donkey's over my own, or wrote about my nose or my "ugly uncovered face." The posters attacked me for my "scandalous attempts" to drive and for disrupting Saudi society. I was called a "whore," "immoral," "Westernized," a "traitor," and a "double agent."

The comments hurt. Some left me shocked, others simply disappointed, but I learned a valuable lesson. I saw that people preferred scandals to the very real plight of Saudi women. I saw too that people criticized me and the other women behind the Women2Drive campaign because they were afraid, afraid of any real change. I had miscalculated how much effort our opponents would put into switching the focus to me and away from the movement. I trained myself to ignore them.

The other girls would send me links to the pages that attacked me and Women2Drive, but I told them, "Forget about these people. They are just noise." Day by day, I toughened myself. I kept all my thoughts and emotions inside, I stayed quiet, and I moved on. I think that's one of the things that puzzled our opponents. They thought they could break me with what they said, with what they posted. Even at work I was harassed. But I always stayed polite. I always kept a smile on my face. I kept saying respectful things, emphasizing that I am a Saudi, that I am proud to be Saudi, and that I love my country. I just want to change this custom. My strategy was never defend and never attack. Educate people and get more supporters, that's what I told all the girls.

I began to see that there would be a price for standing up for my rights, as there had been for Saudi women before me. But I could not have foreseen the full consequences. I would soon learn that nothing upset Saudi men and the entire Saudi ruling order more than the simple act of women driving. The decision to take action in real life was what *really* scared our opponents. There had been talk of driving before, but women across the country had never just picked a date and said, "That's it. We've had enough. We are going to drive."

———

We were still trying to get media attention. One of the first journalists to reach out to us was Maysa, a TV host and blogger; she is Saudi but was living in the United Arab Emirates, a collection of seven principalities bordering Saudi Arabia. The friend who had convinced me to get on Twitter grabbed my phone one day and sent Maysa a message saying, "This is Manal from the Women2Drive campaign. I'd like to speak with you." Maysa called me immediately, and later I realized why. Maysa had publicly stated that she would not return to Saudi Arabia until women were allowed to drive. (Her father had died before her eyes because when he fell ill, no other man was at home and Maysa couldn't drive him to the hospital.)

One contact led to another. As well as interviewing me, Maysa put me in touch with Abdullah Al Alami, a retired Aramco employee who had been the head of employment. Mr. Al Alami had many contacts among Saudi journalists and officials and had been very involved in previous struggles to change the culture, particularly regarding women's rights. He and I arranged to meet at the Aramco dining hall near my office. For nearly an hour, the older, elegantly dressed Saudi man, who came prepared with a thick file of papers, listened carefully as I explained the goals of the campaign. He didn't interrupt once, just repeatedly nodded his head.

After I had finished, he said, "Listen, Manal, I want to tell you what happened in 1990 to those women who challenged the driving ban."

At first I was put off, thinking, I don't want to hear about those women again. I wanted nothing to do with them. But, as he continued to speak, I realized he was trying to offer me his insights. He relayed in great detail what happened to the forty-seven women who attempted to challenge the ban on driving, showing me a stack of old newspaper clippings. Sitting there, listening to him, I realized I had been wrong. Instead of blaming these women and accepting the lies that had been told about them, I saw that they were my sisters, my role models. They had understood, long before I did, that the only way to challenge Saudi restrictions was to organize and demonstrate; the only way was to drive.

After he was finished, he said, "You must be prepared emotionally and politically for what might happen if you go through with this. We have to go through some possible scenarios. You must be ready for the worst possible reaction."

Mr. Al Alami explained that serious mistakes had occurred in 1990 and tried to tell me in detail how to avoid repeating them. After we discussed some of the potential outcomes, he looked me in the eyes and asked, "What is it you want, Manal?"

With no hesitation, I said, "I want to challenge the ban on women driving. I want women to drive in this country. I want to write a letter to King Abdullah."

He looked down at his two phones, searching for prominent people to introduce me to. By the end of our meeting, he'd given me the numbers of some lawyers, people on the Shoura council (an unelected advisory council for the king), and several other high-profile individuals. He didn't discourage me from writing a letter to King Abdullah, but he told me to expect two possible reactions: either a resounding no or no response at all. Despite his cautionary words, I did not feel discouraged. I left feeling supported and reassured.

I began in earnest to try to meet with anyone who had connections or had some kind of public profile and an interest in women driving. I knew that if we had supporters, especially if they were prominent Saudis, we had a greater chance of success. I spent nearly every day trying to arrange meetings with people who could help us promote the June 17 campaign. My meeting with Mr. Al Alami had convinced me that there was enough public support among common Saudis, including forward-thinking men, to achieve a very different result from what happened in 1990. Though there were still people telling me that I needed to be careful, I pushed all that aside. I believed in this campaign.

One of the people who gave me moral support was Wajeha al-Huwaider, the Saudi woman and seasoned activist who had posted a video of herself driving back in 2008. Wajeha and I both worked and lived in the Aramco compound, yet we'd never met. I sent her an email, asking her to meet for coffee. I didn't tell her the purpose of our meeting: she'd probably heard murmurings of our campaign, and she said yes. We were to meet at the café inside the compound. As soon as I arrived, I realized I didn't know what she looked like. I searched the faces of everyone sitting at the tables outside the café: a few women in full abayas and hijab and one lone woman in jeans and a blue T-shirt, her hair tied back in a ponytail with thick bangs across her forehead. I finally texted, "I'm here, where are you?"

A second later, my phone buzzed, "I'm here outside, wearing a blue top." It was the woman in jeans, with the ponytail.

We started off talking about conditions for women working at Aramco, but before the hour was over, I summoned my courage and told her about Women2Drive. As soon as I began talking, her face lit up. "How did we not know of each other, right here in Aramco, living and working in the same space?" she asked me, reaching over to squeeze my hand. From then on, all our caution fell away. Wajeha was younger than I had expected, and despite all she'd been through, was clearly committed to the struggle for women's rights. Since 2003, she had faced harassment: death threats, email threats, ugly comments in cyberspace. She'd been working at Aramco longer than me, but because of her activism, she'd been unable to advance in her career. Her boss had made it very clear that if she continued to agitate for women's rights, there would be no opportunities for promotion; her goals were not "conducive to the policies or the position of Aramco." She'd accepted these restrictions—she was glad to have a job—and she said that she would "never stop fighting for the rights of women."

Wajeha cautioned me, "Prepare yourself for it, Manal. You're likely to get arrested."

I nodded but casually dismissed her concerns. Wajeha had already filmed herself driving and had posted the video to YouTube. Granted, she had driven inside the Aramco compound at Dhahran Beach, a place where women were allowed to drive, but in the video she hadn't specified her location. I did know that she had been arrested more recently for holding up a sign on the Bahrain causeway that read, "Cars want to be driven by Saudi women." Under Saudi code, this act was considered a protest, punishable by jail time. When I told her that I had read the traffic code thoroughly and was sure that there were no legal obstacles to driving, she smiled slightly and winked at me. "Of course, you're right, Manal," she said, "but that is not all that stands in the way of our rights."

"Don't worry," I told Wajeha, as we parted at the door of the cafe. "This time will be different."

We had a Twitter presence and a very active Facebook account, but inside Saudi Arabia, the local media ignored us. One reporter told us that the paper would only publish a story about us if the event happened on June 17. But if we were to have an impact, we had to get attention from the press. We needed that attention to recruit more drivers. We would have to start with the international press.

The Saudi friend who had convinced me to join Twitter now said that I needed to use it to initiate contact with other activists and with journalists. I increased my tweets about the campaign's calls for women drivers and began reaching out to reporters outside Saudi Arabia. Almost immediately, they responded. One of the first to contact me was Donna Abu-Nasr from Bloomberg News; a few days later, Atika Shubert from CNN asked me for an interview. I was giddy with excitement and felt reassured to have that kind of attention. In other parts of the world, press coverage and public awareness offered a unique kind of protection. In Saudi Arabia, it also guaranteed that our day of driving would not go unnoticed.

The Bloomberg story was posted online right away, but the CNN interview, which I did over Skype, did not appear. There were new uprisings in Libya, which pushed our efforts off the air. I was giving up hope when one morning the official Saudi government foreign-language newspaper published a small mention of the June 17 event. It was just a mention, but it was presented neutrally. I thought we had been given a quiet nod to proceed. That night, CNN International finally aired the interview. We posted screen shots to Twitter and Facebook, and for the first time, many of our wary supporters grew braver. All of a sudden, June 17 and Women2Drive were everywhere.

The CNN interview ended with me saying, "The rain begins with a single drop," a quote which went viral and is still repeated today.

———

That week, it became clear that one of the most daunting aspects of our efforts would be logistics. Many women who wished to participate did not know how to drive. When we put out a poll on Twitter, only eleven percent of the women who said they wanted to drive had any kind of license. More than two thousand women said they wanted to learn how. We began trying to locate women who could drive and were willing to teach others, either in parking lots or other safe spaces like the desert. One woman who came forward to help teach was Najla Hariri, a Saudi woman who had lived in Egypt and Lebanon and was licensed to drive in both countries. She not only offered to teach, she began driving herself around the streets of Jeddah. I put a BBC news crew in touch with her, but they had no film footage of her driving, so many Saudis in their online comments claimed that they didn't believe her. The government did, however, and she was later questioned and referred for trial.

Now, in addition to the logistics of driving, we had to find new ways to deal with the rising backlash to our plan.

I had an idea. I thought that if, prior to the event on June 17, someone posted a video of a woman driving, it might "normalize" the experience and show Saudi citizens that there was nothing dangerous about women driving. I also wanted to prove that many of us already knew how to drive—that we had licenses and even cars. And I wanted to prove that the Saudi authorities would not stop a woman driver. For weeks, I had heard people say, "If you drive, the man-wolves will eat you alive." I wanted to show that there were no "man-wolves," and a woman could drive without fear. So I decided to film myself.

But deciding to do it was one thing; actually doing it was another. I was filled with a combination of excitement and anxiety. I was about to become even more of a public face. I hadn't slept much in the pre- ceding two weeks and my small town house was bustling with ener- getic people who wanted to help with the campaign. It had become our de facto headquarters. We posted updates, but we also delegated. A Brazilian artist, Carlos Latuff, created a logo for the campaign that depicted a Saudi woman wearing a niqab sitting behind the wheel of a car with her hand raised in a victory sign. But I knew that we and I had to be careful. Women2Drive couldn't be seen as an actual protest movement. I clung to the belief that if I could just show Saudi society that no harm would come if a woman drove, many of the other issues surrounding the campaign would simply vanish.

I selected May 19, just a month shy of the June 17 Women2Drive day, as the day to make my video. I got up early that morning, after hav- ing once again slept very little. I didn't have my son with me—he had spent the night with his grandmother at his father's family home, which made it less stressful. I hadn't told anyone in my family other than my brother what I was doing. Neither my parents nor my ex-husband knew, because they would simply try to discourage me. But my brother had supported me unconditionally. Since I had begun working on Women-2Drive, he'd been to my house to offer his solidarity and support. I, in turn, felt fortunate to have a male relative who was in my corner, who understood that this cause was much bigger than me.

I called my brother almost as soon as I got up, but didn't reach him, so I made myself a strong cup of coffee, dressed in the most conservative outfit I owned, and laid my black hijab on the bed. I looked at myself in the mirror, and made a decision not to put on my usual kohl eyeliner. I knew I had to do everything to minimize my appearance so that people would focus only on the driving. After a few minutes, I left the bedroom and sat down at the dining room table, reviewing my driving plan. It would be simple but very visible, and the more I imagined it, the more I excited became. I dialed my brother's number again. When he didn't pick up, I texted him: "Where are u? Waiting for you to come. Time to drive!" Although we'd agreed to meet that day, and he had offered to accompany me, we had not arranged a definite time. I was a bit worried because in one of my tweets, I'd announced that I was going to drive that day and post the video on YouTube. I needed to drive, with or without my brother. And then I had an idea. I would ask Wajeha to accompany me.

Without hesitating, I texted her, "What are you doing? Can you drive with me?" She texted back immediately that it was the fortieth day after her mother's death and she needed to travel to a city about an hour away from Dhahran, where the ceremony would be taking place. A driver would be picking her up. I assured her that we would be finished before she needed to leave. She immediately answered, "Okay."

In the meantime, Ahmed, one of my campaign friends (the friend responsible for our Twitter account), had come to check on me. Because my brother was not available, I decided to ask Ahmed if he would accompany Wajeha and me: we needed a male driver to clear the security gates at the Aramco exit. Wajeha would be the film crew and Ahmed would be our designated driver until I slid over and took the wheel of my purple Cadillac SRX. I had spent several years saving my money for the car, a car that I would now for the first time be driving on actual Saudi kingdom streets. Ahmed smiled and agreed, promising, "I'll drive you to my favorite café, get myself some ginger lemon tea, and leave you two ladies alone." The more I thought about it, the more I liked the idea of another Saudi woman filming me. I told Ahmed that we should tweet about it.

After about an hour, Ahmed and I left my house. We drove through the neatly groomed streets of the Aramco compound, past perfectly green lawns. Wajeha lived on the other side of the sprawling golf course, in a part of the compound where many Saudi employees had their homes. By the time we arrived at her house, it was almost eleven o'clock. We honked the horn and I texted her that we were out front, and she practically ran out the door. She looked very different from the day we had met for coffee, and yet she still made a statement. Her hair was neatly concealed beneath a black hijab, but she had on a bright pink abaya. Saudi women rarely wear anything but black abayas in public. When I saw Wajeha in pink, I giggled, thinking that she was even more fearless than me. No doubt she was thinking that if we got arrested, at least she'd look stylish.

As she approached the car, Ahmed moved from the passenger's side to the driver's seat so we could exit the Aramco gate. I got out of the car and walked around to the passenger seat. Wajeha sat down in the back, and just as soon as she closed the door, she opened it again. "Oh, I forgot my ID card," she said. "I better have it with me, just in case we get arrested."

Ahmed looked at me nervously, and I knew what he was thinking. "Don't worry, Ahmed," I said, "we're not going to get arrested."

After Wajeha came back, she spoke excitedly. "Manal," she said, "you're a genius. This is great, filming yourself driving outside and posting it. I wish I had thought of this."

Ahmed smiled, looked in the rearview mirror, and turned the key

in the ignition. After he turned onto the main street, I twisted my
head slowly and looked back at the buildings behind us. As the neat
Aramco skyline receded, it was as if I was leaving the safety of all that
I knew.

Outside the compound, Ahmed drove nervously, looking at the
speedometer and then over at me and up at the mirror to see who
might be behind us on the road. His anxiety was contagious, but I also
felt a growing sense of exhilaration. After several blocks we passed
the local police station, and then at last, we reached the café where
Ahmed would get his ginger lemon tea. He pulled into the parking lot
but didn't park until we were well behind the building, out of sight.
He got out of the car, but then spent a few minutes chatting with us.
Finally I said, "Okay, Ahmed, go drink your tea. We have some places
to drive to."

I moved to the driver's seat and Wajeha moved to the front passenger seat, laughing. I took a deep breath and sat down inside the
car and put my hands on the steering wheel. I still vividly remember
the feeling of pulling the door closed and locking it. Although I was
enclosed, at that moment, I felt like one of my father's songbirds, let
out of its cage and flying around the room. "Thank you, my friend,"
I said to Ahmed out of the rolled-down window. "We'll be all right,
don't worry."

As I fastened my seat belt, I could feel my hands shake slightly.
I placed the key in the ignition, adjusted the rearview mirror, and
pulled my black hijab close around my face to make sure no hair was
visible. I reached for my sunglasses from inside my bag, placed them
on my uncovered face, and took one last look at myself in the mirror.
Then I looked over at Wajeha and asked, "You ready?" I didn't wait
for her reply.

My heart began to beat faster as I turned the key, heard the engine
catch, put my foot on the brake, and switched the car into reverse. My
decision to drive had been made in a moment of anger, but now I felt
pure calm rise up inside me. I was committed to driving because I
was convinced, after having read and understood the traffic code, that

there was nothing actually forbidding me from doing so. I believed it would be okay. So it was an odd combination of fear *and* fearlessness I felt as I pulled out onto the main road.

I had already handed my iPhone to Wajeha and showed her how to turn on the camera and shoot the video. As the car glided down the street, I began to compose my thoughts for the video's introduction. I wanted to declare in a clear, loud voice, "This is my right, the right to drive." But instead, I turned the wheel of the car and gazed straight ahead, feeling the iPhone hovering close to my face. After chatting casually for a few minutes in Arabic, I said, "There's something to be proud of in this country. There are people doing volunteer work, doing it without pay, to help the women of this country. We are ignorant and illiterate when it comes to driving. You'll find a woman with a PhD, a professor at a college, and she doesn't know how to drive. We want change in the country."

As I turned the steering wheel, I could feel the words slip out of my mouth. It was hardly the stuff of protest; it was a conversation I had started simply to keep myself calm. At that moment, the driving did not feel all that different from the driving that I did on a daily basis inside the Aramco compound. But it *was* completely different. I felt Wajeha's eyes on me and her presence as a witness. I felt the gaze of the camera as a witness. Like other people of my generation, who had been gathering in city squares and on street corners across North Africa and the Middle East, who were raising their voices and their hands and using their cell phones and cameras to stand up to repression, authoritarianism, and tradition, we were at that moment pushing back against one of Saudi Arabia's most enduring cultural taboos. We were taking a chance to express the basic aspirations of Saudi women. With Wajeha beside me, I felt that we were now in "the driver's seat of our own destiny."

As I kept driving, adjusting my hijab and sunglasses again, Wajeha added, "Today there was a report in *Al Riyadh* newspaper that a sister took her brother to the hospital in her car. But a woman is not just for an emergency. A woman has the same right as a man to live her daily life—in dignity," she said. I nodded, even as I kept my eyes on the road.

We continued, speaking about women who pay as much as a third of their monthly salaries to hire a private driver. Many of these drivers work for multiple women; what would be a ten-minute trip can take one or two hours as the driver circles the area, picking up all the other women. We talked about the hour-plus wait for a taxi during rush hour, about standing on the roadside as hired drivers humiliate us because they want more money than we are offering. We talked about mothers who cannot drop their children at school when their husbands are away, about mothers who put their ten-year-old sons behind the wheel so they can leave their homes. As we spoke, I negotiated the traffic, obeyed the lights and signs, and rounded the roadway's curves.

I looked left and turned down Corniche Street, heading toward the supermarket where I shopped for groceries each week—and where, previously, I could only go with a male driver. I let the steering wheel glide smoothly in my hands as I made the turn, looking out so I could make eye contact with any oncoming drivers. A silver Toyota SUV approached, and I saw the male driver lean slightly to his right and speak to a woman seated next to him. They looked at each other and then back at me. I smiled, and Wajeha asked, "Why are you smiling, Manal?"

For a second, I turned to face the iPhone in her hands, smiled even wider, and said, "Because I am driving."

For several minutes, I circled the parking lot, watching as various drivers noticed me, until finally I slowed the car and turned into a parking space. Then I said, "Come on, Wajeha," I said. "Let's go shopping." Wajeha turned off the cell phone, and together we exited the car.

The parking lot was crowded with foreign male drivers, standing outside their cars, waiting for their female clients. Their eyes widened and followed us; I could hear several whisper to each other in Hindi or Urdu. But no one confronted us. I felt a bit like a child breaking the rules, but I also knew this was far more serious than a childhood prank. Every gaze seemed to burn into my skin.

"Wajeha, let's get some groceries," I said. "I'd like to get my son a treat." She nodded and waved her hand, indicating that I should enter the supermarket first. I pulled my hijab tight around my head and didn't remove my sunglasses. From just inside the store, I saw a man lean over and whisper something to his coworker. We moved through the aisles, placing items in our shopping basket: a bottle of water, a piece of fruit, a candy bar for Aboudi. At the checkout counter, the two of us stood side by side, saying nothing as I pulled out my wallet. We walked proudly through the parking lot, opened the car doors, and got back in. Only then did Wajeha and I look at each other and break into spontaneous laughter, calling out together, "We did it!"

I placed my slightly sweaty hands on the wheel, turned on the ignition, and said, "Okay, Wajeha, let's keep driving." She began to film again, but I barely spoke. Instead, I took in the space and power of the car and the undeniable sense of victory. I knew then that no matter what my future held, I had done something important and meaningful. That day, I felt I was driving for all Saudi women—and in a sense, I was.

As I drove, I contemplated what route my driver usually took after leaving the grocery store. But I also knew that I did not yet have that freedom. After a few more miles, I guided the car back in the direction of the café where we'd dropped off Ahmed. I drove neither fast nor slow, but I could feel myself looking at the familiar streets and buildings that I had never seen from a vantage point other than the passenger seat. I couldn't help glancing in the direction of the police station as we passed, wondering if any policemen would catch a glimpse of me.

It was the same police station where two days later I would be arrested and detained.

12

In the Kingdom of Saudi Men

I drove on Thursday, May 19, on what was then the first day of the Saudi weekend. That night I uploaded the video to YouTube. It was completely in Arabic, with no subtitles, my hair was covered, and I was wearing big sunglasses. It was like someone's home movie. I hoped that most of the people who had watched the previous video might see this one too, but not leave so many nasty comments. The next day was Friday, Islam's weekly holiday, a time for prayer, for sermons from imams, and for whatever public punishments the kingdom might mete out. The following morning, Saturday, I went to work as usual. Except that nothing would ever again be the same.

One of my colleagues walked into my office and, holding on to the lip of my desk for support, he told me that my video was the most watched YouTube video in all of Saudi Arabia and one of the top videos in the world, with more than 700,000 views and a 20:80 like:dislike ratio. At first I thought he was joking, but then I checked online. Someone living in Australia had posted in the comment section, "I have no clue why the hell everyone is watching this." But every

Saudi knew exactly why he or she was watching. And the reaction was quickly overwhelming.

Aramco publishes a private directory listing the names and contact information for its employees. It didn't take long for angry strangers to find me. My inbox was clogged with messages calling me a "whore" or worse. "If I ever see you in the street . . ." one began. I immediately deleted it. Another started with the words, "We are digging your grave." A third, "You have just opened the gates of hell on yourself." I began forwarding the worst ones to Aramco security. Even after reading only a few words, I could feel the writers' anger seething across cyberspace. The phone on my desk was ringing constantly, some callers doing nothing but breathing on the end, but some screaming, "You drove a car! Your face was uncovered!" It didn't matter that a group of Saudi clerics had acknowledged a woman's right to uncover her face or that there was no statute explicitly banning women from driving. I endured rants about my bringing chaos (*fitna*) to the country. On YouTube, I disabled the video's comment section because about half of the four hundred comments were vile. At lunchtime, two strangers stopped at my cubicle and read my nameplate. They stared, but said nothing and then left. I felt nervous that someone would try to hurt me.

Not long after, I went to my boss and requested two weeks off; I didn't want to cause any trouble at work. My request was verbally accepted, but I was determined to finish out the current day as if nothing had changed. Soon the department manager came to my door.

"I want you to listen, Manal," he told me. "I want you to be very careful with the things that you are doing. We don't like it, and we don't want the company's name involved, in any way." And then he asked this: "How are you going to change anything by doing what you're doing?"

I looked at him and replied, "It's 2011. It's time."

He asked me again to be careful, to think of my son and my family, and to think of all that I was risking, including my job.

"Don't worry," I said. "I have things under control." But I also did not want anyone to doubt my commitment.

The chaos of that morning had thwarted one key piece of my plan. I had intended to go to the local traffic station during my lunch break and apply for a Saudi driver's license. I had already checked; there was no statute prohibiting me from doing this. I still had my valid American license, and I had completed the Saudi application form. All I needed was my younger brother acting as my mahram to accompany me. But he was unable to leave work, I couldn't find a taxi, and I was occupied by angry emails and harassing phone calls. The license application waited, folded inside my bag.

After work, I picked up Aboudi, got into a taxi, and together we headed to my brother's house. I told him about the video and the responses. But now I had a new concern: how could I be certain the women who drove on June 17 would be safe? After the forty-seven women who had driven in Riyadh in 1990, only the occasional woman here and there had dared to drive. In each of those instances, it appeared that the woman had been brought to a Saudi traffic police station and her guardian summoned. The women were forced to sign pledges agreeing never to drive again.

When I had driven two days before, I hadn't encountered any traffic police and I hadn't been stopped. I had hoped that no one would stop any woman driving on June 17, but after the reaction to the video, I was worried. "I need to find out," I told my brother. "Let's go now and I'll drive by the traffic police."

My brother agreed. He told me, "I will be with you until the end," and handed me the keys to his car, a Hyundai Azera sedan. But my sister-in-law was upset and begged us not to go. I told her that it was late in the day, the officers would want to go home quickly, and there was no rule that made my driving illegal.

My brother suggested that I drive down Corniche Street again, the biggest street in the city of Khobar. There were always traffic cops on that street. So my brother, my sister-in-law, their baby, and five-year-old Aboudi got in the car. I got in as well, but unlike every other time that we had ridden together like this, I was behind the wheel. I was excited but terrified. I hoped having my family with me would offer some protection if I was harassed. As I drove, I asked my sister-in-law to take out her cell phone and make another video. I was already thinking about how I could post it on YouTube, a Part 2.

I drove for about thirty minutes until we reached Corniche Street, the steering wheel feeling comfortable—easy and familiar—in my hands. Right away, I saw the first traffic cop. I held my breath as we passed. But he did not wave me over. Nothing happened.

"We have the green light!" I shouted. "We have the green light! It's okay!"

I kept on driving, watching the faces of the other drivers on the opposite side of the road. All of them stared, even swiveling their necks around as we passed. Some glanced down or looked away and then looked back, as if they could not believe what they were seeing: a woman driving. I looked them straight in the eye and smiled, as if to say, Yes, you are seeing a woman behind the wheel. Time finally to get used to it.

I continued until I reached an intersection. There, directly facing me, standing in the middle of the street, was another traffic cop. I came to the horrible realization that perhaps the first traffic cop had not reacted simply because he had not seen me. This time I was in full view. As the traffic cop looked at my vehicle, our eyes locked. When the light changed, I made a left turn, directly in front of him. I was barely through the lanes for oncoming traffic when I heard the command blaring over the police address system: "The Azera, pull over."

"That's us, Manal. Stop!" my sister-in-law called, her voice rising from the backseat.

"No, wait a minute," I said. Perhaps, I rationalized, he meant a different Azera.

But then the police address system blared a second time, "The Azera, pull over."

I jerked the car to a stop. I blew out a big breath as I saw him striding up to my window, the driver's-side window. Then I saw that he was smiling.

"Are you from Saudi?" he asked. "Do you know, in Saudi, women don't drive?" He looked at me, completely amused.

I smiled back and asked him his name. Then, caught up in the moment, I made a huge mistake. I told him my name. I handed over my brother's Saudi license, my Massachusetts license, and the car's registration. And then I added, "Sir, there is nothing in the traffic police code that says I cannot drive."

The traffic cop inspected the documents, all of which were valid. With a surprised look and a big smile, he told us to wait and then called for backup. While we were waiting for the second officer, a black car stopped in the middle of the road and the man inside looked over at me, still sitting in the driver's seat. "Who is this woman?" the man demanded.

The traffic cop answered. "Manal al-Sharif."

The man in the black car must have known about the YouTube video, because he made a call that would change my life. Within ten minutes, a huge GMC vehicle raced up, its tires squealing as the driver hastily applied the brakes. I was now surrounded by vehicles on all sides, but this last one was the most terrifying. Painted on its side was the insignia of the Mutawa—the Saudi religious police. Two men quickly emerged, one was very heavy, the other thin. Their names, I would learn, were Abu Abdullah and Faisal, and they were from the Commission for the Promotion of Virtue and the Prevention of Vice.

My brother immediately hopped out of the car and went to talk to them. Trying not to panic, I awkwardly shifted myself over to sit in the passenger's seat.

The Mutawa are like an unmarked army, invisible and yet everywhere all the time. They are best described by one word, brutal. They patrol malls and markets to make sure shopkeepers close for prayer, and are known to shout at ordinary Saudis for wearing the wrong clothes or being insufficiently covered. The religious law is left to their own interpretation, and their application of that law arbitrary and unchecked. The Mutawa have chased vehicles when they believed the occupants have violated religious requirements, resulting in several deadly car crashes, including one in 2012, when a man died and his wife, five months pregnant, and two children were badly injured. Several news outlets reported that a member of the Mutawa demanded that a woman cover her eyes, because although every other part of her body was covered, her eyes were "too seductive." When her husband asked them to leave her alone, a Mutawa officer stabbed the husband twice in the hand. The Mutawa severely beat a British man and his wife for using a women's-only automatic teller machine inside a supermarket in the capital city of Riyadh. All of this the Mutawa do—and are allowed to do—in the name of God.

The two Mutawa officers began insulting my brother, calling him every horrible name they could think of. As the minutes passed, it was clear that the situation belonged to them. The first traffic cop and the second one who had joined him stood off to the side, powerless. The Mutawa were yelling that they would not permit such an "outrageous mixing of the sexes" as had apparently happened when I, a woman, sat in the driver's seat next to a man.

"But I'm that man and she's my sister!" argued my brother.

Eventually, the Mutawa grew tired of harassing my brother and approached me in the car. People stopped in the street to watch. I triple-checked that the doors were locked.

The fat Mutawa tapped on the car window and called me "bint"—a pejorative term for "girl."

I cracked the window and called out to them, "First of all, pay your respects. You may call me Umm Abdalla"—meaning Abdalla's mother, the appropriate form of address for a mother in Saudi society. "Secondly," I said, "this is a traffic issue, not a moral issue. I was driving with a valid license, there's nothing immoral about that. This is an issue for the traffic police, so I'm not going with you." I closed the window.

Abu Abdullah and Faisal from the Commission for the Promotion of Virtue and the Prevention of Vice were enraged. The heavyset one pounded on the passenger side window, inches from my face. Like a furious, thwarted cartoon character, he pulled repeatedly on the handle of the locked door. Then he banged on the door. Spit flew from his mouth and collected on the glass as he bellowed at me over and over, "Get in our car! Come with us!"

I had seen countless videos online of the Mutawa harassing and assaulting sobbing women and children. I had watched them pull women by their scarves into Mutawa vehicles, like the GMC that was parked beside me. Many met with awful fates: detention, jail, and worse, scandals. "Over my dead body," I said through the glass.

In the backseat of the now very hot car, my sister-in-law was crying. The children bawled, terrified. And the battery on my cell phone was dying. Before I shut it off to save what little power was left, I sent texts to two friends. "I've been stopped by the religious police for driving, please tweet about it."

Traffic up and down the largest street in Khobar was at a standstill. Everyone had stopped to look at us. People were taking their own photos and videos. I felt like an animal in the zoo, captive and with no choice but to endure the endless stares.

For nearly an hour, the Mutawa tried to intimidate us. Finally, as dusk approached, my brother and I agreed to sit together in the backseat of his car and allow the two Mutawa to drive us to the traffic station. But that was not enough for them; they wanted my sister-in-law and the two children to come as well.

"They have nothing to do with it," my brother insisted. He quickly hailed a taxi and placed his wife, their son, and Aboudi inside. It all happened so fast, I didn't even get a chance to say goodbye.

The next thing I knew, the Mutawa were driving my brother's car. Beside us, stopped at the light, was the taxi with my sister-in-law and the two boys. My sister-in-law was holding her son on her lap, but Aboudi was in a seat by himself, looking so panicked and alone. And I could do nothing. I could not take my own son in my arms and rock him, whispering to him that everything would be okay.

I thought, in that moment, of my own mother. I was here, in this seat, because despite all the years that she had fought for us to be educated, fought for us to have a future, my mother still could not change some of the most fundamental aspects of my present situation. But if I had courage, perhaps I could change my son's. "So help me God," I thought, "I will stick to this."

I sat up as straight as I could and spoke directly to the Mutawa. "You know this is illegal. You know you have no right to drive our car," I told them as we drove to the station. "After this, I can file a complaint against you. And I will."

———

It was sundown when we reached the gates of the Thuqbah traffic station, which meant that it was prayer time. Within the compound, there was only a place for men to pray; no women were allowed. I saw a small window of opportunity.

"Can I sit in the car and wait?" I asked.

"Yes," they said.

Once the men had walked off, I powered on my phone. Holding my breath, hoping the battery would last, I dialed one number. As quickly as I could, I explained where I was. "Please," I said, "get the word out."

On the other end of the line was a newspaper reporter from *Al Riyadh*. At least now I believed that I would not disappear without a trace. When the Mutawa, the traffic police officers, and my brother returned, we went inside the station. I was surprised to find the traffic police colonel waiting for us. I now was the only woman among six men.

With the workday over, the station was empty. The phones were silent. There were no fingers typing on keyboards, no papers being shuffled and restacked on desks; the only sounds were our footsteps as the colonel led us to his office. He unlocked the door and turned on the lights. When everyone was seated, he looked at the Mutawa and asked, "What's going on?"

The men told him to ask my Wali al-Amr, meaning my male legal guardian. They assumed it was my brother. This is the standard treatment for Saudi women. We are expected to sit in silence while our male keepers speak for us, act for us, and ultimately decide for us. But I had not come this far to stay silent.

"He's my little brother," I said. "I should be *his* guardian."

The Mutawa were shocked. I'm sure they wanted to slap me.

I explained to the colonel what had happened, and asked why, when this was a traffic disagreement, the Mutawa were involved.

"Do you know that what you did is illegal?" the colonel asked.

"Sir," I replied, "I did not violate any traffic code. According to Section 32 of the Traffic Statute, there is no gender specification in the driver's license application. In fact, there is nothing in the statute anywhere that says women can't drive."

He leaned back in his chair. "You can cite the statute?"

"Yes. I've been studying the code for days, sir."

He sat still for a moment, silently assessing me. Finally he said, "Well, you need a Saudi license to drive here."

"Sir, true, but," I said, without blinking, "I am allowed to use my valid foreign driver's license for up to three months until I get a Saudi one." I reached into my bag and handed him my completed driver's license application, glad I had been carrying it with me. I could nearly hear the colonel think, *Oh my God, who the hell is this woman?*

Waving his hand as if he were shooing off flies, the colonel said, "Put your papers away." Then, turning to question my brother, he asked, "Did you give her the keys?"

"Yes, I did," my brother answered calmly. "I am fine with her driving."

"Are you for women driving?"

My brother was no longer just my brother at that moment, he was my friend and my ally. He told the colonel that as a petroleum geoscientist, he is often stationed in remote locations for weeks or longer, far away from his family. Because his wife can't drive, she's stranded. They don't have a driver and he doesn't trust a stranger around his pretty young wife and child. His car sits parked outside his home, worthless. Once, his wife got very sick and suffered for days until he returned.

"So, yes," my brother answered, "I totally support women driving in this country."

Looking over, I could see the clenched jaws of the Mutawa.

The colonel left the room to make a phone call. I turned to my brother, tilting back in my chair to face him, when one of the Mutawa snapped, "Look how you are sitting! Change how you sit! Behave!"

And so began the five hours my brother and I would spend at that station.

My bag was confiscated. We were taken to another room, and this one had a landline. I wanted to use it to check on my precious Aboudi. It was nearly bedtime. I wanted him to hear his mother's voice wish him sweet dreams, so he might sleep soundly after everything that had happened. But when I asked to use it, the phone was ripped from the wall and taken away.

The day had long since ended. My brother and I performed our evening prayers as officials from different authorities began arriving at the station. We could hear their voices and the clipped sounds of their shoes as they moved across the hard, slick floor.

"Manal, they're planning something," my brother said in a low voice. He motioned with his eyes toward a few men who wore no uniforms. They were standing slightly apart and spoke only among themselves, monitoring everything else.

"Are those the Dababees?" I asked him under my breath.

"Yes," he said grimly. It's a nickname Saudis use for the Mabahith, the "domestic intelligence agency," or secret police. *Dababee* literally means pushpin or tack—something with a sharp point that can stab you in an instant.

Panic was beginning to creep into my voice. "Why, why, why, why are they here?"

"I don't know," he answered. "Let's not even talk about it."

After some time, the colonel reappeared and introduced me to the chief of the Khobar Police. "Aren't you Manal of June 17?" he asked.

So the head of the police knew about Women2Drive.

"Yes," I answered.

"Why didn't you wait until then? Why did you drive now?"

"There is no traffic code banning women from driving," I said. How many times had I repeated that line? He didn't reply, so I asked, "May I go now?"

"Not until we get orders from the governor's office."

"What?" I asked.

"We can't release you until we get approval from the governor."

I resumed sitting in silence. There was no reply I could make.

Around 10:00 p.m., the provincial governor's office finally sent over a pledge for me to sign: *I, Manal al-Sharif, will never drive on Saudi land ever again and I will stop the event on June 17.*

The police chief asked that the part about June 17 be removed, and the governor's office reissued the pledge. Now it simply said: *I, Manal al-Sharif, will never drive on Saudi land ever again.*

I looked at the pledge, at the blank lines awaiting my brother's signature and mine. I hadn't eaten. I hadn't slept. My throat was hoarse. I wanted to see my son. It would have been so easy to sign it and leave.

"I don't accept this," I said. "I broke no code." I made sure to speak slowly so they couldn't miss my words.

"You . . . you have to sign it," the police chief gently urged.

"If I don't?"

"Then I fear we will have to hold you in detention until you do." I think at that moment the police chief was very worried about precisely that.

"Sir, I broke no statute," I said again. "Tell me now what code I broke, and I will sign. What code did I break?"

After a minute he said softly, "You broke *orf.*" In Saudi society, *orf* means tradition or custom, a practice or convention. It is not the official code.

I turned to the chief and said very deliberately, "I want to hear both of you say it, please repeat it."

"You broke orf," the chief stated.

"Say it again."

"Orf. You broke orf."

"Good, we agree. I broke no traffic code." It was a small victory, but I wanted to prove to at least the men in the room that I had broken no Saudi statute by driving.

"Still, you have to sign the pledge. Or else, sadly, we must put you in detention," the police chief said.

My brother signed the pledge. I signed the pledge. I said to myself as I wrote my name, "I'm going to use the fact that I broke orf and no code to keep going." Orf was not a reason not to drive. When it was done, I asked for a copy of the pledge. The answer was no.

———

It was after eleven when we were released from the station.

"I had no idea it would turn into this, I am so sorry. We didn't mean to keep you here this late," the chief said. His face and his words seemed genuine, and I wondered for a moment if he was sorry for more than the five hours that had passed.

We were halfway out the door when we were told that we couldn't go home in my brother's car. It had been impounded. If he wanted it back, he would have to plead his case at the governor's office. Exhausted, my brother and I decided we would return in a few days to deal with his car and to file complaints. The traffic police called a taxi for us.

Just behind the taxi were three unfamiliar cars packed with men. We got in the cab and the driver sped off, with the three other cars following in close pursuit. One pulled near to us, and I watched as a man leaned out the window and pointed a long, probing camera lens at me. I never heard the click of the shutter, but I saw the explosion of the flash, lighting up the darkness, blinding me. I put on my scarf and sank as low as I could in my seat.

Saudi roads have checkpoints, where authorities can randomly stop you at any time. As we neared the checkpoint before the Aramco compound, we lost two of the cars, but the third one flashed its high beams, signaling that it wanted us to stop. My brother told the cab-driver to pull over at the checkpoint, and he got out of the car. The reporter following us was from the paper *Al Yaum*. He told my brother he wanted to talk to me. Pointing to the time on his watch, my brother said no. I squeezed my brother's hand when he got back in the car and said thanks.

I never expected my detention to be national news, and I thought that I would come home to a silent house, but instead there was a small crowd waiting. After my one furtive phone call from my brother's car, not only had the local papers reported on what had happened but Ali Alalyani, the host of the 8:00 p.m. *Ya Hala* show on the Rotana Khalejia channel, had broadcast news of my detention to the entire nation along with these kind words: "We pray that Manal will get back home safe."

Another Saudi activist, Kholoud, had gone with her driver to the traffic police station and waited outside of the walled compound for hours, phoning in updates. My sister-in-law had contacted Ahmed, who managed the Women2Drive Twitter account. He tweeted out what had happened, thousands more retweeted it, and international press outlets picked up the story. Someone else had put up a "Free Manal" Facebook page, and within a couple of hours it had more than five thousand likes.

My friends were giddy. "The entire world is talking about you!" they exclaimed. "They're calling you the Saudi Rosa Parks!"

My eyes were watering with emotion, but I couldn't help laughing. "You are all so silly to worry about me!" I said. I explained that the police chief had crossed out the line about cancelling the June 17 event. I thought that was significant. We had tacitly been given the okay to drive that day. "We won!" I said. "I told you! My dears, you are scared over nothing! We won!"

After such an exhausting day, I wanted to pass at least a few easy hours before dawn broke and a new day began. That, however, was not to be. Before I ever went to bed, the secret police were at my door.

When I finally got to sleep, it was nearly twenty-four hours later, and I was locked inside Dammam Women's Prison.

━━━

My first morning in jail, it was the smell that woke me, the overwhelming stench of cooked food, stale sweat, and human waste. Then I felt the hard surface beneath me and heard the clucking and rolling of unfamiliar vowels, trilling consonants, and sharp, truncated sounds. Any slight pause was filled with the rough buzzing of the overhead lights, which made it always daytime in the windowless room. I closed my eyes tighter: I knew the artificial brightness would stab even more than if I looked out across the gleaming golden desert sand at midday.

Only one thing could get me to sit up that morning: the belief that in a few hours I would be leaving and going home.

I quickly discovered that just as everywhere else, jail had a hierarchy and a routine. There was a woman called Umm Misha'an, who collected our ration coupons and our orders for breakfast. The better-off women refused to eat the prison food; Umm Misha'an would order them freshly cooked falafel sandwiches. The rest of the women were forced to eat the horrible food from the prison's very dirty kitchen. After Umm Misha'an had gathered up the coupons and the requests, she passed them to a guard who would go to the tiny grocery store next to the prison gate. The guard would return before the gates opened at 9:00 a.m. with everything from feminine hygiene products to shampoo and toothpaste and plastic plates and spoons. At nine, prisoners were allowed out into a very tiny yard with high walls. It was outside, but not open: there was a ceiling that stretched across it, covered with metal shingles.

The first day, I refused to order anything to eat. I kept insisting that I would be leaving. I remember saying, "They are going to open the door now, and I am going to ask about my lawyer. I don't even know why I am here. I want to leave."

Umm Misha'an shrugged and said, "Just sit and have breakfast with us."

So I sat with them. On the second day, I ordered the falafel.

One woman, Maha, was already outside most mornings. She was locked in solitary confinement, but each day, the guards opened the door to her cell and let her into the tiny prison yard. I believe she had been jailed after being accused of murdering her own daughter, but her daughter's actual murderer was already inside the prison. That's why Maha asked to be in solitary confinement. Umm Misha'an and Nuwayer would go out and sit with Maha on the ground and eat falafel. In an odd way, it reminded me of my school days and how I would sit with my friends and we would all eat breakfast together.

After breakfast, I asked to see the prison administrator. I had to wait outside for the metal doors to be unlocked and could not even knock. I just had to wait, standing, until I was allowed to enter the office wing.

The administrator, whose name was Dina, was a pretty woman. She wore her hair short, near her shoulders. She wore makeup and had a nice smile. Her clothes were good quality. She was, in short, a professional woman, like me. Her office was small, but it still held a large desk, a sofa, and a place to hang your abaya. She had a phone on her desk as well as a computer. It was another world from the central prison room, where women hung up small pieces of cloth to try to separate their cockroach-infested space from the cockroach-infested space next to them.

I didn't have to introduce myself. She practically interrupted me to say, "Yes, they told me about you. I don't know what to tell you. I have no information about your case. They just said, 'This is Manal al-Sharif, the one who drove. She's here in jail until further notice.'"

"Please," I said, "I need to call my family, but I don't have their numbers. They are all stored in my phone. I only have the number of my sister-in-law."

"Yes, you can use the phone," she said, "and you have a visitor."

The woman waiting for me was a representative from the Saudi National Human Rights Commission. She did not cover her face, and the dark skin of her eyes and cheeks was covered in heavy, bright makeup, so much so that the color stood out in the drab visiting room. She said very little, and offered no words of consolation, no hope. She opened the visit by asking me, "Tell me your story."

"I think everyone knows my story by now," I said. "I just drove and I was sent to jail. They interrogated me and suddenly I'm in jail. No one explained to me why I'm here." Then I told her, "The story you need to hear is the story of those other women inside. Did you see this jail? Did you see how filthy it is?"

She looked at me and said, "Yes, yes, I know. What can we do about it?"

Suddenly, I was so mad at her. It was absurd, sitting here going through the motions. "How could you know the conditions of the women living here, being treated like animals, and not do anything about it?" I asked. "Aren't you for human rights?"

She just said again, "Yes, yes, I know, but what can we do about it? We complain, we say something, but what can we do?"

I sat there feeling confused and hopeless, at the situation and at her. With a bit of a bite in my voice, I asked, "So how do I join your group if I want to volunteer with you?"

"No," she said. "You have to quit your job. We don't accept volunteers. You have to leave your work and be full-time with us."

At that point, I gave up. No one would leave a good job to work for a powerless institution for a small salary. I also realized she was not going to leave until I had told my story, because she was required to write up some formulaic report, so I went back over everything that had happened. She listened but did not take a single note. We were both trapped in our roles until the visit was over. In fairness, looking back now, I can only imagine how many other stories she had heard over the years, knowing that long after the stories were told, nothing would change. Domestic human rights groups in Saudi Arabia have little authority and even less sway. Major international groups like Amnesty International and Human Rights Watch can speak out, but even then the kingdom picks and chooses whether or not to listen.

Even so, I believed I would be leaving prison soon. I believed that the reporters and bloggers who had followed me would agitate to secure my release. I believed this until one of my good friends, Hidaya, arrived. Even though it was not a visiting day—those were Saturdays and Thursdays—the prison staff let her in. I was grateful to see her, but then I realized that she was carrying a change of clothing, a book, and a photo of Aboudi, which the guards confiscated.

"Why did you bring me clothes and a book?" I asked. "Do you know something I don't?"

"I just didn't want you to think you'd been forgotten," she said, "I wanted you to know we're thinking of you."

Before she came to see me, Hidaya had asked her mother's permission. Her mother, who is very conservative, had told her yes, and added, "Ask the authorities to put you in jail with Manal, so that you can stay with her and she is not alone." Of course, that didn't happen, but I was grateful. It is particularly humiliating to go to jail as a woman.

Hidaya told me that Aboudi was being cared for by his father's mother, that she had my sister-in-law and her son at my house inside the Aramco compound, and that the whole country was shocked to hear I had been arrested and sent to the women's prison in Dammam. She said that the Arab press had reported my arrest, but that many national news outlets had been characterizing both me and Women2Drive negatively. Only *Al-Hayat,* the major newspaper of the Arab world, had portrayed my actions in a positive light. Saudi newspapers wrote in their headlines that I had broken down in tears and "confessed" to the charges against me. The five charges that the press had stated as the reasons for my arrest were: 1) inciting public opinion; 2) driving without a license; 3) operating as a traitor and spy on behalf of foreign enemies; 4) posting a video of my driving on YouTube; and 5) contacting the foreign press. And yet I still had no idea who or what entity had ordered my arrest and detention.

As Hidaya told me everything, I grew increasingly furious unt'

my emotions erupted. "Those liars! How can they charge me with violating statutes that don't exist?" I cursed. "Wait until I get a lawyer!"

In the middle of our visit, the prison warden entered and interrupted us. She held a piece of paper in front of me and without looking at me said, "Sign this." It was another pledge not to drive. This
time, I did not argue. I simply signed the document and handed it
back. I wanted to get out.

The days passed agonizingly slowly. All we could do in the cell was
stare out through the bars, count the cockroaches, or wash clothes.
There was nothing to read, nothing to watch, nothing to occupy our
minds. I could see the boredom and helplessness that had settled over
these women. It was etched in deep lines across their faces, in a vacant
dullness in their eyes. Like most everyone trapped inside the space,
I slept little. It was hard to sleep because of the noise, because of the
cockroaches that crawled across our beds, and because the lights were
on twenty-four hours a day. Often I felt on edge, constantly alert for
sudden eruptions of violence. The women would fight over the water
for tea, or who got to use the bathroom. Because many of the women
now trapped in these cells had been abused themselves, they would
often abuse each other and their children. Living inside with all of us
was a six-year-old boy named Abdulrahman. Some of the prisoners
regularly pinched, hit, or shouted at him. Remembering Aboudi, I
tried to play with and comfort him. After several days, he followed me
around like a little duckling. Later I heard that he and his mother were
deported back to their home country, Indonesia, and I felt a sense of
relief that he was out of that place.

I started keeping track of everything I could. I read the inmate
statistics on a whiteboard in the prison guards' room: 168 total inmates, 152 female prisoners, and 16 children. All 168 of us lived together in seven small cells with bunkbeds. Each cell was about ten
by fourteen feet. No one ever came to clean them. There were seven

bathrooms for all those women and not one of them had a door on the stalls. None of the toilets worked properly; the smell was repulsive and overwhelming. There was no dining room, the prayer room was locked at all times, and there was no space for anyone to have a shred of privacy. Some nights, I could hear women having sex with each other.

Even growing up poor in a poor neighborhood had not been nearly this bad. The conditions in the prison were deplorable by anyone's standards, and looking at the small children forced to live in these spaces with their mothers made me cry. No mirrors were allowed, and so, after a few days, you forget what you look like. You forget your identity. The differences between humans and animals become so small you start to wonder whether perhaps there is almost no difference at all.

I tried to find ways to keep myself from going crazy. I bought a small notebook from Umm Misha'an and began to record the names and stories of the women in prison with me. I already knew something about the stories of abuse of domestic workers; Saudis employed hundreds of thousands of women, mainly from Asian countries, to do their cooking, their laundry, and to take care of their children. Saudi Arabia has no domestic labor codes, so any rights these women have are determined solely by their employer. We hear stories of foreign women who are mistreated or not paid, making them virtual prisoners in the homes in which they worked. (Ironically, their male counterparts, often employed as drivers for Saudi women, usually enjoy good wages, housing, and benefits.)

Now I found myself in a jail cell surrounded by many of these poor, frightened women, who were completely alone, spoke very little Arabic, and had next to no resources. Maysara, a widow from the Philippines with six children, had not been back to her country for eight years. She had been sentenced to one year in jail because she had run away; her sponsor had not paid her wages for months. She made space for me around her few things and gave me her bed. Other

incarcerated women had done nothing more than confront their employers for mistreating them and the employers had them arrested
and thrown into jail.

My arrest was in some ways an education: I was learning about
domestic slavery.

By transcribing the personal histories of these women and trying
to figure out how I might help them, I became a kind of impromptu
therapist. I listened to the women's problems and wrote letters on
their behalf—like my father, many were illiterate. My interest in their
lives encouraged them, but at the same time, they also encouraged
me. Their problems became a distraction from my own.

Hana was twenty-six years old and had been jailed because she
was caught with a man who was not her husband. She had finished
her sentence the year before but was still in prison; her father refused
to receive her and, as a Saudi woman without a guardian, she could
not be released. The prison wardens were trying to marry her off to
one of the inmates from the men's prison so that she could have a
guardian and leave jail.

"Why are you doing this, Manal?" one of the prison guards finally
asked me. "Why do you care? You should worry about yourself, and
not these women."

Some of the more aggressive prisoners mocked me, calling me
the UN Ambassador, but I just ignored them. As long as I was there,
I wanted to do something.

13

Abouya and the King

Since college, my life has revolved around the science and certainty of electronic communication—the ping of email, the click of a keyboard, the vibrating of a cellular phone. Even in my personal sphere, when I gather with my family or friends, more and more often, instead of sharing stories and hearing the rhythmic conversations that were the background music of my childhood, there is only silence, accompanied by the faint glow of each person's individual screen. We are connected by wireless signals as much as we are by the faces and voices in front of us. But once I entered Dammam Women's Prison, I became literally and figuratively trapped in the dark. My world was largely frozen, as if I were a bee trapped in amber on May 21, 2011. Even the constant noise all around me could not pierce the silence outside the prison walls. I wanted to know everything, but I knew almost nothing. A few of the guards shared what they had read in the press, but even that was sometimes second- or thirdhand. I was left to my imagination.

On my second day as an inmate, I was allowed to make two phone calls in the prison administrator's office, likely because of the visit from the Saudi human rights representative. One call was to one of my best friends from Aramco, Abdullah. He had come to the prison gates with Hidaya, but because he was a male and not a close relative, he had not been allowed to enter.

"Manal, what happened?" he asked. "They said in the paper that you broke down yesterday, they said that you told them who was behind Women2Drive and to start interrogating those who were behind your actions." I did not understand how the press could spread such lies, or even where they were coming from.

I thought with my logical, computer-information-systems brain. "I need a lawyer," I said.

Abdullah responded with a name, Adnan, and a phone number. Two of my friends had been calling lawyers. But whenever they mentioned my name, each attorney said no.

Adnan had said yes.

My second call was to my sister-in-law, Muneera. My brother had been detained for twenty-four hours, until his friends had bailed him out. Thankfully, my son did not know what had happened. When Aboudi woke the morning, after I had been taken away, my sister-in-law had told him, "Your mommy is on a trip, fixing a big computer." I asked her if the campaign had tweeted about my detention.

"Yes," she said, and added, "Manal, we had to shut down the Facebook event."

I was overwhelmed by fury and frustration. There had been more than 120,000 people signed up to attend that event. Why had I gone to prison if this was to be the outcome? Why did the authorities always get to win?

I started shouting at my poor sister-in-law with the prison administrator sitting right there, listening. "How could you do this? I'm here in jail and you are outside. You are supposed to keep that up." During my interrogation, I had promised to remove my name from the campaign. I had promised to step aside. But I didn't want the other girls to stop. "You're giving away everything that I had to sacrifice for," I railed into the phone. "You're just giving that away."

"We received phone calls from strangers saying, 'You should turn the event off, take it down,'" my sister-in-law explained. One of the people working on the campaign had already put the YouTube driving video on a private setting, accessible only by a password. The group had also changed the name of one Twitter account from @Women2Drive to @FreeManal. But eventually, the Twitter account was also taken down.

I felt betrayed. My sister-in-law tried to soothe me, saying, "No, no, we're doing this for your own safety. It's actually good. Now all we care about is that you leave the jail soon."

But I was having none of it. "You cannot stop the cause because I was sent to jail. You should continue the cause because you have to pay the price."

———

I had half expected those two calls to be my last, but instead, unlike other prisoners, I was allowed to make a phone call to my sister-in-law each day, rather than once a month. The call always took place in the prison administrator's office. No one told me that I was allowed a daily call per some official policy. It simply happened, like so many other things, made up as we went along. Saudi society is highly rule-bound, but many of these rules are unwritten and, at arbitrary moments, some rules are changed. The same system that allowed me to be arrested and imprisoned without knowing under what authority also allowed me a daily phone call. Somewhere, someone had decided to apply different rules to me. This gave me hope that someone, somewhere else, might suddenly decide that enough was enough and declare me free to go.

On my next call to Muneera, she started to cry when she heard my voice. She told me that Aboudi was in the hospital with a high fever. He had fallen ill at his dad's. Muneera was at the hospital with Aboudi's grandmother. At first I couldn't believe it. I kept asking if he was there for a checkup, saying he had been fine at home. But when my ex-mother-in-law got on the phone, I couldn't hear her voice. She couldn't speak at all. She just cried.

I kept calling into the phone, "What's going on here? What's wrong with Aboudi? Can I talk to my son?"

She held the phone up to his ear. I couldn't even hear him.

I kept saying his name, "Aboudi," and finally, in a voice that barely made a sound, I heard him ask, "Mommy?" I had never heard my son sound like that before. I kept saying, "Aboudi, stay strong." I have only talked to Aboudi in English. I struggled for so many years to learn the language that I didn't want my son to have to do so too.

He managed to ask, "Mommy, where are you?"

I never cry in front of Aboudi. When he falls or hurts himself, I don't run up and fuss all over him. I just stop and tell him, "I want you to be strong. I don't want you to be crying." And he doesn't cry.

"Mommy, where are you?" he said to me again.

I heard him but I did not cry. I said, "Aboudi, Mommy is fixing something and she will come back very soon, baby. I want you to be strong, Aboudi."

After that, he was too exhausted to speak anymore.

When I turned off the phone, I broke my own rule: I started sobbing. I sobbed until I had no more tears.

—

By the second and third days, I realized that I would not be leaving prison anytime soon, so I created a routine. Every morning, at 9:00 a.m., when the guards opened the door, I would go to the prison administrator's office, ask to make my phone call, and say that I needed to see my lawyer. For days, the prison refused to allow my lawyer to come and see me without a guardian or mahram or to speak to me on the phone. Instead, they allowed me to call my sister-in-law. In retrospect, I suppose that I was trading one for the other.

The next day, I learned that Aboudi was improving. He had become ill from a cat parasite. Our cat was completely vaccinated but it must have become infected from another animal in the neighborhood and passed the parasite to Aboudi. No one told me until later about how at the hospital the doctors had packed his body in towels and ice. Even my ex-husband had been down on the floor, on his knees, crying, as Aboudi's body burned with fever and nothing seemed to bring it down.

Thursday arrived, my first official visiting day. Muneera came to the gates, and so did my mother. There had been no flights available, so Mama had ridden the bus for eighteen hours from Jeddah to Dammam and come directly to the jail. She must have been sobbing the entire time; she was still hysterical when she arrived at the gates of the prison. I was brought into the visitors room, which had two double Plexiglas panes with holes on either side. But the holes didn't line up. You had to put your ear to one hole to hear and then turn and speak into another hole. Your visitor had to do the same. The room was noisy with so many people, hot without AC, and had a horrible smell of piss and shit. It was the same room where I had been strip-searched. When I undressed, I had not realized there was a clear window behind me.

I did not want Mama to see me like this. I did not want her in this place with these noises and awful smells. Looking back, I think seeing me in prison must have been the most heartbreaking experience of her life. I was determined not to upset her more and kept smiling the whole time. Mama's face was red, and she was drenched in sweat. She could barely speak; she had lost her voice from crying. She put her ear on one hole, and I put my mouth over another and tried to reassure her, shouting into the hole because there was no other way to be heard. I made up my mind that I did not want her to return. I was starting to feel as broken as she was. All around us, visitors were turning to stare at Mama and me. They were much more interested in me than in the prisoners they had come to visit.

During Friday prayers at mosques across the country, the imams stood up and applauded my arrest. In fiery sermons, they denounced me as a bad influence on other women. They condemned me for "corrupting the society" and they accused me of blasphemy and seeking to destroy Islam. I was referred to as a "whore" and a "prostitute."

According to the imams, prison was the only appropriate place for Manal al-Sharif.

———

I wrote and signed an official complaint about being denied a visit with a lawyer. After that, the prison head said I might meet with my lawyer in the presence of a soldier rather than a guardian or mahram. So on Saturday, the next official visiting day, I made my one phone call to a lawyer whose number I had been given.

"Is this Mr. Adnan?" I asked, hoping he would not hang up and my call would not have been wasted.

"Yes, who is this?"

"This is Manal al-Sharif, I'm calling you from the women's jail in Dammam. Is there any chance I could meet with you today?"

"Oh, my God, at last we have made contact," he said. "I have come several times to the jail and tried to get in to see you. I tried to get them to show me the documents relating to your admission and in-terrogation, but no one would allow me to see anything without a power of attorney. I'm in Al Hasa [about ninety minutes away from Dammam] now, but I can get over there in no time. Are you sure they will allow me to meet with you?"

"Yes, we will be able to meet this time. Thank you. I will wait for you."

Our morning break in the sun finished at 11:00 a.m. and, like sheep, we were herded back into the dark, smelly cells. I kept watching the clock on the wall. I calculated the drive, how much time it would take Adnan to leave his office, how much time to show his papers at the gate. I couldn't take my eyes off the clock. I waited to hear the guard's announcement, telling me, "Your lawyer is here." But the hours dragged by and no one came.

At 5:00 p.m., my lawyer still hadn't appeared. Finally they called my name and told me that my family was here. I had a sudden, night-marish vision of Mama's tear-stained face looking out at me again from behind those glass windows. "Please, God, not now," I prayed.

I didn't think I could bear seeing her pain again or watch her face crumple up as she wailed. But the guard didn't take me to the visiting room with glass windows this time. Instead, she walked me out of the first gate to the second gate, and then the third. "Are they releasing me?!" I thought. She led me to a small room in a building next to the women's prison.

All she said was, "Wait here."

I sat down on an aluminum seat next to a small desk, exactly like my teacher's desk back in school.

A soldier walked in with a pile of papers and a pen in his hand. He asked my name and started interrogating me. There were new questions this time. They all came from the false articles being published in the Saudi newspapers *Al Yaum* and *Alwatan*. I had heard the same allegations from my friend at Aramco and later from the prison guards. The articles made it sound as if I was a foreign infiltrator, and that my driving was a plot to destabilize the kingdom.

The man rattled through his list of questions: "Do you have any connections with foreign organizations? Who helped you talk to foreign media? Where are the locations of the demonstrations?"

It seemed that Saudi intelligence was now relying on sensationalist newspapers for information. I wanted to comment, but I held my tongue. I answered everything patiently and signed another statement. Just as I was signing, Muneera walked into the room. Her face was covered and she was completely obscured in black, but I recognized her voice. I felt the most wonderful relief. But when she uncovered her face, I saw sweat on her forehead and that her cheeks were red, as if she had been running.

"Is everything okay?" I asked.

Muneera assured me that she was fine. "Your mother insisted on coming with me to the jail," she said. "I remembered how you asked me not to allow her to come in, but what can I do? She cried and shouted hysterically. When we arrived, I asked the guards not to allow her in. I know how painful it is for her to see you like this." She shuddered just slightly, saying, "I had to keep my face covered, but even so as you pass by the male prisoners' yard, you feel they are eating you with their eyes."

"Thank you, Mannori," I said, using her nickname. "I really owe you a lot."

As the soldier watched us, we sat there calmly talking about normal things—how the family was doing, if my brother had gone back to work, whether Aboudi was getting better—when I leaned in and took her hand. In my palm was a thin sheet of paper torn from my notebook. While pretending to straighten my abaya and my scarf, I had hastily scrawled a few lines on it with the pen I had used to sign the statement. She felt the paper, cupped her hand slightly, and slipped the note through her abaya. Then, as if making a slight adjustment to her clothing, she maneuvered it through her blouse and into her bra, without the soldier noticing. At least in the prison, the soldiers usually didn't stare.

On the note, I had written, "Abouya should meet the king. If he doesn't ask for his pardon, I will be here forever."

———

The day I was arrested, almost as soon as he learned the news, Abouya had flown from Jeddah to Dammam. He didn't know how to book an airline ticket; he had never done so before in his life. My friend Israa got him the ticket and told him that her driver would meet him at the airport. When Muneera told me on the phone that my dad had come, I thought, "Oh my God! Abouya is here. It's getting bigger. It's serious." Now not only was I terrified for myself and my son, I was terrified of what could happen to my dad.

My father did not bother coming to the jail to wait. Decades of living with Saudi customs and unwritten rules had taught him the need for direct appeals. My impulse had been to seek a lawyer; Abouya's was the opposite. Codes, courts, and even lawyers are very much foreign constructs. In the Saudi kingdom, justice is just as often whatever a person in power decides it is. It varies from situation to situation, and it can be swayed by tribal and family ties and lineages.

Accordingly, my father began making a daily pilgrimage to the door of the governor of the Eastern Province, Prince Muhammad bin Fahd, the nephew of King Abdullah and the son of the former King Fahd. Each morning, Abouya would go and wait at the gate to the Imara, the governor's house in Dammam, until the gates closed at 2:00 p.m. He would be the last person to leave, and each time, he would beg to see the prince, to ask for forgiveness on my behalf and for my release. But the prince refused to see him.

Instead, my father spoke with the Imara's social worker, a man named Ghazi, with the title of Family Relationship Adviser. He was a religious man with a large beard and he would ask Abouya how he could allow his daughter, a divorced woman, to live alone in a compound with Americans and non-Muslims. "They drink," he would say. "The women walk around without their abaya." He would go on to list every religious and cultural transgression to which I was exposed and was presumably also committing. And then he would ask how my father could allow me to live alone without a man.

Ghazi was supposed to be a resolver of disputes and a healer of families, but here he sowed shame. He was also leaking false information to the press. It was Ghazi who said that I had "broken down" and "confessed the names of the people behind [me]." Ghazi was the one who said that there were five charges against me, including driving without a license, inciting public opinion, and operating as a traitor and a spy on behalf of foreign enemies. He called for my trial and said that I had embarrassed the country in the international media.

On my fourth day in prison, Ghazi came to the jail. When his visit was announced, I had no idea who he was. The prison guards told me to cover my face because he was a religious man. At first I refused, but eventually I did pull a veil over it, but a thin one so that he could see through. I also had on red shoes.

In our meeting, he accused me of being "egotistical," of calling for a second "Day of Rage," and inciting demonstrations against the king. (The first "Day of Rage" had been in March, when Saudi pro-democracy protestors promised demonstrations: nearly all were squelched.) Ghazi claimed that more than three hundred citizens had come to Imara calling for my trial, and others were prepared to bring cases against me based on my violations of Saudi moral codes. "You want to move your Aramco life outside the compound," he said.

I listened to this diatribe, and the whole time, I remained very calm. Then I spoke. "You don't know me," I said. "We didn't call for demonstrations. I have a driver's license. And I love my country. I disagree with you saying that my ego is doing this. The only people involved in this effort are Saudi girls."

Whatever Ghazi had expected, it wasn't this. He finally conceded, "You are different from how I pictured you," he said, "angry and wanting to break the law." Then he told me that he had called for my flogging in a public place to set an example. When I heard that, I asked to leave.

He did call for my flogging in the press, and that was his undoing. His words embarrassed the Imara and the whole Saudi government in the international media. After that, they shut him up—but they never disavowed any of the earlier lies. Sadly, this is a typical tactic. In Saudi Arabia, when they want to break someone, they spread lies about them, making them appear to be a coward or a traitor. Saudi students in the United States who had put up a Free Manal Facebook page took it down once they read the five supposed charges. I lost supporters because of the falsehoods Ghazi spread.

My father sat at the gate to the governor's house and I sat in prison while in the press and online, each day, articles, news reports, and postings sought to shame me, to assassinate my character, and to so thoroughly humiliate me that no other girl or woman would want to drive. On social media, Saudis were divided on whether I was right or wrong. It was more than a generation since the drivers of 1990, and yet so very little, if anything, had changed.

Except for one thing. Rather than being a small story, my arrest had become a big one. My story was broadcast all over the world, and this international press was causing a great deal of embarrassment for the Saudi state. The flogging comment was the final straw. Even the king was embarrassed when the United States criticized Saudi Arabia for jailing a woman for driving.

As soon as Muneera shared my note, my father flew to Jeddah, where the king lives. My best hope lay on the other side of the kingdom.

I can only imagine my father, the man who had ferried pilgrims in his hot Corolla year after year, now dressed in his cleanest robe, arriving at the lush royal court complex, perched on a corniche that looks out over the glistening Red Sea. The compound stretches for eighty-five acres and includes helipads and boat berths, a vast garden and many tents. Palm trees rise from holes cut into the edges of the vast stone plaza, but even the towering royal palms seemed smaller beside the soaring, futuristic architecture and tall, gushing fountains. Even though the chief of our family's tribe and two cousins accompanied him, Abouya must have felt small indeed.

Although the Saudi capital is in Riyadh and the king has a palace there, the royal palace in Jeddah was built to receive visitors. In spite of its modern trappings, some traditions remained as ingrained as they were in the days when kings received visitors inside their tents. The king still held a royal *majlis,* sitting to receive visitors and subjects and to listen to their concerns, which were delivered by formal petitions. The gleaming entrance to the complex was crowded with scribes, men who for 100 riyals would write a petition to the king. It was a tradition no doubt dating back to days when a large majority of the kingdom was illiterate. But even today, the well-educated still hire scribes, who have learned how best to state a case or pose a request. In my father's case, though, a scribe was a necessity, as he still had not learned how to read or write.

Accompanied by his three fellow tribesmen, my father approached a scribe seated at his desk. He was not particularly interested until my father spoke our tribal name. Then the man raised his head. Abouya had his full attention. Scribes are trained to follow the news, and even the most casual observer could not have missed the story of my arrest. Abouya told my story, the scribe retold it, and after some back-and-forth, they settled on a final version, which the scribe then copied in his best calligraphy onto paper that would be presented to the king. When he had finished, he read the appeal aloud one last time to my father, who pressed his thumb into an ink pad and then pressed it against the paper. That was his signature. It was done. The petition was sealed in a large envelope. My father handed over 100 riyals and received the envelope in return. The transaction was complete. It was still early morning,

Document in hand, my father walked toward the royal court gate, where a security guard asked him what he wanted. As Abouya told me later, "As if he was expecting me, he eagerly took the envelope from my hands and asked me to wait. He was gone for some time. I was standing there in the sun, just outside the gates, and for the first time I was full of hope. After a while, the guard came back, saying, 'Oh, good man, His Majesty's secretary says you may come in today, but you must wait your turn.'"

The king—whichever Saudi monarch is in power—receives people in his palace in Jeddah. Friday is the traditional reception day. Anyone (so long as he is male) can walk into the palace that day without an invitation. Hundreds of people line up in long queues in front of the main gates for a turn to meet the king. But even on a Monday, there was a long line of people waiting to conduct business with the king and one of his chief advisers. My father, his chief, and his cousins took their place at the back of the line.

When it was time for the al-Sharif tribal representatives to present themselves, the four men moved forward one by one. The green-and-gold meeting room was vast: it was a long walk to the far end of the room where King Abdullah himself sat, supported by cushions on a low sofa covered with green silk. He was wearing a soft brown woolen robe with gold brocade trim, and though his trademark goatee was neatly trimmed and dyed a shiny, youthful black, up close, my father thought that the nearly eighty-seven-year-old king looked tired and rather frail.

The king did not rise to greet them. He had done away with the old custom of bowing and hand kissing. Visitors were instead told to kiss his forehead and wish him long life and health, the same type of greeting that Saudi children give their fathers and grandfathers.

As each visitor had before them, the four al-Sharif men approached the king one after the other, kissed his forehead, and wished him a long life. Then the al-Sharif chief spoke. He opened with praise for God and the Prophet Muhammad (PBUH), which was followed by a reaffirmation of the tribe's loyalty to the king and to the country. Then came the heart and the purpose of his words: an apology for my actions, which had disturbed the public order, and a promise that this would not happen again. He concluded with one last elaborate formal apology from the tribe for my driving. After the recitation was finished, there was a brief pause, and then the king spoke. Abouya told me that the king uttered two words: "Advise her."

He said those same words three times.

But my father, the chief, and his cousins left with the promise that they would hear good news soon.

———

At 5:00 p.m. that same day, Monday, May 30, 2011, I was called from my cell and escorted to the guards' room. The prison head was waiting for me behind a desk, dressed in civilian clothes. A soldier in uniform stood next to him, holding some papers.

"Manal," the general said. "Are you enjoying your stay with us? Would you like to stay here longer?"

Immediately I was wary. I did not know if this was a trick, but I was determined not to sound weak or groveling. "I don't like to sound offensive," I replied, "but if you might join us for one day inside you would know the answer."

"I know these buildings are old and falling apart, but this is all we have right now," the general said. "I promise you, in a few months, we are moving to newer and cleaner facilities. I wished you had delayed your driving campaign a few months. But I can tell you, you are a free woman now. I just received the orders to release you."

I had been rehearsing for this moment every single hour I had spent behind bars. I had been imagining it, anticipating it, waiting for it. Every day, I had dressed in my abaya to show my belief that *this* was the day I would be released. And yet, in that moment, it felt like any other routine bureaucratic transaction; it was as if I had been kept waiting an extra thirty minutes to file a set of official papers. I smiled slightly, and asked, to be sure I had heard correctly, "You mean I can leave this moment?"

"Unless you would like to enjoy another day here?"

"No, sir," I said. My body felt almost weak from the combination of adrenaline and relief.

"Can I ask you something before you go?" the general added, almost as an afterthought.

I nodded. "Please go ahead, you have been good to me."

"I know you talked a lot to the other prison guards about the prisoners' conditions here, and I promise to do my best, maybe with your help, too, to make the prisoners' life better. You can't blame us for all the limitations we have here—we are trying our best with whatever we have. I know you want to go out and talk about those women, but I ask you please not to, it's embarrassing to everyone."

"Will you allow me to help the women who need plane tickets to go back home?" I asked.

"If you find people who are willing to buy them tickets, you will be helping us a lot by making this crowded place better. I will do my best!"

The prison head gave his orders to the female prison guard standing outside to bring me my belongings. Then he wished me luck.

"Stay away from trouble" were his last words to me.

After he had walked out, I let fall my tears of joy. I made *sujood*, a special prayer thanking Allah. I thought of Aboudi's face. I thought about removing my dirty, filthy clothes, taking ten hot showers, and sleeping with Aboudi in my arms.

When I lifted my head up from the prayer, my eyes still filled with tears, I saw the prison guard crying, too. She gave me a hug. "Manal, you will be missed," she said.

———

I had to call my brother to ask him to come and sign my release papers. As a Saudi woman, I needed a guardian's signature to be able to leave jail, but because my release had come from the king, in my case, a mahram was acceptable. He was very quiet when I told him I was free.

I couldn't leave without going inside the prison one last time to say goodbye. By then I knew the story of almost every woman—or at least of those who were willing to tell me theirs. I remember the joy and the tears, the goodbyes and the hugs and the requests: "Don't forget about us, please." I couldn't take my clothes with me, so I gave them to Maysara, the woman who had given me her bed on that first dreadful day. I gave her my unused phone cards and my food booklet, too. I later bought her a plane ticket home. I never heard from her again, but I will always remember her kindness toward me.

When my brother arrived, he was wearing the traditional white *thobe,* although without any head covering. I couldn't remember the last time I had seen him wearing traditional dress. At Aramco, he always wore Western clothes to work and he did the same at home. He was smiling and gave me a hug, oblivious to the surprise of the male guards around us. (Saudis are not known for showing affection in public.) After signing some papers, the last gate opened. I gave a final look back at those high towers, the guards with guns, and the dirt yard.

Then I turned my head, and it was gone.

I asked my brother if I could use his phone. Mine had been returned to me, but the battery was dead, and anyway I was nervous about my number appearing on the recipient's screen.

The phone barely had the chance to ring. "Abouya," I said, speaking as soon as I heard his voice, "It's me, Manal. I'm out of jail."

I paused, waiting for a lecture or the recriminations. Instead, I heard my father's excited words, "Daughter! Are you fine?"

"Yes, Abouya," I replied, "I'm fine."

"Then I'm fine. Goodbye."

That was it, every word that passed between us, a very short phone call. In my mind, I had prepared myself for a long speech, laced with scoldings and accusations. "How could you do this to your family?" I expected him to shout. I had prepared to defend my actions and apologize. But he was "fine."

I leaned back, watching the highway pass on the way to the Aramco compound, watching my brother steer the car. It was not his car, the Azera, which was still impounded by the police. It was my car he was using to drive me home.

14

The Rain Begins with a Single Drop

On Friday, June 17, 2011, about three dozen women drove in the Kingdom of Saudi Arabia. Some drove for less than an hour around the streets of Riyadh, the capital. Others got behind the wheel in Jeddah and Khobar and elsewhere. Many weren't stopped, even when they passed police officers on the road. Those who were stopped were escorted home and sternly told not to drive again. At least one woman was ticketed for driving without a Saudi license. But none was arrested.

I did not drive that day, I stayed home.

The day after my release from prison, I was back at my desk at Aramco. The company had a policy that if you missed ten days of work, you could be let go. I had frantically put in for vacation time, but I was close to the edge of being terminated.

I returned to work in the same unit, at the same cubicle. But nothing else would ever again be the same. People at work were as divided in their opinions about me as they were in the society outside. Some were carefully supportive, and some were aggressively critical, while the majority were quiet.

Every person I knew in the office came by my desk, and I said the same thing to each of them, "The vacation was nice, thank you for asking." I smiled each time. Some female employees left bouquets of flowers and cards saying "We are proud of you" on my desk. Omar al-Johani, my Aramco colleague who had tweeted the details of my arrest from behind the bushes by my house at 2:00 a.m., posted his personal PO box number online and encouraged people worldwide to send me letters and cards. I received piles of them; the most beautiful was a computer mouse in the shape of a car.

Eventually, after the initial uproar was over, the executive director called me into his office. He asked, "Manal, are you okay?" I told him, yes, I'm fine. He said that for eleven days, he had been getting up and looking at the news. The day I was released was the day that he "breathed again." Later in the year, I was even nominated to be one of Aramco's one hundred youth leaders and to sit on a company advisory board. I told the director, "I'm proud to work for you," and his reply was, "We are proud that you work for us."

But many other things changed. I was told that I could not mention Aramco in public—indeed, that I could not speak in public. I was also told that I was under surveillance: my phone, my email, my texts, my home. It was clear to me that the company was watching everything that I did, said, and wrote.

One colleague accused me of being an agent for Iran and other Saudi enemies and sent an email demanding my termination from Aramco. The email was addressed to Aramco's CEO, and cc'd a company vice president, the IT executive director, as well as my department head, my group leader, and himself. He cc'd me as well.

What hurt the most were the people who shunned me. On my team, one colleague refused to speak to me. In every meeting or interaction, he treated me as if I did not exist. One of Aboudi's best friends was the son of an American woman who lived in the compound. They played together at her house and at my house twice a week. When I got out of jail, I emailed her to set up the next playdate. She said the two boys could no longer be friends. "I don't feel safe for my son to be around your son," she wrote.

I never used the word *jail* in front of Aboudi. I instructed everyone to say "the vacation" or "Hawaii." I didn't want him to know about it; I didn't want him to worry. But one night, after his bath, as he was brushing his teeth, he suddenly asked, "Mommy, are we bad people?"

I held my breath for an instant and then asked, "Why?"

He told me that two boys had hit him and choked him at school that day, adding, "They said they saw you on Facebook and they told me, 'You and your mom should be in jail!' " I could see the bruise on his neck where their angry fingers had left their mark.

I told him that we were good people, adding, "Sometimes other people don't understand and say horrible things. You mustn't listen to those boys." But there was nothing more I could do. The boys' school was outside the Aramco compound. I could not enter it. When I complained about Aboudi's being bullied on the bus, two fathers accused me of violating the rules forbidding women from entering the bus and forced me to sign a pledge that I would not trespass on the boys' domain.

A few days later, I told the story to one of my friends at Aramco, whose son also attended the same school. She looked away awkwardly and said that she hadn't wanted to tell me this, but "my son's religion teacher told his class, 'Manal al-Sharif is crazy! She should be locked up!' "

But the person who suffered most at Aramco was my brother. After three months of continuous harassment by his colleagues, he quit his job and moved his family to Kuwait. He was the first casualty of my determination to challenge the system.

———

While my brother lived one extreme, my father lived another. Four days after my release on Friday afternoon, my father, the chief of our tribe, and my father's two cousins returned to the royal palace in Jeddah to wait with the other visitors for a brief audience with the king. They had come to thank him. It was, my father recalls, a warm and pleasant meeting. At the end, the king bestowed good wishes and gifts upon the four men. So it was that my father, a taxi driver with no formal education, was redeemed in Saudi society, even as his children have left, one by one.

———

When I got out of jail I discovered that a new group of girls and women had started a Facebook page called Women2Drive—the earlier effort had only been an event, not an actual page. I didn't know anyone involved, but I contacted the group. We worked together for months without meeting in person. Most lived in Riyadh, and I decided to fly there and see them. One girl was fourteen years old; I met her with her mom and sister. Her mom was separated and had been abused by her husband and brothers. She couldn't ask for a divorce because she was afraid of losing her daughters. She was fully veiled and I couldn't see her face, but she gripped my hands and pleaded, "Don't give up to fight for my daughters' rights. I lost all hope until you came." The mom eventually bought a small car. A Sudanese woman taught her fourteen-year-old daughter how to drive. The girl drove her mother and sister everywhere. They were caught several times, but the mother begged for mercy and promised that her daughter would not drive again, so they were released.

Among all the pledges that I signed was one not to give interviews, not to speak about my driving, and not to discuss my time in jail. And initially I held fast to that pledge. I said no to everyone.

What I did do was try to help some of the women I had left behind in prison. I had made a promise to God to give away one month's salary and I did that. I bought a plane ticket home for Maysara, the woman who had loaned me her bed, and gave her money to help her start over. I held a collection among my Aramco colleagues to buy plane tickets for other women who could not afford to leave prison, and we were able to send twelve inmates home.

But, as the months passed, the story of women driving did not fade away. In September, a woman named Shayma Jastaniah who lived in Jeddah was found guilty of driving through the city streets and sentenced to ten lashes; the sentence was later overturned on orders of the king. And the Saudi press would not leave me alone. The final straw was an article accusing me of being an Iranian agent inside Aramco, working in the company's most sensitive department, information security. The article contained many pieces of accurate information—my birth date, where I had gone to school, details about my family—so everything else it said seemed true as well.

I felt I had to respond. I gave one interview to a pro-government journalist, Turki al-Dakhil, with the television network Al Arabiya. One of my friends told me beforehand to stick to the facts, just say what happened, not to make accusations, and not to play the victim. I tried to do that. The government intervened and wouldn't let the show air in its usual slot, but they apparently forgot to ban the radio broadcast of the audio. It played on a major Saudi radio station, uninterrupted, and thousands of people heard it. When the televised interview was shown for the first time during what was supposed to be a slot for reruns, tens of thousands more people watched it. It was seen in beauty salons, car dealerships, and cafés. My friends texted me to tell me that people had stopped what they were doing and were clustered around the televisions to watch this Manal al-Sharif.

After the interview aired, I met with the deputy prince of the Imara, Prince Jalawi bin Abdul Aziz. He told me that he saw my interview and that it "shows you are a patriot and an educated woman. We are honored to have you as one of us." At Aramco, I received a verbal warning for having given the interview. If I did something like that again, I would be fired.

In the weeks that had followed my arrest, a slew of royal decrees were released. The first in June allowed women to work in shops and malls as cashiers. It took a pronouncement from the king for me and millions of other women to be able to buy our lingerie and underwear from another woman.

━━

In October, the king gave his annual address to the Shoura council, in which he said, "We will not accept marginalizing women." He announced that women would be given a chance to stand in municipal elections and to participate in the Shoura, an unelected advisory council for the king. It was the first and last time he spoke about women in this context when addressing the Shoura, and even though he didn't mention driving, it seemed like a victory.

Outside the kingdom, the driving movement had gained attention and support. In June, six US congresswomen, led by Carolyn Maloney of New York State, wrote a letter to me expressing their admiration. Secretary of State Hillary Clinton spoke out in favor of Saudi women being allowed to drive. There were sympathetic campaigns in Italy, and in the States a group called Honk for Saudi Women was formed.

In November, six months after my arrest, I filed a lawsuit in the Saudi courts challenging the government's refusal to grant me a driver's license. At the start of December, academics from Saudi Arabia's highest religious council, working with a retired professor from King Fahd University of Petroleum and Minerals, presented a graphic report warning Shoura members that if women were allowed to drive, prostitution, pornography, homosexuality, and divorce would "surge." The report also stated that if women were allowed to drive, "within ten years, there would be no more virgins" in Saudi Arabia. It cited the "moral decline" that has occurred in other Muslim countries where women drive.

In January, news outlets reported that I had been killed in a car crash in Jeddah, and that I had been driving at the time. My phone lit up with family and friends calling me. I could not believe it. The story of my death on the roadway made headlines around the country and around the world. Of course, it wasn't true. The woman killed was a member of a desert community. She was driving, but she had not been part of Women2Drive. I believe that whoever distributed this misinformation wanted to prove that driving was too dangerous for women, and they wanted people to believe that God was specifically punishing me.

Then I made a big mistake. I was still fighting in the system to get a driver's license. The government kept saying that I needed a mahram or my guardian to prove my identity, but my brother had moved to Kuwait and my father lived on the other side of the country. I brought two male colleagues from work to vouch for me, as well as my phone, which I used to record the audio of the conversation in the Notary Public Service office. Saudi code prohibits recording government officials. But that was not my error. My error was that I posted the entire absurd audio conversation on YouTube and used my Aramco laptop to do it. (When I was released from jail, the first night I was home, I opened a Twitter account under my own name. Almost overnight, I had ten thousand followers; soon it was more than ninety thousand. But I had done that on my personal computer.)

One of the Women2Drive members reposted my audio on the movement's official YouTube channel under the heading "Manal al-Sharif records violations against Saudi women." As soon as our opponents found out that the recording was mine, the audio went viral, springing up like a mushroom on site after site and screen after screen. I took it down soon afterward, but it didn't entirely go away. Aramco was furious. The company came for my computer. They read every one of my emails; they went through everything. I was hauled off to be interrogated by an American man—I presume he was an ex-CIA agent, judging by his behavior. He hollered at me, asking me who outside the company had assisted me and where else I had sent the video. Finally, I was brought in to meet with the public prosecutor. He informed me that someone had filed an official complaint and they were preparing to file a court case against me; if it went forward, I could face two years in jail. My only recourse was to go to the prince and apologize. Aramco management scolded me, and the personnel department gave me a final, written warning and told me if I ever stepped even slightly over the line, I would be dismissed.

"Stay quiet," they added. "This one passed. The next one won't."

Not long after that, *Time* magazine named me one of its 100 most influential people of the year. The honor included an invitation to a gala dinner in New York City. I had never been to anything like it before. Everyone in the room was famous. I sat next to actress Mia Farrow, though I had no idea who she was because I had never seen her movies. Famous musicians wanted to have their pictures taken with me, but I had never heard their music. I met Hillary Clinton and had my photo taken with her; she told her assistant to get my contact information and "stay in touch." People were comparing me to Rosa Parks. The evening was incredible. Then I returned home.

After the YouTube incident and the *Time* magazine honor, Aramco moved me from information security and dropped my name from the specialist development program. I was placed in the procurement department. My job was essentially remedial data entry. But even that would not last long.

The Oslo Freedom Forum, an annual gathering of human rights activists from around the world, invited me to speak in Norway and to receive the first ever Václav Havel Prize for Creative Dissent—I didn't know what the word *dissent* meant when I was awarded the prize. I had to look it up. I was named as a laureate, along with Aung San Suu Kyi, the Burmese Nobel Prize winner, and Chinese artist and political activist Ai Weiwei. I asked Aramco for four days off to travel to Oslo. My manager approved it, but the upper-level Aramco executives did not. Their response was swift and sure. "You are not allowed to go," I was told. "We don't want Aramco to be associated with you." The choice was clear: if I said yes to Oslo, I would lose my job. I said yes and resigned, which meant not only leaving my work but giving up my home in the compound by the end of May. And it meant that I was unemployed for the first time since I had graduated from college. But I felt that I had to speak out. I packed up what little was left at my desk and flew to Oslo.

Appearing at the Freedom Forum involved giving a speech. I was very nervous, but as I spoke, I grew calmer. The speech received two standing ovations, something that had not happened for years. The YouTube video of my speech was watched by 250,000 people in a matter of days.

My time at the Oslo Freedom Forum was a reminder of how sheltered I had been. I knew nothing about many of the struggles in other parts of the world. The award I received was a replica of the *Lady Liberty* statue built by Chinese students during their Tiananmen Square protests. Except I had never heard of Tiananmen Square. All my life, I had only read about events in the Muslim world, about Bosnia, Chechnya, Afghanistan, and especially the Palestinian conflict with Israel. There was so much more I needed to learn, so many more amazing people to discover.

My seventeen-minute speech in English had gone viral on YouTube, but inside Saudi Arabia, it was mistranslated, with misleading subtitles and commentary that depicted me as an enemy of Saudi Arabia and a traitor to Islam. Almost immediately, I began receiving death threats. People even went to my father's home in Jeddah and threatened him. A Saudi sheikh condemned me in a fatwa.

Then a television news segment aired during Saudi prime time, after *Juma'a* prayer, on the country's leading channel, MBC. It accused me of being trained by CANVAS (The Centre for Applied Nonviolent Action and Strategies), a nonprofit organization based in Serbia that advocates nonviolent resistance against dictatorships. I had appeared on a panel in Washington, D.C., with one of the heads of CANVAS, Srdja Popovic—we had both been named on a list of 100 Global Thinkers by *Foreign Policy* magazine. The Saudi TV report used footage from the event and footage of an interview with Popovic, where he praised me as "inspiring," to "prove [I] was a CANVAS trainee."

The pressure became so intense that I locked myself inside my home on the Aramco compound, while packing to move from my town house and trying to figure out what to do next. Vital Voices, an American NGO started by Hillary Clinton and former secretary of state Madeline Albright and dedicated to supporting and empowering female leaders, gave me a global leadership award. But I could not make the trip to Washington, D.C., due to the threats and fears for my safety. I realized I had no choice; I had to leave Saudi Arabia.

I thought first of Bahrain, which is just on the other side of the causeway from Dammam, but there was too much political unrest and instability. I settled on Dubai. But I would not be going alone.

In 2010, a Brazilian consultant joined my division at Aramco. His name was Rafael. We were nodding acquaintances for two years until one day when I started talking with a small group of friends, planning a barbecue. He was standing nearby and said, "You should try Brazilian barbecue."

I said, "Okay, you come over with us and make it." We stayed friends, but I never thought he was interested in me.

Almost every day, I went for walks on the paths around the compound, usually with Aboudi. Rafael started showing up on my doorstep to join us. He was scheduled to leave Aramco in the spring of 2012. On one of our last walks, he told me that he had fallen in love with me "the first time I saw you at that barbecue gathering." He was moving to Dubai to start a company and he wanted me to come with him. He added, "I don't treat women like my girlfriend, but like my wife." But I could not go to Dubai without being his wife.

Rafael asked what he would have to do to marry me. My answer was simple: become a Muslim. But the reality was more complex. As a Saudi citizen (man or woman) you must have special permission from the interior minister to marry a non-Saudi. I asked for permission to marry Rafael, and the Saudi authorities refused. We could not marry in Dubai, either; its government said I needed permission from the Saudi embassy. So, Rafael took me to his home in Brazil to meet his family. He converted to Islam in the Rio de Janeiro Islamic Center, speaking the required profession of faith. We did not have a formal wedding because there was still no place to get married legally. Instead, a cousin of Rafael's who is a lawyer in Montreal helped us get a civil marriage certificate from a law court in Canada.

Rafael's family already knew about me; they had followed the news of my driving and arrest. They were warm and welcoming. But there was also the pain of leaving my own family and country behind. And my second marriage was stunningly close to an arranged marriage. Rafael and I knew very little about each other; we had to wed because the rules left us with no other options.

By far, the hardest part was leaving Aboudi. My ex-husband would not allow Aboudi to travel to Dubai. And although he initially said that he would permit Aboudi to visit me in Dubai at least two times a year, he quickly reneged on that promise. If I wanted to see my son, I had to buy a ticket on my own and fly back to Saudi Arabia. Because I had no house, I had to stay with Aboudi's grandmother in their family home whenever I visited. I did that every or every other weekend, and I do it still.

After I had moved, my ex-husband took Aboudi to Dubai on a trip, but he did not tell me and he did not allow me to see our son while they were there. Later, I found photos from the trip on Aboudi's iPad. I was furious. I hired a lawyer to contest the premise that I could not have my son with me in Dubai.

We spent two years in the Saudi court system, and I spent tens of thousands of riyals. I had to fly my father from Jeddah to appear in court; my own lawyer told me that I shouldn't attend, saying, "Your presence could create complications." My father signed a pledge promising that he would go to jail if Aboudi didn't return after visiting me. In the end, the court's verdict was no. The basis for their decision was a tenth-century text that denied children's right to travel because of the "risk of the child dying en route on such a dangerous distance." That legal premise dated from the time of camels and caravans traveling over hot desert sands. The trip from Dammam to Dubai was one hour by plane. Flights arrived and departed all day long. My lawyer suggested an expensive appeal. I found a woman, Dr. Suhaila Zain Al-Abdeen, who specializes in interpreting old legal and religious texts. We spent a week writing a twelve-page appeal citing passages from the Koran and the hadiths that justified my right to have my son visit. I handed the appeal to my lawyer and waited. But I lost again.

In the eyes of the Saudi Arabian government, I am also still not legally married. When I gave birth to another son, Daniel Hamza, in 2014, the government would not grant him a visa. I could not take him into the country with me. While I was pregnant, Aboudi won a stuffed animal that he gave to the baby. My two boys have big-brother and little-brother T-shirts, but they have never met. Aboudi cannot leave Saudi with me; his brother cannot enter Saudi with me. They only know each other from photos and from waving on screens across an Internet feed.

———

I did not understand the consequences of leaving my job at Aramco until I started looking for work again in Dubai. I went on forty-seven interviews in two years, almost always getting to the final rounds of the application. Then my file would go to Human Resources, they would look me up, and I would not be hired. My name and my history preceded me and negated any other skills on my résumé. In the meantime, I accepted every invitation I got. I spoke at the Institut du Monde Arabe in Paris, gave a TED Talk, and spoke at a UN event, a WIRED summit, Harvard University, and many others. I paid many of my own expenses just so that I could speak out. I wrote in newspapers and blogged. I took up the cause of a five-year-old Saudi girl, Lama, who was beaten with a cane and electric cables. She suffered a crushed skull, broken ribs, and a broken arm and died in a hospital. Her father was a well-known Saudi preacher. He had reportedly been "concerned" that his five-year-old daughter had lost her virginity. After her death, he paid $50,000 in blood money to his wife to avoid punishment; if Lama had been a boy, the sum would have been $100,000.

I started a campaign called I Am Lama, which helped pass the first Saudi code against domestic violence. Efforts to criminalize domestic abuse had been under way since 2008, but nothing had happened for four years. When a group of young men posted a YouTube video in which they cut off a cat's tail, an animal cruelty statute was passed within two weeks. I wrote that Lama's father would have been punished more harshly if Lama had been a cat.

I also started Faraj, a Twitter campaign to release the Saudi, Filipino, and Indonesian female domestic workers who were being held in the Dammam prison. This activism had become my job; more than that, it had become my mission.

In the intervening years, there have been other attempts by women to drive inside Saudi Arabia. On October 26, 2013, hundreds of women drove in Saudi Arabia, and an online petition that circulated on Twitter and Facebook received some sixteen thousand signatures in a few days before it was officially shut down. I lent my support to their effort—and drove in solidarity along the roads of Dubai. But women continue to pay a high price for driving. In December 2015, Loujain al-Hathloul, then twenty-five, was arrested as she tried to drive into Saudi Arabia from the United Arab Emirates border—with a valid UAE license. Arrested along with her was Maysa, the journalist who had interviewed and helped me back in 2011. Maysa had rushed to the border to help Loujain. Both were detained for more than seventy days, and their cases were referred to Saudi Arabia's specialized criminal court, established to try terrorism cases. (They were released several days after Great Britain's Prince Charles visited the Saudi king and raised the case of a male blogger, Rafi Badawi, who had been sentenced to one thousand lashes and ten years in prison for "insulting Islam through electronic channels.") After they were freed, Loujain and Maysa were banned from traveling and faced the threat of renewed prosecution. Their travel ban was lifted and their cars returned only after the intervention of Germany's foreign minister. There has not been another concerted effort by Saudi women to drive.

As I traveled and lived outside Saudi Arabia, my eyes opened, not simply to all the people and the news that I had missed, but to smaller, more personal things. I watched as a friend flew to Spain to watch his daughter play competitive basketball. All those years when I was studying at the university in Jeddah, my parents never knew that I played basketball. I never showed them my team medals or told them about our tournaments. I never told them because I knew that they wouldn't have approved. They might even have insisted that I quit. There were so many moments that we missed because the rules didn't allow it.

Between visiting Aboudi and traveling around the world, I did not make it back to Jeddah all that often to see my parents. When my second son was born, my mother came to Dubai, but she stayed only three days. As soon as she arrived, she got into a fight with some of the airport personnel. At our apartment, she was fighting, shouting, and driving us crazy. After three days, she went home. I insisted that she be evaluated by a psychologist, and the diagnosis came back that Mama was bipolar and likely schizophrenic—her illness had gotten worse with aging and stress. All our lives, my brother and sister and I had been told that Mama was possessed by demons. Mama herself often believed that we were the target of witchcraft or claimed that people or cars were following her. Instead, she suffered from a mental illness, one that was treatable and could be controlled. None of us had a clue that this was the problem. But after she was diagnosed, she refused to take the medicine that might help her symptoms. In frustration, I stayed away, longer than I should have.

On July 17, 2015, the day of Eid al-Fitr, Mama was diagnosed with stage IV breast cancer. I was visiting my parents with Aboudi for Eid, and when I saw her, I realized the mom I knew was gone. She had lost half her body weight and was lying in bed, too weak to get up and move around. And she was coughing up blood but refused to see a doctor. I was mad at Abouya for not telling any of us how bad her condition was. She couldn't even take a shower by herself, so I guided her to the bathroom, and for the first time, I bathed her as if she were a child. When I saw her breasts, I started crying. I knew, but it was the emergency room doctor in the hospital who told me for sure. It took me a month to get Mama to complete the medical tests. She would lock herself in her room and wish herself death rather than go back to the hospital. Some days, she accused us of trying to harm her and refused to take any medicine. I spent hours outside her room, crying and begging her to allow me to take her to her doctors' appointments. It was the most difficult and emotional time of my life. Mama's cancer was very advanced. Finally, I got her to an oncologist, and we also started the shots to treat her mental illness. After the third shot, she was a changed person. It was only in the last months of her life that I got to know my true mother.

She was pleasant, warm, cooperative. I had been afraid to have Mama come to my university graduation for fear that she would make a scene. Now I could go anywhere with her. She came with me to Dubai, and we went to the movies, to restaurants, to the aquarium. I read the news to her, and we laughed a lot. She played and sang to Hamza. My brother was able to sit with her and talk for hours. We learned all about her past. She told us about her parents—about her own mother, who had died when she was four—and about her grandparents. Without knowing it, I had named both my sons the same names as each of her grandfathers, Abdalla and Hamza.

I told my brother that I felt as if I was losing Mama twice.

Mama wanted to go back home, she told me she missed Mecca and the Grand Mosque. It took only a few months for the cancer to grow stronger than Mama. She told us that she had seen a vision of her own mother in a dream and that her mother said, "I miss you."

"I'm going to die before the end of the year," Mama said. The woman who had been unhappy nearly all my life, who had always spoken about how she wished for death, had one last wish: to see my toddler son, Hamza, again. But she was too weak to come to Dubai, and even my father could not persuade the Saudi authorities to grant this eighteen-month-old boy a visa.

On February 28, 2016, she took her last breath. Her lungs literally collapsed from the cancer. But she was tough to her last day. She woke up, took a shower, did her laundry, and even arranged the guest room for a friend's visit. When my father called the ambulance because she was suffering, she sent them away, saying she wanted to die in her own bed. She died lying on my father's arm. The same ambulance came back to collect her body.

As a Muslim woman, I had one final obligation to my mother: to wash her body before burial. I told my father to have the body stored, that I would come. I remember standing in the Dubai airport, crying, and the passport control man asking me, "What, did you not enjoy

Dubai?" and I replied that my mother had just passed away. I washed my mom and saw her dressed one last time in a pink dress with black flowers. Her own mother had been buried in Mecca (she died from heat stroke when she was performing the hajj, sixty-two years before my mom's own death) in a cemetery next to the Grand Mosque where the Prophet Muhammad's (PBUH) wife had been buried centuries ago. Mama's one wish was to be buried next to her mom.

In the Saudi practice of Islam, women are not permitted to attend burial ceremonies. I could not even ride in the car with Mama's casket. But I went on my own to the Grand Mosque to pray. The mosque has 2 million visitors a day, so the crowds for prayer are always huge. At the end of my prayers, my brother texted me, "We buried Mama," and I felt at peace.

At the same time as her burial, a little baby was being buried. The baby's father asked if it was okay to bury their baby with Mama, in the same grave. In Islam, babies, unlike adults, are considered to be without sin. A lot of mercy comes to the grave of a baby. Babies can go straight to God and ask for forgiveness for their parents. Mama, who left her oldest son behind in Libya, who lost two babies with Abouya, and who did not get to see her little grandson one last time to say goodbye, was buried with this poor baby. We believe that now she has a baby's soul with her as a friend.

For three days after her burial, friends came to Mecca to pay their respects. Mom's old cell phone didn't stop ringing with people calling to say how sorry they were. In Libya, there was another funeral for her that lasted three days, and the same in Egypt. In Libya, my oldest uncle's house was crowded with people who came to offer condolences. The entire time we knew her, Mama gave away everything she had. She always wore the worst clothes and no gold jewelry; whatever she was given by her brother or that she later earned, she gave away. I would bring her gifts, and she would give them away. Now everyone was coming to speak of her generosity. Grown women came and said, "She was our other mother too." They spoke of how she taught them to sew or to cook. One family that had lost their own mother talked about how Mama would send food to them. She never told anyone about this. She knew my father wouldn't approve, and she didn't want anyone to know.

She was an amazing woman who will always be my inspiration.

———

Some things about Saudi Arabia do not change. It is a country roughly three times the size of Texas, with vast natural resources and a strategic position in the Middle East. Today it has a population of about 20 million Saudis, and nearly 10 million of these people are under twenty-five years old. The current king, Salman bin Abdul Aziz, is a son of the kingdom's founder, Abdul Aziz Ibn Saud, who was born in 1876 and had more than thirty sons who lived to reach adulthood. Every Saudi king since the founding of the kingdom has been a son of Ibn Saud. But King Salman will be the last; when he came to power in 2015, he removed his younger brother from the line of succession. The next king will be either King Salman's nephew, Crown Prince Muhammad bin Nayef, born in 1959, or, some rumors suggest, Salman's son, Deputy Crown Prince Muhammad bin Salman, born in 1985 and the current defense minister.

Commentators, journalists, and essayists are now sifting through tea leaves, trying to conjecture if and when a transfer of power takes place, what inside the kingdom will change. There is talk of rolling back religious control; in April 2016, the religious police were stripped of their ability to make arrests. There is an effort under way to privatize a portion of Aramco, creating an initial public offering of up to five percent of the company's stock. There are proposals to remove government subsidies and to have more Saudis work—somewhere between ten and twenty percent of the men in the kingdom are unemployed. (Women are excluded from unemployment statistics. And while unemployment is a major issue in the kingdom, at least eighty-five percent of the employees working at all levels of the Saudi private sector are non-Saudis, meaning they are foreign-born workers.) Yet there are changes for women. Four female athletes represented the kingdom at the 2016 Olympics in Rio. A women-owned law firm opened in Jeddah in 2014, and four female lawyers are licensed to practice in the Saudi system, rather than simply serving as "legal consultants." In December 2015, nineteen women won seats in local councils, although with 2,106 total seats, that is less than one percent. Widowed and divorced mothers are finally able to obtain family identity cards.

There is even talk of one day, far in the future, letting women drive.

On November 29, 2016, Prince Alwaleed bin Talal took to Twitter and wrote: "Stop the debate. It's time for women to drive." He also posted a four-page letter to his personal website, where he stated, "It is high time that Saudi women started driving their cars." His reasons were primarily economic, particularly the cost of employing foreign drivers, about 3,800 riyals, or roughly $1,000 a month, which is a drain on household budgets. He also said it prevents women from participating in the workforce. But the prince, while he is wealthy and owns considerable business interests, is not part of the official government. Even the young Deputy Crown Prince Muhammad bin Salman has said that he is "not convinced" that women should be allowed to drive. So we wait. (When I moved to Dubai, I shipped my car and I kept my Saudi license plate, because someday, I want to drive my car across the border into my homeland.)

———

These are all hopeful developments, but there is still a very long road ahead, literally and figuratively, for Saudi women. Saudi Arabia's government is now the largest investor in the transportation company Uber, having provided $3.5 billion in funding from the Saudi Arabian Public Investment Fund. The director of the fund, a member of the royal family, was given a seat on Uber's board. But, while Uber helps Saudi women get from place to place, it is not a way for women to drive themselves. Saudi Arabia is using a modern smartphone app as a means to enforce the long-standing ban. In fact, about eighty percent of Saudi Uber's users are Saudi women.

Or consider this story of a Starbucks in Riyadh. Early in 2016 a sign was posted on its door in Arabic and English: "Please no entry for ladies only send your driver to order thank you." Starbucks's official reply was that while it "welcomes all customers, including women and families," this particular store had been "built without a gender wall," meaning that it could only accommodate men. Starbucks added that it was working to receive approval from local authorities to build a permanent gender wall. As one American female radio talk show host noted, it's like in Greensboro, South Carolina, when the Woolworth's in 1960 said we like all our customers, but the black ones can't sit at the lunch counter because it's tradition.

The third story is of a call I received from a friend of mine. She had been married for eighteen years and had two daughters when her husband announced that he was divorcing her to marry another woman. He took the girls, as is his right under the Saudi divorce code, took the things from their house, and moved to another city. She was left with the loans that he had taken out in her name, unbeknownst to her. At the age of thirty-six, she would have to return to having her father—a drug addict whom she has not seen or spoken to in thirteen years—be her guardian. Now he must be the one to give her permission to travel, to work, to open a bank account, to find housing, to do almost anything.

———

There can be no modern Saudi kingdom as long as women are still ruled by men. It may take a long time, but I do believe that kingdom will come. I think of my father, sitting in the mosque in Jeddah, listening to the Friday sermon and hearing the sheikh say, "Manal al-Sharif has committed evil. If we allow women like her to drive, we lose control over our women." And then I think of another section of Jeddah, home to the Al Shallal theme park, which, one night a week, is open just for women. The most popular attraction at the park? Bumper cars, where for five minutes, women can drive freely, even if it is only in circles, around and around.

The rain begins with a single drop.

Epilogue

*I*t was 5:00 a.m. in New South Wales (NSW), Australia, on the morning of September 27, 2017, but it was still the evening of September 26 in Saudi Arabia. I woke up to give my son, Daniel Hamza, his medicine after a recent ear surgery. I quickly double-checked the time on my mobile phone. At that very moment, a BBC breaking-news alert flashed across the glowing screen: *Saudi Arabia to lift driving ban on women.* I thought my sleepy eyes must have made a mistake. I refreshed my phone and read it again. And then I read it one more time just to be sure, after which I broke into tears of joy. Within a minute, my phone went crazy, and my email was swamped with interview requests from all over the world. Almost everyone I knew, and many people I didn't know, contacted me.

But the only person I wanted to talk to at that moment was Mama. I always knew deep inside me that this day would come. What I didn't know was that she would not be there to celebrate it with me. She had passed away with so much pain in her heart, because her daughter had driven a car and was publicly shamed throughout Saudi Arabia. Now like a veil, that shame would be lifted. In that moment, I missed Mama more than ever.

It took twenty-seven years from the first attempt to protest the driving ban until that historic day. We all must pay our respects to the women and men who have waged this struggle. Women campaigning to end this ban have lost their freedom, their jobs, have jeopardized their safety, and had their cars confiscated and held. They have been harassed and jailed, their families have been targeted. They have been called every degrading name and been viciously attacked. They lost their lives as they knew them for daring to drive on the streets of Saudi Arabia.

But no more. Things started to change in 2011, with the start of the #Women2Drive movement. The struggle continued with additional campaigns, including the 2013 campaign led by the Saudi blogger Dr. Eman Alnafjan. In 2014, another activist, Loujain, attempted to cross the Saudi border from the United Arab Emirates by driving her car. She was joined by Saudi journalist Maysa Al-Amoudi. Both were arrested and sent to jail for seventy-two days. Now I hope a woman will never be jailed again for the simple act of driving a car.

Women's rights activists must continue to observe how the law is implemented and continue to campaign to abolish the male guardianship law, which forbids women to travel, marry, or even leave prison without the permission of a male relative. We must ask for nothing short of full equality for women. Driving is only the start to ending other unjust laws, which treat Saudi women as minors, not trusted to direct their own destiny.

———

The official date when the driving ban will be lifted in Saudi Arabia is June 24, 2018. Women2Drive, the movement I led, had called for women to drive on June 17, 2011. My book, *Daring to Drive*, was released on June 13, 2017. June is my new magical month.

———

It has been interesting for me to listen to reporters' questions and to read their analyses of why the driving ban was lifted. There are many theories: One is that it's a way to distract international media attention from the crisis in Yemen and a Saudi economy that is on the brink of bankruptcy. Amid this speculation, I will add my own: It's part of a power game. I cannot ignore the irony that the Saudi king who has lifted the driving ban is the same man who was the governor of Riyadh when the forty-seven women drivers protested the ban in 1990. He took harsh actions against these women by turning a blind eye while the religious establishment destroyed their lives and reputations and most of society condemned them for challenging the ban.

But this time, I do believe Saudi is changing. The current leader of the power game is Crown Prince Mohammed bin Salman, best known by his initials, MBS. In the spring of 2017, I had the chance to meet with members of his signature 2030 Vision team, which is in charge of the kingdom's modernization. I was very skeptical, but after a few hours of heated discussions and many more hours of studying and reading, I became a supporter and a believer that this young man can finally bring change. When he was named crown prince, I tweeted: "Now my hopes for a better Saudi are bigger than the sky." MBS has reined in the religious police, which choked us, literally and figuratively, and has lifted a long list of restrictions on music, art, and cinemas, as well as on women working and attending public sporting events, and even the practice of closing shops five times a day for prayer. It's also the first time that someone in a major leadership position is younger than me and is part of the age group that makes up the majority of Saudi Arabia's population.

But these changes may not be permanent. The Saudi Arabian political system is very complicated. To most of the outside world, it might seem as if being a king in an absolute monarchy gives the ruler the absolute power to make any decision and execute it. In fact, the Saudi political system is riddled with many small powerful groups, each with conflicting interests. Nothing is absolute.

I do believe that allowing women to drive will be a permanent change. Few things have brought more shame to Saudi Arabia than this draconian ban. And there is more: Saudi Arabia cannot succeed economically if women who are highly educated are kept, literally and figuratively, in the backseat. My hope is that economic reforms will be combined with political reforms, leading to a constitutional monarchy where people have representatives and, one day, full freedom of expression.

——

When I was very young and something would bother me, Mama used to say: "My daughter, the only tight place in this world is our grave. Life is vast and big, if you don't like someone or someplace, move away."

After five years of living in Dubai, Rafael and I decided to move to Australia. The Emirate authorities would not consider us married because the Saudi authorities would not consider us married. It was an impossible position. We thought that change, total change, would make it better. We arrived on Australian soil in March 2017. I spent the following months traveling for my book, and rarely made any connection with this new home. Each time I did return, I missed my country and friends more than ever. From Australia, a round-trip ticket to Saudi cost ten times more, and required a whole day of travel, whereas before, it had been less than an hour from Dubai. I felt isolated and lonely in a place where I had no ties other than my visa status. But being so alone created another kind of revelation: I knew Rafael and I were not right for each other, that it was time for us to go our separate ways.

Rafael was completely supportive of me while I worked on this book; he kept me grounded, and I felt safe and cherished for first time in my life. But I had believed what my society told me: "Marry a man who loves you. Don't marry who you love. Love comes after marriage." But love didn't come. I loved him dearly as my companion and friend, but we never had that spark that I had at the start with my first husband, or my second love, whom I met in Boston after my divorce, but never spoke of in this memoir. I knew what love felt like, and I didn't have it in my marriage. Over the course of two years, we broke up and then tried to come back stronger together. But each time that we returned to each other, we did not find love. We only became more hurt and more miserable.

If love and chemistry aren't there from the start, you cannot create it. Moving to Australia made me face this truth. It was one of the most difficult decisions in my life. I told Rafael between my tears the day I left our home in the rural New South Wales and moved to Sydney: "You are the best man I have met in my life, which makes it very difficult for me to leave you. Whoever ends up falling in love with you will be the luckiest woman alive. I'm sorry it wasn't me." I know I left him with a broken heart, but I believe time will send him love again.

——

I learned another lesson moving to a liberal country that is proud to support women's rights: support of women goes only so far. I thought I could return to my career in technology and information security. Recruiters were excited to place me, but the offers never materialized. The companies all appreciated activism, but none of them wanted to hire an activist. This realization was bitter at the start, but ultimately very liberating. For speaking up, for putting everything at risk, I'm unemployable. What a price to pay, to give up a career that I invested my life in building. But I decided to let it be. This will be my new path. I didn't choose to be an activist, but I can choose to remain one.

——

I'm writing these pages from my new apartment in Sydney, overlooking the Parramatta River and listening to Buena Vista Social Club, a Cuban band. I've been working on travel papers for my younger son, because Saudi officials have finally promised me that, one day soon, he will be given a Saudi entry visa.

I am also building my own business, working with an amazing professor and her students at Macquarie University in Sydney. It is a social enterprise called Women2Hack. My vision is to inspire women within Saudi to become leaders. The academy's mission is to facilitate education, training, networking, and employment opportunities for Saudi women in information security. It is created *for* women in information security *by* women in information security. Through this platform, I will finally be able to reach girls and women in my country and speak to them in person. I could never do that solely through activism.

I'm still overwhelmed by the wonderful response my memoir has received. But the best and truest bliss for me is that, for the first time in my thirty-eight years, I'm completely free to be myself, with no societal or religious constraints or expectations. There is no box that I must fit into. No one to call me disrespectful for wanting to follow my dreams and aspirations.

I have decided to split my time between two countries, Australia and Saudi, with Sydney as my base. But rather than feeling like a partial nomad, I have at last finally found my true home: Home is the place where you are free to be yourself, without anyone's permission.

Manal al-Sharif
Sydney, December 2017

Acknowledgments

My very special and first thanks go to Rafael, who, when I had lost all hope, believed that this book should be finished and seen by the world. Without his belief in me, I would have given up a long time ago. The second person I'd like to thank is Wajeha al Huwaider for putting herself at risk to document my driving in public so that it could be posted on YouTube. You are the most courageous Saudi woman I have ever met.

After my speech at the Oslo Freedom Forum (OFF) in May 2012, someone in the audience asked me: "When are we going to read your book?" I was taken aback by the question; I wasn't sure if it was a joke or meant seriously. I thought, "Why would anyone want to read my story?" To give that speech, I had to quit a job that I had held for a decade. Ten minutes before I stepped on stage, I learned that by quitting, I had forfeited the financing for my house. I was jobless, homeless, and broke. I was overwhelmed to be in Oslo and to have won the first Václav Havel Award for Creative Dissent. I didn't even know the meaning of the word *dissent* and didn't understand why everyone was calling me an "activist." I was just a mother who worked as information security consultant and was inspired by the Arab Spring to start a movement to gain a basic right: the right of mobility, for the women in my country. I owe the idea of writing this book to the woman who asked me that question, even though I don't know her name. And my thanks to Thor Halvorssen, Alex Gladstien, and Christian Paul of OFF for giving me a podium to speak.

This book would not have come to life without the insights, patience, persistence, and guidance of my wonderful, caring agents, Peter and Amy Bernstein. Peter and Amy have been amazing champions, supporting and sustaining this project. I originally wanted the book to tell the story of Women2Drive, but after looking at a sample chapter, Peter and Amy gently but firmly told me that the book needed a personal story, that it should tell my life story. Coming from a private culture where houses are built with small, covered windows and high walls, I thought it was crazy to share the details of my life. In California, Persis Karim agreed with Peter and Amy. Her proposal led Priscilla Painton at Simon & Schuster to offer me a book contract. I'm grateful that Priscilla believed my story was worthy of a book. Without each of these people I would never have been willing to share my world, even though I do not yet know what impact publishing this book will have on my life back home.

I am deeply indebted to Lyric Winik, who agreed to be my fifth collaborator in three years, when I had all but given up the hope of finding the right writer. Lyric took more than one thousand pages of transcriptions of my interviews with previous collaborators, as well as videos and speeches and lengthy, rough chapters, and then conducted more interviews, read books and countless supplementary materials, and worked tirelessly to transform a badly organized manuscript and materials into a well-organized and finely polished book. I'm deeply in your debt for your care, professionalism, and dedication. Thanks to Trisha Calvarese for her contribution.

At Simon & Schuster, I am grateful to the wonderful insights and support from my editor, Priscilla Painton. She had always believed passionately and unwaveringly in this book. My thanks to Megan Hogan for her very careful work on the manuscript and very thoughtful questions. I am grateful as well for the support of publisher Jonathan Karp, for his very kind words and excellent advice on a title. My thanks to the entire talented team at Simon & Schuster, who have worked so hard on behalf of this book, especially Al Madocs, the production editor; Lewelin Polanco, the designer; Alison Forner, who did the cover; Beth Maglione, the production manager; and Kristen Lemire and Amanda Mulholland in managing editorial, as well as Erin Reback and Nicole McArdle in publicity and marketing, respectively.

My deep appreciation goes to Hannah Campbell, my talented translator, who captured and maintained my voice when translating my Arabic manuscript to English. Your work, dedication, and attention to detail, along with your feedback, kept me going.

Very special thanks are due my family and my friends. For my mother, Mama, for all the times you gave up the chicken thigh, your favorite part of the chicken, for me and my brother; for how you ate the leftovers of the lunch that you had spent the whole morning cooking for us. For the dresses you sewed for us, for saving bits of money the whole year so that you could take your children to spend the summer in Egypt; for the times that you shut the kitchen door in my sister's and my faces and told us to spend our time learning physics and math instead of cooking. For all those suitors whom you rejected so we could finish our college educations, for all the things you gave up, the new clothes that you didn't buy so that you could sew new clothes for us to wear on Eid or take us to the Funfair. For that precious pearl necklace your favorite brother gave you, which you sold to pay our house expenses, for that, and for all the other things we took for granted, forgive us, thank you, and may you rest in peace.

For my father, who never had a father, but tried his best to be a father, for coming home every night, for never forgetting my school allowance or my favorite magazine every Wednesday, for taking me to buy my favorite books every summer, for the times you let me score a goal while playing soccer when were kids. For trusting me to work away from home and to marry the man I chose. Thank you.

For my brother, Muhammad, who is always proud to have me as his sister, thank you for giving me your car keys and sitting next to me on the day that I drove, for getting me out of jail, for being my driver, my mahram, and my biggest fan. Thank you.

For Bahiya Almansour, the girl who started the Facebook event Women2Drive and inspired a movement, for Eman Alnafjan, Najla Hariri, Huda, Eman, Ameenah, Hidayah, Ahmed, Muneerah, Shakir, Talal, and all my first supporters.

For Maysa al-Amoudi, for believing in Women2Drive and putting us in contact with influential media figures to support the movement. For Abdulla Al Alami, Women2Drive and Right2Dignity's godfather, for his guidance, for his time and money, for putting us in contact with the officials, for not giving up on me even when I was in jail and everyone else had abandoned the movement. For Omar al-Johani, for risking his own safety and bravely tweeting about my 2:00 a.m. arrest and letting the world know. For Abdullah, Muneera, and Hidaya, again, for being the only ones who had the courage to visit me in jail when everyone else was scared. You are my heroes. For Ahmed, our Twitter expert, thank you for keeping #FreeManal in the Twitter account favorites, forgive me for misunderstanding you. For Abduljalil al-Nasser, the talented photographer and filmmaker who took that photo that went viral online upon my arrest. Thousands around the world used that photo to show solidarity with Saudi women's rights.

For Talal al-Ateeq, Tarfah al-Ghannam, Amjad al-Amri, Rasha al-Duwaisi, Madeeha al-Ajroush, Suaad Alshammari, Kholoud al-Fahad, Hutoon Alfasi, Dr. Badrya Albishr, Khalaf Alharbi, Turki Aldakheel, Maysa Almane, Dr. Aisha Almane, Aziza Alyousef, Bashayer Alyami, Geenan al-Ghamdi, Raneen Bukhari, and many other activists, journalists, and writers who supported the movement when everyone else attacked it or stayed quiet. Your courageous voices have made a difference for generations to come.

For Donna Abu Nasr from Bloomberg and Atika Shubert from CNN, for letting the world know about the movement. For my dear friend and true feminist Constance Piesinger and Pedro M. Burelli, who both helped me craft my TED talk: you made an important difference in my life. For Carlos Latuff from Brazil, thank you for the amazing icons you designed to help make our movement known

worldwide. For Mohammed Sharaf from Kuwait, for the amazing posters and banners to support a women's rights movement in Saudi Arabia. For all my friends and all the people around the world whom I have never met but who changed their social media profile photos to my photo to call for my release from jail: thank you!

And thank you to my honorable friend and journalist Alaa Brinji, who has been jailed for five years for his honest tweets about extremism. Your article defending my name while I was in jail, when so many had tried to smear me, was a great consolation to my family.

This book took five years. Many times, I almost gave up. But after my mother was diagnosed with stage-four cancer in June 2015, and I spent months with her until her death in February 2016, I understood why this book took so long. I was still learning my mother's story and my own. Deep inside, I have always wanted to tell my story. What I could not have known was that after May 22, 2011, my story would be of interest to millions of people simply because I, a Saudi woman, drove a car.

About the Author

Manal al-Sharif was born in Mecca, Saudi Arabia, in 1979 and grew up poor in a religiously devout society. After earning a computer science degree, she was the first Saudi woman to work in information security in the kingdom and was hired by the Saudi-Aramco oil company. In 2011, she was imprisoned for driving a car, charged with "driving while female." The mother of two sons, Manal is now a leading women's rights activist, She has been lauded by the Oslo Freedom Forum, *Foreign Policy*, *Time*, and *Forbes*.

Simon & Schuster Paperbacks
Reading Group Guide

DARING *to* DRIVE

Manal al-Sharif

This reading group guide for Daring to Drive includes an introduction, discussion questions, ideas for enhancing your book club, and a Q&A with author Manal Al-Sharif. The suggested questions are intended to help your reading group find new and interesting angles and topics for your discussion. We hope that these ideas will enrich your conversation and increase your enjoyment of the book.

Introduction

Born to struggling parents in Mecca, Manal al-Sharif understood from an early age that she would never experience the same freedoms her male peers enjoyed. In keeping with Saudi custom, from the onset of puberty, Manal had to remain fully veiled and become virtually invisible; wearing perfume and leaving the house unless absolutely necessary were considered sinful. She faced an abrupt separation from her male cousins, and she was discouraged from any self-expression.

As an adolescent, Manal found herself drawn to the incendiary teachings of her radical Islamist instructors, and she became a religious zealot herself, eagerly exposing the forbidden activities of her own siblings. But by her twenties, after earning a university degree, Manal was a computer security engineer, one of a few women working in a desert compound that functioned more like suburban America than the Saudi kingdom. With her eyes wide open to the opportunities and liberties that had previously been denied to her as a female citizen, Manal al-Sharif found herself in a unique position to advocate for women's civil rights and make her mark on Saudi Arabian history.

Topics & Questions for Discussion

1. Manal grew up in relative poverty. What facets of her upbringing surprised you most: that her family was not rich? That her parents had both been divorced? That her father could not read or write? Why?

2. The Saudi Rule of Guardianship: The Saudi rule of guardianship exists because the Saudi system does not recognize women as adults for their entire lives. "Even a woman in labor will not be admitted into a hospital without her guardian or at least a mahram. Police cannot enter a home during a robbery, and firefighters are forbidden from entering a home during a fire or medical

emergency if a woman is inside but does not have her mahram present." (7) To your mind, which would be more difficult to live with: Saudi rules requiring male guardians for everything from emergencies to travel, schooling, and employment *or* forbidding women from driving? Could one policy change without the other changing as well? As a result of the guardianship rule, what advantages and disadvantages might women encounter in their everyday lives?

3. Virginity: At eight years old, Manal gets circumcised against her will, after which her mother warns her repeatedly not to participate in any physical activity that might damage her hymen and call her purity into question. Were you surprised by the emphasis on virginity and sexual purity in book? What would you say to a person who was defending these practices in Saudi society?

4. "As soon as a girl reaches puberty . . . she is obliged to enter a state known in Arabic as *khidr* ('numbness'). She must be outwardly devoid of emotions and feelings. In public, she must veil herself from prying eyes and avoid speaking." (89–90) What do you think is the primary objective or purpose of the veiling of women in Saudi Arabia? What do you think explains Manal's ever-changing feelings about the coverings she wears? What does the onset of veiling for girls in Saudi Arabia suggest about society's views of girlhood, womanhood, and female sexuality?

5. How does Manal's embrace of religious fanaticism as an adolescent affect her relationships? When Manal betrays her siblings and exposes their *haram* (forbidden) activities—her brother's clandestine listening to Western music, and her sister's secret conversations on the phone with a man—to their parents, to what extent does she believe their punishments are justified? How did you respond to these punishments and conflicts? Are they similar to basic family issues around the world, or are they fundamentally different?

6. As a young student, Manal al-Sharif receives instruction in the Doctrine of Loyalty and Disavowal, a tenet of radical Islam that compels Muslims to hate anyone deemed infidel, or faithful to

a religion or creed other than Islam. Manal later rejects these ideas. Do you think that Manal's views might have changed anyway if the terrorist attacks of September 11, 2001, had not happened?

7. "It can be difficult for people living outside of Saudi to understand why so many in our culture, women in particular, submit, stay, and suffer . . . physical violence. But the price of resisting can be even higher." (183) In light of the physical violence that she endures over the course of her life, to what extent does Manal al-Sharif embody a stereotypical Saudi woman? By serving as the face of a grassroots campaign aimed at changing Saudi attitudes about female drivers, how does she expose herself to the possibility of violence? To what extent do you think this makes her a hero?

8. When Manal al-Sharif gets arrested and jailed for driving outside the Aramco compound, Saudi authorities claim that she disobeyed *orf*, or tradition—not the law. Given that official Saudi code does not prohibit women drivers, why do you think the police chose to incarcerate Manal? What do the distinctions between tradition and the law reveal about the Saudi Arabian criminal justice system and the power of its religious police?

9. "In Saudi Arabia, your patriotism is measured by how much you love the king. The king is revered like a father, and we are considered his daughters and sons." (13) Consider the Saudi concept of patriotism and discuss how political dissent is viewed in Saudi society. To what extent does the Women2Drive campaign seem patriotic?

10. Discuss the impact of developing technology (satellite dishes, the Internet, cell phones with cameras, and social media) on the daily life in Saudi Arabia. To what extent is this kind of disruption inevitable for all societies? How is it uniquely threatening to insular societies like Saudi Arabia?

11. Of the many rich details of Saudi Arabian life detailed by Manal al-Sharif in *Daring to Drive*, which did you find most memorable or eye-opening and why? Discuss and compare your reactions and reflections with members of your book club.

Enhance Your Book Club

1. In a fifteen-minute TED talk she delivered in 2013, Manal al-Sharif asks her audience to consider whether battling oppressive governments or battling oppressive societies is more difficult. You may want to use al-Sharif's question to her audience as a prompt for your club's discussion about *Daring to Drive*. At a break in your discussion, screen Manal al-Sharif's TED talk with your group. How does the experience of seeing and hearing Manal al-Sharif articulate her views online differ from the act of reading about them in *Daring to Drive*? You may want to ask your club to examine the emotional impact of different types of media, and consider why Manal al-Sharif chose to upload a video of herself driving and talking about the Women2Drive campaign rather than merely blogging about it. Have members of your club compare and contrast their reactions to Manal al-Sharif's ideas in both audio/visual and literary genres.

   Hyperlink to Manal al-Sharif's 2013 Ted Talk:
   https://www.ted.com/talks/manal_al_sharif_a_saudi_woman_who_dared_to_drive#t-31600

2. In *Daring to Drive*, Manal al-Sharif describes her family's elaborate preparations for Eid al Fitr, the annual holiday celebrated by Muslims worldwide to mark the end of Ramadan, the Islamic holy month of fasting. Discuss the family's holiday customs, including the types of food prepared and procured, the distribution of gifts, the carefully chosen clothing, the relatives included in the event, and the traditional decorations used to mark the joyous occasion. Ask members of your book group to reflect on significant holidays they celebrated as children and to share some of their most vivid memories with each other. If members of your group are so inclined, they might want to prepare traditional dishes from their own childhood celebrations for a potluck feast. Alternatively, ask members of the club to choose

one of the treats Manal al-Sharif describes and prepare it for a shared Eid-themed meal.

3. The veiling of Muslim women in conservative Saudi society continues to fascinate and repel people throughout the world. While some Saudi women consider the veil to be an outward sign of their inner piety, others rebel at their imposed confinement. Manal al-Sharif likens her own experience of wearing a *niqab* to a kind of disorienting blindness. Have members of your book club voice their thoughts about the veiling of women in Saudi Arabia. At any time in their lives have members of your club felt "veiled" either figuratively or literally—kept hidden or separate from others because of their gender, race, sexual orientation, or religion? How does the veiling of women uphold the aims of the Saudi kingdom? You may want to reflect on the recent controversies that have arisen in socially liberal countries regarding their treatment of Muslim citizens who choose to wear veils.

A Conversation with Manal Al-Sharif

Q. Your imprisonment for breaking with Saudi convention and driving a car in public became an international cause célèbre. What are some of the impressions that people have of you because of this act of civil disobedience? Are they right or wrong?

A. I have two images: one inside Saudi Arabia and one outside of the country. Most people back home see me only as evil or, as some imams called me in their Friday sermons, a whore who should be lashed in public and shamed, so no other girl will follow in her footsteps. Most people abroad see a hero who stood up for what she believes in. I can give a small example with my own mother (God bless her soul). Mom was a very simple woman. When she was inside Saudi Arabia, I was dealing with her tears when she read or heard something bad about me, and there were plenty of bad things and plenty of tears! People criticized her, saying that she didn't know how to bring up a good Muslim woman. But all this changed when my mother went on her annual trip to see her family in Egypt. She would call me with so much joy and pride in her voice, telling me that people in Egypt saw me as a hero, and that many women there look up to me. People would ask my mom to send me their regards, and girls would ask if they could talk to me or have my email. Her family and friends showed her articles and TV shows that spoke highly of me! But it took all that to change Mom's view. And she is my own mother! Imagine a complete stranger who knows me only from what other people say!

Q. How do you reconcile your mother's extraordinary generosity and her unfailing encouragement of her children's education with the brutal physical attacks she inflicted on you and your siblings? To what extent have those childhood experiences influenced the way you parent your children?

A. I feared and hated my mother as a child. We were taught all those *anasheed* (Islamic rhymes), Quran and *hadiths* (sayings of the Prophet Muhammad, PBUH) that speak of how we should love and respect our mothers. But I was confused, because my mother did not behave in the ways that those songs said about other mothers! But as I grew up and went to college, and Mom stopped beating us, I started seeing a broken woman who tried to do everything to make sure we got an education, clean clothes, food, and the encouragement to finish our education by rejecting marriage suitors. Slowly, I also came to understand why my parents were okay with my and my sister's circumcisions, although Mom told us the story of her own circumcision and how she ran away from the house, bleeding, before the woman could finish her job. She hid in their neighbor's house for days. But she still did the exact same thing to us. The society puts so much pressure on parents that they submit to. Mom came from a very rich family but accepted to live in poverty and worse conditions, because she wanted her independence from her family. In many ways she refused to submit to anyone. She made her own money and taught us how to be financially independent. And for that, I love my mother dearly. It all comes down to putting yourself in the other person's position and trying to see the world through their window. Things really look different once you understand the whys. Mom was truly my hero.

Sadly, beating was considered—and still is—a normal practice. If parents beat their kids, it's a way of discipline. Beating remains a controversial topic in Saudi society.

Q. How did the many individual freedoms you experienced as an employee and resident of the Aramco compound contribute to your decision to challenge the restrictive order of the Saudi kingdom outside its gates?

A. I think it was a culmination of many experiences—not only the freedoms in Aramco, but before that, the freedom of choosing my own clothes and working for an hourly rate at the University of Jeddah. That contributed to my self-esteem. And it gave me more liberty to make my own decisions, such as buying the satellite dish and getting the Internet connection in our house. These small things, put together, created in me a realization that there is something wrong with the way women are treated. And although I could drive and didn't always have to be covered, there were many parts of the Aramco experience that weren't all that nice, because I was a Saudi woman. It was nice only with the non-Saudi women. For example, as a Saudi, I was under continuous scrutiny from my male colleagues. Women from other countries were not under the same scrutiny. They had different rules.

Q. What prompted your decision to start a Facebook group called Saudi Female Employees of Aramco, and how much of a risk were you taking by doing so?

A. It was an undercover group. The frustration of so much discrimination in the company policies, especially the policy to deny housing to female Saudi workers, brought it up. I could have lost my job if I was reported as the person who started it.

Q. To what extent did your year in the United States serve as the catalyst that transformed you into a political activist for women in Saudi Arabia?

A. I never understand when someone calls me an activist! I think I'm the type of person who won't accept wrongdoing, and over time, I have found the guts to speak up. I remember when I was working at Aramco and brought up the issue of being excluded from the training just because I was a woman. I kept fighting and eventually prevailed. After that, my colleagues called me a troublemaker. It did upset me but didn't stop me. I also think after turning thirty we change, we become more mature and more sure of ourselves. My thirtieth birthday happened the year I was in the United States. Living there felt normal! Everything I needed to do I could do by myself. When I returned to Saudi Arabia, I felt disabled, as if they had cut off my hands and feet but gave me no wheelchair. It was so frustrating to know that all the extra steps, restrictions, and difficulties that I had to go through every day back home were all man-made. There was nothing wrong with me except that I was a woman. My colleagues in Aramco said that I came back a different person."

Q. How important was your brother's support when you wanted to drive?
A. My brother changed as I changed. Before he was married, he was far less accepting. He couldn't really understand my divorce and my situation. But after he went through the experience of having a wife who couldn't drive, and all the worry and suffering that caused, he saw exactly what I was talking about. Once he finally understood, he became very supportive. I think in any effort to make lives better for women, it is very important to include men and to educate them. It does change a lot when the men are involved with us.

Q. You have characterized domestic human rights organizations in Saudi Arabia as essentially powerless. How has social media impacted the visibility of the most vulnerable members of Saudi society?
A. It is the voice for the voiceless. We finally found a podium where we can speak our views, express views that before were just a few shouts in the dark. We also found like-minded people on social media. People are too afraid to speak up in Saudi in case their immediate circle of people disagrees. With the social media, you create your own circle, and more and more people are speaking up. Many have gotten

into trouble and been jailed, but the government can't jail a whole generation, particularly the Saudis who were born in the 1990s and later. It's funny that my views are accepted and celebrated among this generation, and most of the resistance and criticism I face is from my own generation, those who were born in the seventies and eighties.

Q. You no longer live in Saudi Arabia. To what extent was your ability to write *Daring to Drive* without fear of repercussion dependent on your living outside of the Saudi kingdom?
A. I'm still Saudi; I still travel back to Saudi so often, as my son and my family are still there. I wrote this book and had no idea of what was waiting for me once it was published! But because I go back to Saudi, I had to hold back so many of the views that could get me in deeper trouble. When I wrote the book, I kept in mind that fine line that I didn't cross so as to be able to go back home.

Q. In *Daring to Drive*, you write: "There can be no modern Saudi kingdom as long as women are still ruled by men." What do you think it will take for the male rulers of Saudi Arabia to effect the far-reaching social changes required to bring their country up to speed with the rest of the world?
A. Let women drive their own lives and prepare men to accept and support that. Introduce constitutional monarchy where people have say in their life, promote more freedom of speech, political rights, and liberties.

Q. How do you continue to challenge the social and religious conditions that prevent girls and women from achieving full enfranchisement, both in Saudi Arabia and abroad?
A. "Never, never, never give up." —Winston Churchill.